MW00781020

Colonel Heg and His Boys

Colonel Heg and His Boys

A Norwegian Regiment
in the American Civil War

by WALDEMAR AGER

Translated by Della Kittleson Catuna and Clarence A. Clausen
With an introduction by Harry T. Cleven

2000
The Norwegian-American Historical Association
Northfield, Minnesota

The cover design is by Tom Redman of Redman Illustration in Milwaukee, Wisconsin (e-mail: tomredman@mailcity.com), noted graphic artist and Civil War reenactor. It depicts a desperate moment for the Wisconsin Fifteenth Regiment during the vicious fighting around Viniard's Farm at Chickamauga, Georgia, on September 19, 1863.

> *"A charge was made by rebels and the Brigade to which the 15th Regt. was attached was outflanked and compelled to retreat a short distance. In this retreat the color bearer was severely wounded and dropped the colors, when Jens Hanson noticed it and exposing himself to deadly fire advanced to the front and picked them up thereby preventing their falling into the enemys hands."*
> Award citation, 1867

Based on actual events, the artwork shows Private Jens Hanson of Company K thrusting the flag aloft while holding onto Color Sergeant Anders Urness, with comrades charging to their support. To the right is Captain Hans Hanson of Company C who lies mortally wounded. Above them in Norwegian is the Fifteenth's watchword "For God and Our Country." And before them are the words of Sergeant Nels Johnsen of Company D who, though severely wounded that fateful afternoon, urged his comrades to "Stand by the Flag boys!"

Preface

The Association is pleased to publish in translation *Colonel Heg and His Boys: A Norwegian Regiment in the American Civil War* by Waldemar Ager as volume 13 in its Travel and Description Series. The many personal accounts from the battlefields by the soldiers of the Fifteenth Wisconsin Regiment, penned in letters to family and friends, remain the most evocative and moving contributions. Their value is enhanced as primary source material to a wrenching national experience. These intimate narratives relate both the horrors of the conflict and the loyalty of the young men, many of them recent arrivals from Norway, to what they consistently refer to as "our new fatherland."

Ager wished to convey to a generation of Norwegian Americans rapidly distancing itself from its roots that it was at the time when the Norwegian impulse was strong and fresh that they had made the most significant contributions to America. In 1916 when the original Norwegian version appeared it was precisely the patriotism of foreign-born Americans that was in question as the xenophobic hysteria during the World War I era generated heated anti-hyphen campaigns to eradicate anything that seemed foreign to the dominant Anglo-American culture. Ager admonishes his readers through the voices and actions of the Civil War soldiers to honor their heritage, and not reject it as the nativistic propagandists for "100 percent Americanism" advocated—only by doing so would they become good and patriotic citizens.

The translation begins with Ager's own "foreword" in the 1916 edition; in editing the body of the work some parts of the original have been deleted. None of the numerous portraits collected by Ager could be reproduced. The book's organization—which in Ager's somewhat random procedure in collecting information occasionally assumes the irregularity of a scrapbook—has been retained out of loyalty to the original Norwegian version. To modern readers the work itself may indeed seem like an artifact of the past; they might even experience some confusion in following Ager's eclectic narrative. It is, however, not published as an authoritative history of the Civil War or even of the Fifteenth Wisconsin Regiment, though a few of Ager's most obvious errors of fact and interpretation are noted. The first-hand accounts found in the letters of the soldiers, even though not always entirely accurate, possess great value in themselves as personal documents and should be of interest to a broad readership. The Civil War period is a dramatic watershed event in the adjustment of Norwegian Americans to the challenges they encountered in America and moved them toward integration with the new society. The heroic roles played by the men of the Fifteenth Wisconsin Regiment remain lasting and treasured images in the iconography of the Norwegian-American experience.

The Association is indebted to a number of people in the preparation of the manuscript for publication. Our gratitude goes first to the two translators Clarence A. Clausen and Della Kittleson Catuna, both now deceased.

Clarence A. Clausen (1896–1991) joined the St. Olaf faculty in 1924 and taught history there until 1964, save for the years of graduate work and of government service during World War II with the Office of Strategic Services and after the war as Cultural Attache at the United States Embassy in Stockholm, returning to teach at St. Olaf in 1953. As a member of the Board of Publications he contributed translations of some of the Association's documentary publications and a number of articles.

Della Kittleson Catuna (1906–1999), a native of Wisconsin, received a B.S. degree in 1929 from Gallaudet College for the deaf. For most of the next thirty-five years she worked in the records department of the Hispanic Society of America in New York, where she became an expert photographer. Only after she and her husband moved to California in 1969 did she become involved in translating the Civil War letters of her father's older half-brothers, Lars and Knud Dokken. These letters were published in *Norwegian-American Studies*, volume 28, in 1979.

Robert Kittelson, a nephew of Mrs. Catuna, contributed his detailed knowledge of the Civil War to correct errors of fact. Professor Michael Fitzgerald at St. Olaf College graciously volunteered to read the manuscript and made additional valuable suggestions for improving the manuscript. We are also grateful to Harry T. Cleven for his insightful introduction, a partly revised version of his article published by NAHA-

Norway in 1990 in *Essays on Norwegian-American Literature and History*, volume 2, edited by Øyvind T. Gulliksen, Ingeborg Kongslien, and Dina Tolfsby. Harry Cleven, a resident of Norway since 1979, is currently employed by the Norse Federation in Oslo. His childhood and youth in Madison, Wisconsin, gave him a special interest in Hans Christian Heg and his role in the Civil War.

Ruth Crane, assistant secretary, assisted greatly in the technical aspects of manuscript preparation. Jennifer Bothun, college secretary, typed parts of the manuscript. As in past publications, my deepest gratitude goes to my competent and cordial assistant in the editorial work, Mary R. Hove. She also prepared the index.

Odd S. Lovoll
St. Olaf College
University of Oslo

Contents

Introduction

by Harry T. Cleven

The Fifteenth Wisconsin—a Norwegian Regiment in the American Civil War. Several histories of the regiment, both Norwegian and American, were written, in Norwegian, between 1869 and 1916. They are fairly reliable though not always accurate in detail. It is fortunate for posterity that they were written, though it may be that for historical objectivity they were written too close to the events they describe. Their authors all disclaim them as actual histories. One gets the impression from them that the 15th nearly won the war alone, and that most of its men were great and virtuous heroes. Nor is there much attempt to show how the 15th Wisconsin fit into the overall picture.

Thus, although a great deal has already been written, we are much in need of a new, more complete and thorough history of the regiment. This cannot be our purpose in this context, however.

For the present, only a few basic questions: How did the regiment come into being? Why did Scandinavians join it? What effect did the regiment have on the men who filled its ranks? What effect did the Civil War, and their participation in it, have on Norwegians in America as a whole?

As of April 12, 1861, war between North and South was an incontestable fact. The South was determined to become independent, the North determined to preserve the Union whatever the cost. Neither side, however, was equipped for war.

Congress authorized the recruitment of 500,000 men and Abraham Lincoln, newly-inaugurated president, appealed to loyal Northern states for volunteers.

To the inhabitants of Wisconsin, both Washington, D.C. and Fort Sumter must have seemed very far away indeed. But like the first shots fired in the American Revolution, the cannon fire against Fort Sumter was also heard around the world, even on the edge of the American frontier, in rural communities and hamlets, most of which were inhabited by "foreign" immigrants. Governor Alexander W. Randall and the Wisconsin legislature immediately took action in response to Lincoln's appeal. Land was offered by the Wisconsin Agricultural Society as a camp for drilling troops. The offer was accepted and the grounds renamed Camp Randall in honor of the governor. It was here that the majority of Wisconsin's Civil War soldiers would undergo training.

A nation of immigrants, Americans of varied ethnic and national backgrounds responded to the plea for men, in Wisconsin as well as in other Northern states. There were, in 1860, something over 50,000 Norwegians living in America. They proved to be no less patriotic than any other group. While an eighth of the "original" Americans volunteered, as many as a sixth of all Norwegian immigrants joined the service. This was also the case with immigrants of all nationalities, who enlisted in numbers that more than equaled their percentage of the population. There were more of the foreign-born of an age for military service and many were tempted by the generous bounties offered to those who volunteered. There were Norwegians in just about all the regiments that came into being in Wisconsin, Iowa, Minnesota, and Illinois. One Madison newspaper, the *Wisconsin State Journal*, was interested in the varied national origins of the men of the 12th Wisconsin Regiment: forty were from Norway, thirty-seven from Canada, thirty-five from Germany, thirty-three from Ireland, ten from Prussia, nine from Wales, six each from Sweden and Scotland, three from Switzerland, and one each from Hungary, Belgium, and France. Not all regiments, however, were to be as heterogeneous as the 12th. The Civil War soldier enlisted and gave his first loyalty to company and regimental units that were locally recruited. Because many immigrant groups settled in the same areas, local units were often of homogeneous ethnic composition. Later studies of the contributions of the various foreign groups indicated that their participation in the war marked a transitional step in their identification with the nation's fortunes and ideals.

According to Theodore C. Blegen, when a call came to Wisconsin on August 20, 1861, for five additional regiments, Governor Randall made an official request that one of these regiments be composed of Germans. This may have sparked the idea for a Scandinavian regiment. On the evening of September 15, 1861, several prominent Norwegian politicians met at the Capitol in Madison, where it was decided to establish a Scandinavian regiment. The September 15 meeting ended with a recommendation to the governor that Hans Heg be made colonel and Kiler K. Jones lieutenant colonel. O. A. Buslett in his history of the regiment writes that even though Jones was not himself a Scandinavian, he was married to one, which Jones considered validation enough for his involvement. The recommendation was approved and the appointment of officers was to be left to Heg and his friends. As an immigrant himself, Heg knew a large number of the immigrant population personally, and he was therefore able to use his personal influence to encourage enlistment. In eloquent language Heg discussed in press and on platform the burning issue of the war effort. "The land which we, as strangers, have made our home," he wrote, "has received us with friendship and hospitality. We enjoy equal privileges with the native born. The path to honor and fortune is alike open to us and them. The law protects and befriends us all alike ... Let us prove ourselves worthy of that land and of those heroes from whom we descend." In a speech he asked, "Shall we Scandinavians sit still and watch our American, German, and English-born fellow citizens fight for us without going to their aid?" He closed his appeal with these words: "Come, then, young Norsemen, and take your part in defending our country's cause, and thus fulfill a pressing duty which everyone who is able to do so owes to the land in which he lives. Let us band together and deliver untarnished to posterity the old honorable name of Norsemen."

Historians differ regarding the number of Norwegians who served on the side of the North during the Civil War, but there were probably about 800 from Minnesota, more than 400 from Iowa, about 3,000 from Wisconsin, and a relatively large number from the older settlements in Illinois. The roster of Wisconsin volunteers, 15th Regiment Infantry, originally listed about 850, officers and enlisted men, and included some Danes and Swedes. On a complete roster published after the war, there are roughly 1,100 names.

Why would young men, most of whom could barely speak English, join a war on a new and foreign continent? The motives for taking part in the war were probably different for each individual. Some were undoubtedly idealists who shared Lincoln's vision of an indivisible nation conceived in liberty and dedicated to the proposition that all are created equal. Others may have been attracted by the monthly salary paid in cash. But what thoughts, really, were in the mind of a young boy from a cotter's place at Hovland in Saksumdal or Simen Owren from Lexhus as they marched south through the Mississippi Valley to fight for the Union? Was it the dream of a big farm gained with the help of their earnings, or was it the thought of a free country with endless possibilities that drove them on?

Norwegian-American author Waldemar Ager here gives us an account by Bersven Nelson, a young recruit in the 15th Wisconsin who described some of his reasons for enlistment. They are perhaps not atypical for others. Although he had been in America only a few months, Nelson was eager to enlist. The $100 bounty, $13 a month wages, and free food and clothing seemed a great windfall to him. Also, the army offered him the opportunity to travel and see his new country. Then too he heard reports that the fighting would not last long, a view held by many persons in the early stages of the war.

Enlistment was also a means by which the immigrant showed his loyalty to his adopted country and made him a part of it.

Jens Hanson Eggen, a native of Haltdalen, Norway, who belonged to the 12th Iowa Regiment, wrote to a friend from Camp Benton, St. Louis, Missouri, on December 3, 1861, and perhaps unwittingly revealed reasons for enlistment both for himself and for other young Norwegian men as well. "I want to tell you how much we receive each month. We get $13 a month plus food, not food like the soldiers in Norway, not coarse stuff and the like, but meat and side pork, all we want, and wheat bread, newly baked, and coffee and sugar and other things which are not necessary to enumerate. And clothes for $42 a year—if one needs more he must pay for them himself. And if one doesn't need that much he is given payment. I think it will be enough. And it is fine clothing, too; there is not much difference between ours and that of the officers. And we will be given $100 when we have done our time in the army, money over and above our salary. Payday is every other month, though it can go beyond that up to 3 or 4 months, but it is as certain as the bank. It is the United States Bank that pays us. We are not certain if we will get our own land. We should receive 160 'eker' land according to the law and they say we will get it."

Most of the Scandinavian men were either small farmers or farm workers. They were strong and muscular, accustomed to hard work. They were divided into companies which were given names such as St. Olaf's Rifles, The Wergeland Guards, Norway Bear Hunters, and Odin's

Rifles.* Their patriotism was also reflected in the official recruitment reports from the adjutant general of the United States Army at that time, who in connection with the presentation of a status report added the following words: "All hail, Norsemen, descendants of the Vikings, let your hordes, as in days of old, sweep down upon the South, crushing as with Tor's hammer the Southerner who meets you on the field of battle."

The recruits of the new regiment underwent two months of basic training. Few of them, and few of their officers, had had any previous military experience.

It is not so difficult to understand that the 15th Wisconsin recruits found life at Camp Randall an even greater adjustment than did the native-born regiments. At Camp Randall, Scandinavians were introduced not only to military life but to American life as well. Like many immigrants, writes Carolyn J. Mattern in a master's thesis about Camp Randall from the University of Wisconsin, they had chosen to live among their fellow countrymen both out of necessity and to maintain intact their language and customs. The other regiments present in camp provided the largest group of Americans and other foreigners they had ever encountered. The letters of the James brothers of the 16th Wisconsin indicated that the relations between nationalities were not always smooth and other regiments enjoyed making fun of the "Norways" because of their language and "ignorance."

There were language difficulties not only between the Norwegians and other nationals, but among Norwegians themselves who came from various parts of Norway and spoke their own dialects. Waldemar Ager describes the situation in his novel, *Sons of the Old Country*: "With eight hundred men from all parts of Wisconsin and all parts of Norway gathered in one place, there was no telling what might happen. Oddly, one of the big problems was language. Nearly all of the widely varying Norwegian dialects were being spoken somewhere or other at one time or another, and sometimes the men had to resort to a limited knowledge of English to make themselves understood.

"'God alone knows what kind of people we're mixed up with here,' said Hans. 'They claim they're Norwegians, and they cuss in Norwegian, but when most of them talk I can't figure out what they're saying.'"

Another serious factor was that many of the young soldiers in Camp Randall had come from sparsely populated, remote areas and had never been exposed to childhood communicable diseases. Many of the men got sick and died of illness before seeing combat at all. Even superficial wounds often resulted in death because of poor hygiene and infection.

A love of beer, Mattern tells us, won the regiment a reputation for rowdyism. Whether or not this was true, with Heg's arrival on the scene in January, more stringent restrictions were placed on the men. Only six two-hour passes were issued at a time and at the eight o'clock curfew a patrol of six to eight men was sent out. For those found absent without leave Colonel Heg devised a unique punishment. Sober soldiers had to chop wood for a day, and those who were drunk chopped wood for two days. A soldier who became involved in rowdyism had to carry an eighty-pound bag of sand on his back for a day with a guard watching so that the delinquent did not rest. The guard was relieved every two hours. Christmas Eve provided the opportunity for some unexpected revelry. The Christmas celebration began when a wagonload of beer was relieved of a keg while the driver was making a delivery near the camp. After a while the beer began taking its effect and fighting broke out with the 17th. The 16th was on guard duty, but had not been issued guns and was helpless to do anything. As a result the fighting lasted until the beer was gone. Christmas morning in Camp Randall was greeted with sore noses and black eyes.

As a result, the 15th had won a reputation among the Madisonians for bad discipline in training. Much to the townspeople's surprise, however, regimental and brigade drills were done with amazing precision. Such reports suggest either that the rumors of poor discipline were exaggerated or that the Norwegians were excellent material for soldiers.

The men of the 15th departed from Madison by train on Sunday, March 2, 1862, a dismal, rainy day. The Madison station was thronged with hundreds of friends and relatives assembled to bid goodbye to the soldiers. They had been given orders to go to St. Louis, Missouri, by way of Chicago. Ager describes the day of departure: "It rained and snowed intermittently the morning that the Norwegian regiment left its training camp to start the long journey south by rail. Despite the unpleasant weather, enthusiasm was running high and a large crowd had turned out to bid farewell to the soldiers, because that's what they were now. Hurrahs were heard from all sides, and—as was the custom speeches were made. Madison seemed full of Norwegian farmers who had come to say goodbye to their boys."

Upon the arrival of the 15th Wisconsin in Chicago, where Colonel Heg had recruited a company, it was met by the members of Nora Lodge, a Norwegian society, who entertained the soldiers and presented them with a flag with on the one side the American colors and on the reverse the American and Norwegian insignia united, the Norwegian being the picture of a lion with an axe, on a red field. The flag bore the inscription "For Gud og Vort Land" (For God and Our Country). It also bore the inscription (in Norwegian), "Presented to the Scandinavian Regiment by Nora Lodge, Chicago, March 1, 1861." The Chicago company was Co. A and was known as the St. Olaf's Rifles.

Ager describes the scene in Chicago: "Because of the weather the regiment did not get the reception it had expected upon reaching Chicago. Nevertheless, there was the march to the City Hall, music and shouts of hurrah—and speeches . . . A strong surge of patriotism swept through both the crowd and the regiment, making it an occasion long be to remembered—not least by the soldiers themselves during the hard days to come. Their uniforms were new, their rifles were new, swords and bayonets were bright and shining, and the officers' decorations glistened like pure gold.

"In order to appear as manly as possible, the youngest newcomer boys in the regiment would plunk their heavy shoes down so firmly as they marched that water and spring slush squirted to all sides and even up onto the sidewalks.

"So the people shouted and sang and applauded, and they continued to do so even though they knew inwardly that some of these boys, maybe many, would never return."

As interesting as it is, the military history of the regiment cannot be described in this brief space except to note that the 15th saw action in several major battles at various places including Island No. 10, Perryville, Knob Gap, Murfreesboro, and Chickamauga. Ager compares the somewhat glorious beginnings of the Fifteenth Wisconsin Regiment with the less than glorious conditions it later faced at Murfreesboro: "Nine months later and in the same kind of weather they were in the battle line near Murfreesboro in Tennessee. In front of them stood a formidable foe.

"Although the weather was the same, much had happened and much had changed since that day in Chicago. The regiment had been successful in carrying out the assignments given it. It had taken part in the capture of the strongly fortified Island No. 10 in the Mississippi river, and it had also been involved in several other engagements. It had been fortunate, however, in that up to now the enemy had shown a tendency to take to his heels wherever the Union forces of which it was part showed up.

"But apparently this was not going to be the case at Murfreesboro. The soldiers sensed this, the officers knew it.

"The Wisconsin regiment had been stationed in the front flank of the Union army, and it bore little resemblance to the one that had been cheered and honored in Madison and Chicago. By now the uniforms were faded and threadbare; the shoes were battered and worn through. For days on its way to Murfreesboro the regiment had marched over muddy roadways, and it had been forced to spend rainy nights out in the open without benefit of bonfires. And the men had been living on the rations each carried with them."

As Ager indicates, the soldiers marched and marched and marched, sometimes knee-deep in mud for miles on end. Or they camped. There was either drudgery or boredom—and sometimes great deprivation in addition. The men were often wet and cold. They had been trained for war, however inadequately, and the 15th Regiment saw its share of blood and horror, often with great losses to itself. One of the worst battles it saw was the major Union defeat at Chickamauga with opposing forces of about 58,000 men on the Union side and some 66,000 on the Confederate side. It was during this battle that Colonel Heg lost his life, a fact which was to have dire consequences for the 15th regiment. When the fighting was over at Chickamauga, some 4,000 men had relinquished their lives. Nearly one of every four soldiers became a casualty.

Of the approximately 850 men who had volunteered for service with the Fifteenth Wisconsin during September–October, 1861, only seventy of the men could report for duty on the day following the battle at Chickamauga. It must, however, be noted that only 175 of the 850 volunteers were present for duty at Chickamauga; 150 (Companies G and I) were on route from Island 10; others who were absent were sick or detached for other duties. Practically all the officers had been killed, wounded, or taken prisoner. Among the seventy who could stand on their feet, the majority were wounded and bandaged. It was said that the regiment's banner was carried by seven different men. When an ensign fell or was badly wounded, another man immediately took over the banner, which was carried as long as the battle lasted.

The 15th was later placed with the troops commanded by General Sherman. Its history ends with the taking of Atlanta, with an exemplary record from beginning to end.

The Civil War was to have a permanent effect on the Norwegians who took direct part in it and also on those who stayed home. E. Biddle Heg, a direct descendant of Colonel Hans Heg, has made the following summation: "The Civil War was a major catalyst in the Americanizing of the Norwegian immigrants who arrived here between 1825 and 1860, molding them in some ways very subtly and in other ways more obviously. Few immigrant Norwegian Americans escaped the influence of this upheaval, if not on the battlefield then certainly on the economic and social fronts. Those on the home scene who assumed the duties of business, farm, and family were passively influenced, adjusting to the attendant deprivations and daily changes, not always aware that they were participants in the struggle of their adopted country. Others, more aggressive, were drawn into the vortex of the war on the several battlefields away from home. On whichever front they found themselves, the immigrants came to feel at home in America during these Civil War years."

Many years earlier, Theodore C. Blegen observed that Colonel Hans Heg had become the war hero of the Norwegians and the personal symbol of their contribution to the preservation of the Union.

The Civil War, writes Odd S. Lovoll in *The Promise of America*, "marked a decisive phase in the immigrant's process of adjustment. The enormous conflict created a new patriotism, a sense of having earned a legitimate place in America, for Norwegian blood had been spilled in the defense of the nation. . . . In the Norwegian settlements veterans from the war were listened to and honored . . ."

The 15th Wisconsin participated in a total of twenty-six battles. Many of the men did not return to their homes or live to tell about their experiences. Many of the severely wounded died in Southern hospitals if not on the battlefields. Some died terrible deaths in Southern prison camps. By the end of the war, the regiment's total losses amounted to more than a third of the original volunteers. The sacrifices of those Norwegians who died and of those who survived contributed significantly to the fact that following the war the Norwegians in America had become something more than what they had been—they were now truly Norwegian Americans. "It is a heroic and dramatic period in the history of the

Norwegians in America, idealized by later generations and given great symbolic value."

*The companies were numbered and named as follows:

    A.   St. Olaf's Rifles, also known as The Chicago Company

    B.   The Wergeland Guards

    C.   Norway Bear Hunters

    D.   Norway Wolf Hunters, aka The Waupun Company

    E.   Odin's Rifles

    F.   K. K.'s Protectors (for Lieutenant Colonel Kiler K. Jones), aka The Valdris Company

    G.   Rock River Rangers

    H.   Heg's Rifles, aka The Voss Company

    I.   The Scandinavian Mountaineers, aka The Waupacca Company

    K.   Clausen's Guards

Foreword

In my work collecting pictures and other material for the Wisconsin section at the Centennial Exposition in Norway I obtained some pictorial material and written records concerning the Norwegian 15th Wisconsin Regiment that I felt ought to be preserved.

Those of us Norwegian Americans who try to keep an open window toward Norway are especially indebted to the men of the 15th because they gave the strongest proof possible of the fact that our most Norwegian-minded compatriots in this country are also at heart the best Americans—that is, the most dedicated—the first to volunteer when the war trumpets sound and their adopted country is in danger.

It was also significant how much interest even the Norwegian people took in the Regiment and its old banners. This regiment was in fact the only Norwegian military organization that had been under fire in more than a century. I believe it can also safely be said that seldom if ever have Norwegians faced fiercer fire.

The conduct of the Regiment during the long and bloody war is such an honorable chapter in the history of the Norwegian people that we can not afford to lose anything about it that can still be rescued for coming generations.

It was especially Corporal Bersvend Nelson's war memoirs that I felt should be preserved in a book. There is also much other material of great value.

To supplement this firsthand material I included articles about the Regiment which have appeared in newspapers or magazines.

So it will be understood that this is not an attempt to write a history of the Regiment—that has been done by Mr. O. A. Buslett, who thereby deserves the gratitude of everyone interested. My purpose has merely been to gather between two covers some pictures and records which might otherwise be lost.

Waldemar Ager

The statue of Hans Christian Heg in Madison, Wisconsin. Courtesy of
Richard G. B. Hanson II.

Colonel Heg and His Boys

The Norwegian Regiment in the American Civil War

by Waldemar Ager

The American Civil War is one of the greatest struggles in the annals of world history. It lasted four long years. At first fortune appeared to favor the Southern states, and there were times when the Union cause seemed lost. But President Lincoln's call for volunteers aroused a response in the nation—not least in the West, whence came the soldiers who ultimately brought victory home. It was west of the Alleghenies that the war was decided in favor of the Northern states; and it was on these battlefields that most of the Norwegians fought.

As a result of the Civil War the Union was saved and the slavery question decided once and for all. In a sense it was a fortunate war because the questions at issue were completely and finally settled and the honor of the American people cleansed from the stigma of slavery, although at the cost of much blood.

The casualties were enormous. The Northern forces lost 67,058 troops on the battlefields while 43,012 died of wounds. Furthermore, 224,586 died because of sickness and 24,872 as a result of accidents or other causes—a total of 359,528 men from the Northern states gave their lives. To this number can be added 275,175 wounded soldiers, many of whom remained cripples for life. The Confederate losses also ran to about a quarter million men, of whom nearly 100,000 fell on the field of battle or died because of their wounds. Altogether, more that 600,000 men gave their lives, so we many conclude that war is a serious matter. It has been estimated that the cost of the war amounted to about seven billion dollars.

Many Norwegians were engaged in this giant conflict. From Wisconsin alone between three and four thousand men of Norwegian blood enlisted as volunteers.

Actually, the war revolved around the question of the rights of individual states to independence; but the Slavery Question was the issue that had caused States' Rights to become a bone of contention. And it is certain that for the common man in the North—most especially for the Norwegian immigrant—the opinion prevailed that the war was a fight against slavery. For them it became practically a Holy War, involving moral rather than political objectives.

The thought of organizing a Norwegian—or a "Scandinavian" regiment as it was then called—arose because at the time there were so many newcomers with incomplete knowledge of the English language. On September 15, 1861, several Norwegians gathered in Madison, Wisconsin, and resolved to attempt the organization of a Norwegian regiment. At first the intention was that only Norwegians should be included, but several non-Norwegians were enlisted. Captain [Joseph] Mathiesen, for instance, was a Dane. Captain [Charles] Gustafson of Company F (the Valdris Company) was a Swede and had served in the Mexican War as a volunteer. Lieutenant Colonel [Kiler K.] Jones was an American, but his wife was Norwegian and he could speak the language, so he managed to get along. Lieutenant [Henry] Seigel was of German descent but born and raised in Norway. Major [George] Wilson was born of English parents in Hamburg, but reared in Christiania. However, more than ninety percent of the enlisted men were Norwegians.

At the outset they were very Norwegian-minded. Company A is entered on the official lists as "Saint Olaf's Rifles," Company B as "Wergeland's Guards," Company C as "Norway Bear Hunters," Company D as "Norway Wolf Hunters," etc. Furthermore, in the field the regiment used to be granted a holiday every 17th of May; and that day was celebrated so lustily that, on one occasion at least, they were disciplined afterward.

A Norwegian named Hans C. Heg was chosen colonel of the Regiment. He left a good position to assume this post. Heg was born in Lier near Drammen and came to America with his parents at the age of ten. His father, Even Heg, homesteaded in the Muskego settlement, where the first Norwegian church in America was built and the first Norwegian newspaper in this country was published. The elder Heg was the publisher of this paper, called *Nordlyset* (the northern light). The family lived, like many other early settlers, in a cave dug into a hillside—in this case an Indian mound, an old burial ground. Even Heg also ran a store in the community; and there the lawyer [James D.] Reymert, [Frederick] Fleischer, and many of the so-called "better" Norwegians often appeared. It is reasonable to assume that young Hans was an attentive listener when things

Norwegian were extolled. Hans C. Heg likely lived and died in the belief that the Norwegians were a breed without equal anywhere on the globe. As an officer he was exacting, correct, conscientious, and of unblemished behavior.

On March 1st, 1862, the Regiment was ready to leave for the front.[1] They went by way of Chicago where a Norwegian society, "Nora," Knights of the White Cross[2] (which still exists), gave them a beautiful silk banner decorated with the American and Norwegian emblems side by side and the motto "For God and Our Country" in Norwegian. Evidently Company A also received a Norwegian flag that seems, however, to have disappeared from history. Probably this was the flag which was raised on the steamer that took the Regiment down the Mississippi River. Because of its resemblance to the Confederate flag certain Union men opened fire on them. The banner the Regiment received in Chicago was an American flag with the Norwegian and American emblems in the Union field near the flagpole.

On March 30th the Regiment first engaged in combat when, together with another regiment, it took Union City. This was an easily won victory, as the enemy was taken by surprise. The whole camp with a wealth of military equipment was destroyed and many prisoners were taken. Here the 15th captured its first banner. It bore the inscription "Victory or Death" and belonged to an Alabama regiment.

On April 7th the strongly fortified Island No. 10 in the Mississippi was taken, and the Norwegian boys had an opportunity to get acquainted with heavy garrison artillery. Several thousand prisoners were taken as well as 160 cannons, a number of steamers, and a gunboat. The Norwegians had distinguished themselves and were left on the island for garrison duty.

On the 1st of October the regiment—except for two companies still doing garrison duty on Island No. 10—were on the march to meet the enemy. On October 8 the battle of Perryville took place. It began with some skirmishing over certain ponds but ended with a collision between the two forces. The Regiment distinguished itself here also and pursued the enemy so far that it was in danger of being cut off because the other wing of the Union Army had been pushed back. The battle was indecisive. The Northern forces lost about 2,000 men, dead and wounded.

On December 29th the big battle of Stone's River began. The Confederate forces under [Braxton] Bragg and the Federal under [William Starke]

Rosecrans were about equally strong. The Southerners won; but when they attacked again on January 2nd they were driven back, and this gave Rosecrans a chance to claim the victory. In this battle the Norwegian Regiment took the first cannon with a bayonet charge. Colonel Heg greatly distinguished himself and had a horse shot under him. Lieutenant Colonel [David] McKee was killed and likewise Captain John Ingemundsen. He was from Rygge in Smålenene. From the commanding general came a complimentary letter to the 15th Wisconsin, lauding its excellent discipline and the gallantry it had shown. But the Regiment had suffered great losses. In this battle the North lost 13,249 men, the South 10,266.

On July 3, 1863, Colonel Heg was named Brigadier General and put in charge of the third brigade in Jefferson C. Davis' division. On August 17th the campaign against General Bragg's army began, and Heg's brigade was the first to cross the Tennessee River. The Norwegian Regiment was the first of the whole force to set foot on the southern shore of the stream.

On the 19th and 20th of September the battle of Chicamauga was fought, in which the Regiment lost more than half of its men and where Colonel Heg fell. With him fell also many of the 15th's most capable officers.

The next muster revealed that only 76 men remained of the Norwegian Regiment; and of these there were only a few who did not carry scars from the battle.

On this field the state of Wisconsin has raised a monument at a cost of $26,000 or nearly 100,000 Norwegian crowns in memory of the heroism of the 15th Wisconsin Regiment. Another monument marks the place where Colonel Heg fell.

And here the saga of the Norwegian Regiment might well have ended but for the fact that reinforcements in the form of the two companies from Island No. 10 arrived with practically a full contingent of some 150 men.

When, a couple of months later, the great Missionary Ridge near Chattanooga was to be scaled, the Regiment was in the front line and distinguished itself. At the storming of Rocky Face Mountain, the Norwegians were again in the lead and three members of the Regiment were the first to reach the summit. They arrived too early, however, because one was killed, another was captured, while the third fell into a crevice— the only one of the three who returned safely. This was John W.

Wraalstad from Kragerø, who later became a prosperous businessman in Scandinavia, Wisconsin.

It would be entirely too complicated to discuss all the twenty-six battles and skirmishes in which the Regiment played a part. When it followed Sherman in his campaign against Atlanta there were daily encounters. One of these battles—at New Hope Church—was the most disastrous ever experienced by the Regiment in terms of casualties. The brigade to which it was attached had been greatly decimated during the constant fighting in the Kennesaw mountains and at Resaca. General August Willich, a German, was in command of the brigade. Originally he was a socialist who, together with Carl Schurz and others, had been expelled from their homeland after the abortive democratic revolution of 1848. Willich was highly regarded by the Norwegian Regiment and, in turn, he was very proud of having the—by now—famous regiment in his brigade. He did not utter a "soldiers' damn" even when the Regiment, in dire need of provisions, expropriated, butchered, and ate his cow at a time when he was absent.

During the engagement at New Hope Church the brigade received orders to proceed to the left, and they followed the trumpet signals on a long, tiring march. When the weary soldiers finally reached their destination they saw before them a hill whose crest bristled with bayonets and rifle barrels behind strong barricades. All the dead who lay scattered about told in their way about other troops who had tried in vain to storm this hill.

The signal to advance sounded, bayonets were fixed, and on the run the men charged up the hill. The flag of the 15th was planted on the rampart and the fight went on with bayonets and rifle butts. If reinforcement had only arrived, the victory would have been won; but it was the enemy who received reinforcements and the Regiment was driven out of the already captured trenches. They pulled back some 40 or 50 feet and kept the fight going, still awaiting reinforcements. But neither relief nor orders to retreat came. The men remained in position, as they refused to yield without orders. Only remnants of the Norwegian Regiment survived that day. Five or six standard-bearers were shot; but they brought the flag back with them. The last man to carry it out of the rain of bullets had his right hand shot off; but he grasped it with his left and carried it to safety. This was Major Wilson.

After this battle the Regiment took part in only a couple of minor skirmishes. It had played its part and was now detailed for guard duty until the end of the war.

Much more could be told about "the Fifteenth Wisconsin." Some mention should be made of Andersonville—the horrible prison where thirty-two members of the Regiment starved to death or died of scurvy and neglected wounds.

General Grant refused to exchange prisoners. The Confederates had taken many captives and did not know what they should do with them. Since they lacked clothing and provisions for their own men, they had very little to give to the prisoners[3]. In Richmond a large tobacco warehouse was equipped as a prison; at other places mere fence-like palisades were built. Such a structure was Andersonville. In a Georgia forest an area of about twenty acres was cleared. Some fourteen or sixteen acres were fenced in with high, pointed palings. At certain intervals along the borders, towers or platforms were raised on which sentries were mounted. Within the stockade a "line of death" was drawn. Anyone who ventured beyond that fatal line was shot by the nearest sentinel. The terrain sloped toward a muddy creek from which the prisoners got their water. They lived in shacks or tents, or in caves which they had dug into the ground. Thousands of ragged, sick, and starving men languished their lives away there. During the last months they got a daily ration of corn bran, their only source of nourishment except for some vegetables that were sometimes doled out. The bran was mixed with water and stirred—at times in their caps, as not all of them had cups or other utensils. Some men even used a shoe for this purpose. The prisoners died by the thousands. They were called "stiffs" and were buried in rows in big trenches dug outside the stockade. In so far as they kept a reckoning of the dead, the last man to die in Andersonville was a Norwegian named Knud Hanson of the First Wisconsin Cavalry Regiment. He was laid in grave number 12,848. Osmund Johnson of Company K and Ole Steensland of Company E stayed in Andersonville more than eleven months and are said to have been the two who remained there the longest without dying. Both of them were members of the Norwegian Regiment.

The author of this book asked one of the old veterans how it happened that so many Norwegians were taken prisoners of war. "We did not watch the opportune time to 'beat it' when the others ran," he explained. "We figured we could stick it out a bit longer, and a bit longer, until it was too late to run—and so they took us."

"Ya, that's the way it was with us" said another veteran who had been with the 28ᵗʰ Wisconsin Regiment, which also contained many Norwegians. "We Norwegians in the Regiment looked at each other when the others started to run, and then we did not like to turn tail as long as no one else of us did."

"And then you were captured."

"Not everyone," he answered. "Some were left lying on the field because they stayed too long."

A few saw their chance to escape. Lieutenant Colonel Ole C. Johnson Skipsnes and several others were captured at Chicamauga. They were taken away in a cattle car but managed to cut a hole in the floor, slip out, and lie flat between the rails while the train passed over them. In the process Johnson had the buttons torn off his uniform.

A remarkable occurrence can be mentioned in connection with Andersonville: the spring that gushed forth while 34,000 prisoners were there, faint with thirst. People said this was God's answer to the many prayers for water sent up to Him. The stockade has long since rotted away and the place where the prison was located is covered with dense forest; but the spring is there, still bubbling forth—now beautifully roofed over with faced granite. It is called "Providence Spring."

The Civil War experiences of Norwegian soldiers would seem to indicate that they possessed an innate discipline or a moral conception of what is demanded of a man in the ranks during hours of danger.

Several books have been written about the Regiment. J. A. Johnson's *Det Skandinaviske Regiments Historie* came first [1869]. *Kortfattet Skildring af det 15de Wisconsin Regiments Historie* by Bachelor of Laws P. G. Dietrichson appeared in 1884. Kristofer Janson wrote a book, *Femtende Wisconsin*, which was published in 1893. The best and most comprehensive work is O. A. Buslett's *Det 15de Wisconsin Regiments Historie*, a big, thick volume of several hundred pages. Kristofer Janson's book is more fiction than fact. This is what so far has been published in Norwegian about the Regiment.[4]

NOTES

1. According to both Nelson (p. 12) and Dokken (p. 88), they left on March 2.

2. The Knights of the White Cross was a fraternal order created in Chicago in 1863 to function as a mutual aid society.

3. The more recent literature places considerably more responsibility on Confederate actions for the breakdown of the prisoner of war cartel, particularly over the issue of captured African-American Union soldiers. See James McPherson, *Battle Cry of Freedom: The Civil War Era* (New York, 1988), 565–567, 792–794.

4. To these might be added the following: Theodore C. Blegen, *The Civil War Letters of Colonel Hans Christian Heg* (Northfield, Minnesota, 1936), and Agnes Larson, *John A. Johnson, An Uncommon American* (Northfield, 1969), as well as Ager's own *Oberst Heg og hans gutter* (Eau Claire, Wisconsin, 1916).

Observations from the Civil War

by Ben. (Bersven) Nelson
Company I, 15th Wisconsin Volunteer Regiment

On May 9, 1861, my parents, with eleven children, left my birthplace, Upper Fleskemo in the Målselv valley, Finnmark, and set off for America. The second oldest son had gone across the previous year. The oldest one had also been there, but he had returned. On the 12th we boarded a steamer at Molsnes and arrived at Trondheim in the morning of the 17th. Thus we had the opportunity of witnessing the 17th of May celebrations in Trondheim, which were quite elaborate. That evening we took a boat for Bergen, where we arrived on May 20. There we boarded the sailing ship *Camilla,* which was all set to depart for America with emigrants. We left Bergen on May 25th and arrived in Quebec on July 9. The voyage went well; all of us were in good health, except for seasickness.

Because a great number of English soldiers had just arrived to guard the boundary between the United States and Canada, we would either have to wait a while or take a boat across the Great Lakes. We chose to do the latter, but the trip took much longer than we had expected. We did not get to La Crosse until July 16. There we remained for about two months and then went to Eau Claire, where my father claimed land eleven miles west of the town and half a mile north of Elk Mound. I stayed at home and helped build a house—and soon we could move into our new home, a substantial timbered building constructed along Norwegian lines. Now I decided to go to Eau Claire and look for work or else get a job in the woods for the winter. I got work at Smith and Buffington's sawmill at $18.00 per month. I remained there for three weeks; but then the mill closed down, and I returned home.

On November 8 O. R. Dahl came to the house.[1] He was a sergeant from Norway who had been in this country a while so he could speak tolerably good English. Hans C. Heg had got in touch with him and asked his help in organizing a Scandinavian regiment. Heg had already received his appointment from the governor as colonel of this projected regiment. After we had talked about the war between the South and the North for a while, Dahl told us that a battle had been fought at Fort Henry which the Northern forces had won, so prospects were that the war would not last very long. Furthermore, a bounty of $100 was offered for enlistment plus $13.00 per month in salary as well as free clothes and free food. These terms struck me as rather good; and, on top of it all, I would have an opportunity to travel and see lots of things. My father said I could do as I wished—so I enlisted for three years or the duration of the war. James Anderson, Bjørn Thompson, and Casper Hansen enlisted that same day. Dahl continued his recruiting, so by the middle of December there were twenty-two of us. Then we left for Madison to be trained in military tactics. By now there were several hundred men on the training grounds, which went by the name of Camp Randall. The 16th and 17th regiments were also stationed there, so by the end of February we numbered about 3,000 men. We drilled some two or three hours in the forenoon and similarly in the afternoon. On Sundays we marched up to town to attend church. Our minister there was the Pastor Preus.[2]

Camp Randall

I want to tell a little about conditions at Camp Randall. Both the sleeping quarters and the dining hall were built of plain boards—walls of only a single thickness. We had a large stove, but this was of little avail against the severe cold that beset us. The dining hall was a structure containing ten tables, each large enough to accommodate 100 men. There were no chairs, so we had to stand while we ate. The kitchen was at one end of the hall. The food was not of the best, but it was no use to complain. We had to eat what was dished out or else starve. It was not then as now, where the soldiers have a selection of food ready so all they need do is make coffee in order to get a respectable meal.

Off to the War

On March 2, 1862, the 15th, 16th, and 17th regiments were ready to set off for the front. We were paid in full from the day we enlisted until March 1. At 8 o'clock in the morning we left Camp Randall in a blinding snowstorm and marched to the station where we took the train. A vast number of Norwegians were gathered at the station to say farewell to husbands, sons, brothers, and sweethearts; when the train left, there was waving of hats and handkerchiefs—as one might expect. The locomotive had not gone very far before we got stuck in the snow. An extra engine had to be brought up to help pull us out. In the evening we arrived at Chicago, where it rained, making the streets full of mud. We marched up to the courthouse, where we were met by Chicago Norwegians who presented us with a beautiful silk flag. We already had two flags (regimental colors and battle flag)—so now we had three. This flag was American with the Norwegian lion on it.[3] After these ceremonies we marched back to the train, and there the Norwegians treated us to coffee, for which we were very thankful.

Now we were off again, and came to Alton, Illinois, the next day at 7 o'clock in the evening. We marched through the town to the steamer wharf where, on the morning of March 4 we went aboard a very large boat, the "Alton," which took us down the Mississippi, reaching St. Louis at 11 o'clock that forenoon. There we transferred to another large steamer that took us to Cairo, Ill., where we arrived at 7 o'clock in the morning of March 6. Now we were ordered to cross the Mississippi to Bird's Point, Missouri. After arriving there, we marched a distance of three miles and were then arranged in line of battle, as an enemy regiment was located nearby. We stormed forward but, when we came within range of them, the rebels took to their heels as quickly as possible. Thus there was no opportunity for a fray, but we pursued them seven miles and took several prisoners. We stayed there some days, guarding a railroad that runs south from St. Louis. This first skirmish gave us courage. If the Southern soldiers were all as frightened as these fellows, the war would soon be over!

We marched back to the river and encamped for several days. On March 14 Commodore [Andrew] Foote arrived with his fleet of gunboats for the purpose of opening the Mississippi to traffic. We were ordered aboard a steamer which was to accompany the fleet. The first town we reached was Columbus, Kentucky. We met no resistance despite the fact that a strong fortress was located there. Continuing downstream we came to Hickman [Kentucky] at 7 o'clock, without meeting any opposition. Here the 15th Wisconsin and the 42nd Illinois regiments were ordered ashore. We marched nine miles into the country, where we burned a railway bridge and tore up a stretch of the railroad three miles long, and returned to Hickman the following morning. Three thousand rebel troops were located beyond the said bridge; we burned it to prevent them from coming to Hickman. On the 15th we proceeded down the river and around 11 o'clock we were fired at by some Southern gunboats, and a few shots were exchanged. But then they pulled back to Island No. 10, pursued by our boats until they came within a mile and a half of the island.[4] Our gunboats began firing; but there was no return fire, presumably because the enemy wanted to lure us closer, since their guns could not carry as far as ours. For three days our flotilla continued throwing bombs into the enemy camp. Then our men became impatient with this long wait; one of our ironclads was sent half a mile farther down the river. Now the enemy opened fire, blazing away so we could see water spurting all around the little gunboat; but it returned unharmed. The rest of the gunboats also took part in the bombarding, but apparently it had no effect.

We now had Kentucky to the east of us and Missouri to the west. We were put ashore on the west bank of the river to keep the rebels from coming into Missouri. From our outposts we could see the enemy soldiers and their fortifications; but we could not tell how strong they were. We estimated, however, that there might be between 2,000 and 3,000 of them and that they had somewhere between 20 and 30 large cannons besides some small ones. The Mississippi was very high that spring, so the lowlands were flooded. We had to wade through cold water reaching above our knees in order to find higher ground where we could stand guard. This was tough on us who were not yet inured to such hardships. Many became sick and had to be sent to hospitals in the North. Our men were not inactive on the Kentucky side either. They were busy digging a canal toward Tiptonville [Tennessee], fifteen miles distant, to allow some gunboats to get south of the island. But before the canal was finished, the water-level in the river fell, making their efforts seem futile. . . . On March 31 we were ordered back to the boat that had brought us down. It took us six miles up to Hickman. Here we were put ashore; and we set off on a twelve-mile march inland, where we pitched camp for the night. Everything had to be done quietly and we were not permitted to light a fire.

At four o'clock in the morning, the march continued for three miles. There we found the enemy guard asleep and took him prisoner. We had arrived at a large plain and could see the Confederate camp at the opposite edge. Three cannons we had brought along were put in place and discharged, so we saw pieces of the tents flying in the air. Then we rushed forward. It seemed as if the enemy managed to get one company placed in battle order; but when we drew near and fired a salvo, they took to their heels. We captured several prisoners and seventy horses and mules besides some wagons, and then set fire to the camp. After this engagement, we went back with our booty by the same road we came; but before we reached our camp we were attacked by some of the rebel cavalry, which fired away at us. We held them at bay, however, and arrived unharmed. There we got help from a regiment stationed at Hickman and drove the enemy back. This happened at Union City [Tennessee]. Thus ended the second skirmish with the enemy, and we thought things were going real well—we began feeling like the old Vikings who never shunned a fight. Now we boarded the steamer again and went back to our old camping place two miles above Island No. 10.[5]

April 1862

After our expedition to Union City we remained quiet until April 7. Except for the regular guard duties we did not have anything to do. When on guard duty, we were called out at 7 o'clock in the morning and were relieved at the same time the following morning. Three men were stationed at each post; we mounted guard two hours and then were free four hours. In the meantime our gunboats had been bombarding for three weeks, but there were no indications that the enemy would surrender—something had to be done. Our men had placed a barge or flatboat by the side of a gunboat and piled up a mass of cotton bales to guard its exposed side; and now they waited for an opportune time, or a stormy night, so they could launch an attack. In the evening of April 7 a terrible storm broke loose with thunder and rain. Then [Lucius] Fairchild, who later became governor of Wisconsin, took four men along in a little boat and let it float with the stream until they reached the island. He got up to the fortifications and spiked six of the largest cannons so they could not be fired. All the men came back unharmed. Now we let the protected gunboat float down the river until it got past the island. A hole was shot through its funnel, as the enemy detected it when it was alongside the island, but they were unable to inflict any serious damage. Soon the gunboat fired the predetermined signals and began bombarding. Immediately, the gunboats above the island also opened fire—a pandemonium broke loose, the likes of which we had never heard. This continued until the break of day; then we spied the white flag which signaled that the enemy had surrendered. Thereupon the whole flotilla went downstream. The 15th Wisconsin and the 42nd Illinois regiments were landed on the island. We captured 500 men who had not managed to escape across the river. The 42nd was left on the island to guard the prisoners until we could send them up north. Our regiment was sent across the Mississippi to take care of things there; but some of us marched upcountry and took a number of stragglers captive. Here it may be of interest to note that General John Pope, with 20,000 men, came down through Missouri to New Madrid [Missouri] and Tiptonville, crossed the Mississippi and went into Tennessee, where he met the fleeing rebels from Island No. 10 and took all of them prisoner—about 14,000 men....[6] Our booty on the island was 90 large cannons and ten small ones as well as a large storehouse with provisions, a pharmacy, and a clothing store. We could not use the clothes, but they came in handy for the Negroes. The rebels also left a great amount of ammunition behind them. This happened on April 8th.

After our victory we set up our tents and fixed things up on the campground, which was referred to as the Tennessee Shore. The boundary-line between Tennessee and Kentucky runs here; we were in the state of Tennessee. We began gathering up things the rebels had left, such as guns, shells, axes, hoes, besides some small cannons. The rebels had made the rifles unfit for use and the vents in the cannons had been spiked; but the rifles could be repaired and the vents bored open. Everything was sent up north. Our doctor, Hansen, took charge of the pharmacy.[7] The cannons we had taken on the island had also been spiked by driving steel bars into the vents. They, likewise, had to be bored open before they could be used.

While we were moving the pharmacy, two boys drank from a bottle that they thought contained whisky. They became so sick that we had to bring them to the hospital. There both of them died within a few hours. They belonged to our regiment, but I regret that I remember neither their names nor the company to which they belonged. At that time it did not enter my mind that such facts might later seem important.

We repaired the entrenchments the rebels had left, and cleaned up both there and in our camp. Our only duty now was to take our turns as guards, which did not occur very frequently. Jens Andersen, N. K. Landrew, and I took a trip out into the country to pass the time away. We called on many farmers, who had fine houses and seemed to be prosperous; but they were afraid of us. At first they would not even speak to us, but after a while we got their tongues loosened. We found that there were a couple of brothers in the community who lived only two and a half miles from our camp. They were named Prinze and were of German descent. We got some buttermilk to drink and wanted to pay them; but when they saw our money they shook their heads and said "No good." Silver or gold was what they wanted. At the time we had nothing but paper money—5, 10, 25, and 50-cent bills called shinplasters. We thanked them for their kindness and went back to our lines.

On April 17, which happened to be Maundy Thursday, we were ordered to move over onto the island, because it was rumored that our gunboats had been in an engagement with the enemy down by Memphis and were forced to withdraw up the river. We began building fortifications at the lower end of the island and managed to get six large guns in position. However, we were soon informed that our gunboats had been able to hold the enemy back. Nevertheless, we practiced with the cannons and were prepared to receive the enemy in case they should come. My company (I) had three cannons to man and Company G also had three. The other companies continued digging across the lower end of the island, where several more small guns were emplaced. When this work was practically completed, we had nothing to do but take our turns at guard duty every third day. On Sunday forenoon we had religious services and dress parade in the afternoon.

June 1862

We had a great store of ammunition—which we had taken from the enemy—at the upper end of the island. This we moved to our new fortifications; and now we were ready to receive the rebels if they came. But so far our troops had held them back.

On June 11 eight companies from our regiment went up the Mississippi. Their destination was unknown to us; companies G and I remained behind—for how long, we did not know. We really wished to go with the rest of the regiment because this was a very unhealthful place, and when we had remained in the same location a while we got tired of it and wished to get a move on and engage in some skirmishes with the enemy. We were also bored with the rations we received: hardtack, salt pork, beans, rice, coffee, tea, and sugar. So we got to wondering if we might have a bit of a change—at least some milk for our coffee. Well, Jens

Andersen, N. K. Landrew, and I went out to one of the Prinzes and asked if we could exchange coffee, tea, or salt for milk, butter, and eggs. "No," he said with a gruff voice, "I don't want to have anything to do with those damned Yankees. It's best for you to skip the country." Fortunately, his daughter Annie heard this brusque talk of his. She came and told us that they had milk, butter, and eggs for sale—if they could only get good money for it. But we had only paper money of the sort we had when last we were there. Then she asked if we had flour; if so, they might accept flour, salt, or tea. Well yes, we knew that our quartermaster, Ole Heg— brother of the colonel—had some flour in the storehouse. We figured if we could only get hold of some of that, then there would be a trade. Of course, we could not do anything this time; but we did get three quarts of sweet milk on condition that we would later bring some tea.

Next day it was our turn to fetch rations, and we asked Ole if we could get flour instead of hardtack. Ole could not agree to this; but we could get corn meal: He had lots of that, he said. This was no news to us, because the storehouse was about full of the stuff when we took the place. We told him that we had a good baker in our company and we wished for wheat bread once in a while. Nothing helped, however. We went back to our quarters without provisions—but returned with our rifles and asked what he would prefer, either to give us flour or to sit on the points of our bayonets. He chose the former alternative. Now we fixed up an oven; and Herman Andersen, a baker from Christiania, baked bread for us of the very best quality. We still lacked butter; so we took a twenty-five pound sack of flour, some tea, and a bag of salt out to the Prinze farm and traded for a large lump of butter and an eight-quart pail full of milk. After this, we went out there twice a week for trading, so we had butter, eggs, and milk at all times. Annie had a sister named Kate. A brother of Mr. Prinze lived half a mile away who also had a daughter named Annie and a son who was in the Confederate Army. By now we had become well acquainted and were good friends. They often came to our camp with vegetables—and now our money was good enough for them. Furthermore, they could not secure any supplies except from the northern states.

On the 24th we moved over to Tennessee Shore, where a cavalry regiment was stationed. There were rumors afloat that some "bushwhackers" were in the neighborhood.[8] Presumably this was the reason we were moved. Fifteen men remained on the island to take care of the cannons.

The next day the cavalry and we took a swing of some five or six miles into the country, but we saw no bushwhackers. We did, however, see many slaves plowing with mules in the cornfields. There were so many stumps that they could hardly get between them. This was a forest area with very large woods. The trees were cut down and burned, leaving the stumps standing. A Negro girl was standing looking at us. We asked what her name was, and received the answer: "Topsy Massa Williams."

July 1862

On July 1st I was doing guard duty. This did not happen as often here as on the island. There were six posts, which were alternated between the members of companies G and I and the cavalry, so guard duty did not occur very frequently. During the night of the 3rd two men from Company A skipped jail, where they had been sitting more than a month for having stolen silverware from a house that they had happened upon. Now some of us were to go in search of them. Arne Thorkelsen and I set off with rifles on our shoulders, taking the road toward the Prinze farm where we were acquainted. Here we learned that two soldiers had been there that morning, and we were told which direction they had taken. We went on until we came to a crossroads, where we met some of the cavalry men and told them which direction we thought the fugitives had taken, namely toward the north. They set off northward at full gallop, caught the culprits, and brought them back to camp. They were sent to Cairo by the first boat, after which we heard no more of them.

On the 4th, whiskey was doled out to all of us. We got about three shots apiece; but this whiskey was so bad and evil-smelling that I could not down it. So I sold it for twenty-five cents. That evening many fellows got so drunk and crazy that they had to be thrown into the guardhouse to sleep off their intoxication. Next morning they were set free. On the 9th I was sent back to the island to take the place of someone who had become ill. Our hospital was located on the island—a great number were confined there with sickness while other members of the regiment had been sent to hospitals in the North. It was stupid of me not to get their names. I had to mount guard the evening I arrived on the island. The weather was terrible with rain and thunder; and the heat was so intense that it was impossible to sleep. There were eighteen of us on the island, as three who had been sick had recovered sufficiently to be on duty.

Those of us who remained on the island agreed that each one should take turns cooking for one week, because there was no regular cook. On the 16th day my turn came around. I accepted the challenge; and the first thing I did was to clean up the cook shack and put everything in order. Of course, there was not much to cook: beans, rice, pork for frying, smoked ham, and pork for boiling. But there were two cows that came about quite often. I started milking them, and thus could prepare rice "velling" every noon.[9] The boys thought this hit the spot. We got bread from Andersen on the other side of the river. In the hospital was a woman who had come down to care for her sick husband. She was kind enough to teach me how to make doughnuts and cookies. Now we were living high—and I continued cooking the whole month. While on this job, I was relieved of guard duty and also of drilling, except on Sundays. When the eight companies left, the chaplain went with them. Hence we had no chaplain and consequently no religious services.[10]

August 1862

I continued as cook for the time being. On August 2nd we received orders to dismantle all the cannons at the fort. Our gunboats had sunk some of the Confederate gunboats and driven the rest down the river, so now the island was no longer in danger; and everything was quiet. We had nothing to do but mount guard, and there was very little of this as only one post remained. On the 16th a company of engineers arrived who brought all the cannons and all the ammunition as well as a large supply of cartridges down to the wharf.

On the 19th Jens Andersen returned. He had been home on sick leave but was now well again. On the 21st we were on the Tennessee Shore to receive four months' pay, for March, April, May, and June. The next day a couple of boys and I went to the Prinze farm to buy butter and eggs. We were there frequently while we were stationed on the island, so we were supplied with butter and eggs. On the 27th a steamer arrived, hauled the cannons aboard and took them down the Mississippi to be used at the siege of Vicksburg. Two days later our lieutenant, Finn Gassman, went home on sick leave. The same day we were told that a great battle had been fought at Fort Donelson, but nothing was said about the outcome. We were also informed that some rebel troops were on their way to take our camping place on the Tennessee Shore; so our cavalry set off to meet them and drive them back.

On the 30th, two gunboats and five steamers went down the river to Memphis for the purpose of exchanging prisoners with the Southerners. The following day our cavalry returned with ten prisoners. One of our soldiers was badly wounded and was sent up to Cairo, Illinois. Company G took part in this fight, which lasted two hours. They beat the enemy and put them to flight.

September 1862

On the 7th we moved over to Tennessee Shore, leaving only the hospital and some slave-refugees on the island. From New Madrid came reports that the enemy had taken possession of the town, so the cavalry, the artillery, and Company G were ordered to go there—eleven miles north of the island. On the 11th they returned after having had a skirmish with the enemy and driven them off. The next day six steamers went down the river with prisoners to be exchanged. On the 13th, Company I had a competition in target shooting. Christian Olsen took first prize, Ole Westby second, and B. Nelson third. On the 25th, Company I received orders to proceed up to New Madrid, as it was rumored that bushwhackers had been in the area, plundering and stealing from people. We had a clash with them in which they lost two dead and six prisoners. Two of our men were wounded. We remained there until October 4th, but nothing of importance happened during these days. Our two wounded companions were sent to the hospital on Island No. 10, where they soon recovered.

October 1862

We returned to our camp on October 4th. On the 9th Jens Andersen and I took a little trip out into the country. When we had hiked two or three miles it began to rain, and we went into a house. The only occupants were a woman and a fourteen-year-old boy. In reply to our question as to her husband's whereabouts, she replied that he was in the employ of Jefferson Davis, and when her son was two years older he would serve Jefferson Davis. In a short while, she said, the armies of Jefferson Davis would crush the Yankees and scatter them like dust. We could not agree with her on this point, but it was not easy to say at that time how things would go because the war was still young.

We went on in the rain and decided to return to camp. We walked and we walked; but there was no camp to be seen. Then we met a man on horseback and asked where the island was located. He pointed in the opposite direction and said it was about five miles distant. Naturally, we turned about and took the same road back, past the house where we had visited. Soon we came to a place where the road forked. We could not take both roads; but the one we did take was, of course, the wrong one. After a while we saw a house by the wayside and went in for further guidance. We were informed that the road we were on led to New Madrid and that the camp was three miles away. These people were Union sympathizers and treated us very kindly. We were even invited to eat with them. After the meal we wanted to pay for the food; but no—they would not accept money. They helped us find the right road and we reached the camp toward evening. When a person first gets lost he usually continues to take the wrong direction. We were in a heavily forested area with poor roads and, since it was raining, we did not have the sun to guide us. After this nothing in particular happened until the 17th. The days went by with the ordinary camp routine.

At about four o'clock in the morning of the 17th we were awakened by rifle shots from our outpost. More shots followed, as if a whole army was in action. We were ordered into battleline and marched toward the scene of action; but when we came there everything was quiet. We searched the place and found some pistols and rifles. Fortunately for us, the enemy had made a great mistake. Their force had divided into two detachments, which were to attack us from two directions. But they had not approached close enough to the river; and when the two parties met, they mistook each other for the enemy and started blazing away. Now we took after them with the cavalry, naturally, in the lead. In a little house we found two wounded men—one mortally. The other one was not seriously wounded, so we brought him to our camp and cared for him. After a march of five miles we made contact with the enemy and a violent engagement ensured. They were 500 and we only 230; but still we took 15 prisoners, five of them officers. The rebels gave up and retreated into the woods. This flight took place on a farm with large buildings and much cultivated ground. We used the buildings as cover, otherwise we would undoubtedly have lost more men. As it was, we lost three dead and three wounded. We do not know how many men the enemy lost. In the afternoon we returned to camp with our captives, who were sent by steamer to Cairo. That evening a cavalry company came as reinforcement. On the 18th the two cavalry companies went out into the country to discover whether the rebels were still in the neighborhood, but they found no trace of them. Now things were quiet for several days.

On the 21st we received a report that 3,000 Confederate soldiers were only seven miles away and that they were heading for our camp. We were poorly prepared to receive such a force. There were two cavalry companies, totaling 160 men, besides our two Norwegian companies, also numbering 160 men. We had only one small cannon and poor entrenchments. If our encampment fell into the hands of the rebels, they would also take Island No. 10, and then all transport for General Grant's troops coming down the Mississippi would be stopped. So this was an important point to hold. We were ordered to transfer to Island No. 10. This did not take long, since we had a large steam ferry which took us across. The next day the enemy arrived; but to their great surprise we were over on the island and our little cannon began lobbing bombs at them. They left the place as quickly as they had come.

A couple of days later all the farmers round about came and complained that the rebels had taken away from them everything they had. They only wished that we would come back to the camp again so the cavalry could keep the marauders away. They even offered Companies G and I horses if we would help the cavalry keep the area clear of rebels. The people in the neighborhood had become so friendly toward us that they had more confidence in the Union soldiers than in the Southerners. It was decided that we, in combination with the cavalry, should make a sortie into the area. On the 25th we set off and took time to gather horses; by noon we were prepared. First we went toward New Madrid; but as we did not detect anything there, we continued on to Tiptonville. Some rebels had been there the previous day, so we went off in the direction they had taken but we were unable to catch up with them the first day. That night we pitched camp near a large creek. In the morning we continued on our way and by noon we came to a little town. There we found four saddled horses that belonged to these marauders, but the owners were nowhere to be seen. We then made about-face and started for our camp; but we had not gone far before a mounted man in civilian dress caught up with us and presented himself as a farmer. Our captain, however, and others among us were not satisfied with this explanation, so the man was searched. We found some papers in his possession which proved that he was a courier for General [Nathan Bedford] Forrest, who was in command of a part of the Confederate cavalry and had orders to inflict all the damage possible on the Union forces along the Mississippi.[11] We took the courier captive and shipped him up to Columbus, where he was grilled by a court martial and found guilty of treason as the leader of a band of bushwhackers. We never did learn whether he was hanged—as he probably deserved to be. Late in the evening we returned to our camp.

Now we received orders from Columbus, where our headquarters were located, to move back to Tennessee Shore and entrench ourselves. The move was made and the work begun. A great number of black refugees had arrived and were quartered on the island. Thirty large, husky Negroes were sent over to work for us. Our only responsibility was to supervise the operation. More Negroes came every day—so many, in fact, that we could not make use of them all. By the end of the month we had built barricades around more than half of the camp.

November 1862

The construction of the barricades proceeded rapidly. On the 12th an officer of the regular army came to inspect our work and it evidently met with his approval. In a week the entrenchments were completed, but then we were ordered to move back on the island since to defend our present position required too many men. On the island two companies would be sufficient. All our labors on the fortifications were therefore wasted and worthless.

The two cavalry companies that had been with us were now transferred to their respective regiments, leaving only the two 15th Wisconsin companies on the island. We had a little cannon which we fired every morning and evening—a shot at 5 a.m. to awaken everybody and a shot in the evening, signaling that it was time to go to bed. . . .

December 1862

There were robbers loose in the neighborhood so we were ordered out in search of them. After a march of some 5 or 6 miles we came to a house that six robbers were busy plundering. We took all of them prisoner and returned to the island. The prisoners were sent to Columbus. A fisherman came to the camp and began some petty trading. Things went well for a while, but then the quality of his goods began deteriorating. His tobacco, for instance, was rotten and everything else was of the cheapest kind. This stuff he sold at outrageous prices. He had also peddled beer at times, which was illegal. So we gave him the choice of either leaving the island or being arrested. He chose the first alternative.

On the 8th General [Jefferson C.] Davis, who was in command of this district, came and inspected our camp. He wanted us to move to Camp Pillow, but the captain of Company G, who was in charge on the island, advised against this, so no move was made. Nothing of importance happened for some time. We had lots of rain and one night four inches of snow fell, but it disappeared before morning. We went out to the Prinzes for butter, milk, and eggs, and at times we ate at their place—all of which was very pleasant. On the 25th, Christmas Day, we were told that a great battle had been fought below Memphis in which we had lost several gunboats; and now, so the report went, the remainder of our flotilla was coming up the river with the rebel boats in pursuit. Consequently there was great danger that the island would fall into enemy hands. But these reports were not sound. The next day we learned that the Confederates had lost three boats and our side only one. So we realized that our boats could hold the enemy in check.—About this time a member of Company G was killed by an accidental shot.

Twenty-five men of our regiment arrived in camp, fleeing from Union City, which had been retaken by the rebels. It will be remembered that we had captured this town nine months earlier and that a small garrison had been left there to protect the railway station. Union City was located 25 miles distant from the island.

Otherwise everything was quiet. From time to time boats went up or down the river. Those that went downstream brought provisions and mail to our men, while those that went upstream were usually loaded with prisoners taken from the rebels.—There were many sick men in camp. The most common illness was ague.

January 1863

Now a new year set in for us, and our sincere wish was that by next New Year's we could be at home, safe and sound. On the first day of the year we heard that Vicksburg had fallen, but this rumor proved to be erroneous. There had been a battle, to be sure, but neither side had won a victory. A boat came up the river with captive Union troops who had been released on their word of honor that they would not bear arms against the Confederacy during the remainder of the war.

On the evening of the 5th the 28th Wisconsin and the 32nd Missouri regiments stayed here overnight. They were bound for Vicksburg. In the 28th Wisconsin Regiment there were many Norwegians. They told us that the 15th had taken part in a great battle at Stone's River or Murfreesboro, and that one half of the regiment had been killed or wounded.[12] On the 8th three boats loaded with troops went down the river. On the 9th Lieutenant Christ Olsen and I were out at Prinze's place and had a good time. On the 13th a gunboat arrived to keep watch between the island and New Madrid, as bushwhackers had been firing at our boats plying the river.

The weather was very uncertain. For two weeks rain kept falling, but suddenly it turned to snow—twelve inches of it covering the ground. After that we had clear, cold days, very cold, indeed, for this part of the country. On the 25th another gunboat came and relieved the earlier one, which was sent on to Vicksburg. By now most of the snow had disappeared, as rain had again fallen. On the 30th two soldiers who had been given discharge because of illness left for home. One of them was Olaf Andersen of Company I, but I do not have the name of the other one.

February 1863

A great number of Confederate soldiers tried to come across the river from the Missouri shore during the night between February 1st and 2nd. But our guard heard something out in the water; he could not see what it was, but he shot and sounded the alarm, so we got down to the bank in a hurry and held them off until the gunboat could come to our assistance. We fired a number of shots, and so did the gunboat. In the dark, however, we could not tell whether we hit anything. The rebels fired at us also; but none of us were wounded. We heard later that the gunboat found a little boat in the river with a hole from a cannon ball in it. But none of the crew were found either living or dead. On February 2nd I had to go to the hospital because I too had been struck by fever and stomach trouble. On the 3rd five companies from the 35th Iowa Regiment came to reinforce us, but our captain sent them back the next day. He told them he had no need of them. February 5th—snow again. A member of our company, Jacob Jackson, left for home on sick leave. I remained in the hospital until the 12th, when I was tolerably well again.

On the 13th a steamer was stopped and searched. We found that it carried lots of goods intended for the Confederate army, and also 560 letters bound for the South. Many of the letters were addressed to officers and men in high positions and gave detailed information about conditions in the North and about maneuvers of the various Union armies. Sixteen of us were sent aboard the boat as guards and we took it up to Cairo where everything intended for the South was unloaded and the captain put under arrest. There was a certain suspicious-looking fellow on this boat. He wanted to leave, claiming that he lived seven miles out in the country and wished to get across the river. Our captain was willing to let him go ashore, but first he wanted to inspect the contents of the man's knapsack. This he objected to strenuously; but, of course, he had to give in. A lot of letters, addressed to higher officers, were found destined for Richmond and other places. Furthermore, there were $35,000.00 in gold, also destined for Richmond—the Confederate government there; but he claimed the sum was intended for pupils in certain Catholic schools whose fathers were in the army. Our captain, however, let him know that it was not necessary to smuggle money for such purposes as it could be sent across the line by regular mail. The man was sent up north. The captain took the papers and the money and went with him, together with three soldiers as guards.

On the 22nd a large gunboat went downstream toward Vicksburg. Nothing except the regular activities of camp life happened during the rest of the month.

March 1863

On Easter Day a Methodist pastor who traveled about preaching to the soldiers held religious services here. I suppose it is a mistake to relate that the following night we were over on the Missouri shore and stole a yearling calf which we butchered and took along to camp. The veal tasted excellent, as we had not eaten fresh meat since we left Madison.

On the 6th we had terribly bad weather with thunder and rain. On the 10th Arne Thorkelsen, N. K. Landrew, and I were over in Tennessee to the Prinze farm. We brought along wheat flour, coffee, tea, and salt, besides some cigars because these people smoked and chewed lots of tobacco, as the weed is raised in this area. Even the women smoked what they called "Ladies' Cigars." We gave cigars to the old man; he lit up immediately and blew smoke like a factory chimney. We also offered one to old Ma Prinze, but she said she feared it was too strong. Then she showed us some small cigars. "These are the ones I smoke," she said, "they are milder." The other Prinze with his wife also happened to be there, so we had to give him a cigar too. He thanks us politely and smoked with gusto. Well, we figured that the girls should also have a cigar apiece; they accepted the offer and lit up. Naturally we had to join in; so there we all sat, puffing away until the room was so full of smoke that doors and windows had to be thrown open. The girls thought these cigars were pretty potent, but by taking brief periods of rest from time to time they managed very well. It was too cold to sit outside.

Then we did our trading, and we were ready to leave since it was past one o'clock. —But no—we should stay for dinner. Old Ma said that Annie would soon have the biscuits ready so the wait would not be very long. The flour we brought came in handy, she said, because they had not had any for a couple of weeks. They had lived on cornmeal all the time. —Now the food was ready and we had an excellent meal!

On the 11th a gunboat again went down the river toward Vicksburg. It was built in Ohio and was reinforced with railroad rails while the superstructure resembled a flat-roofed house. On the top was a deck where the captain had his quarters. The boat had a crew of 100 men. The rails were so arranged that they formed a plain wall, causing the balls to glance off when they made contact. Both ends of the boat were similarly protected. There were six gunports along the sides and a large cannon at each end. The balls for the latter weighed 30 pounds while the other cannons took 24-pound balls. The rail reinforcement extended two feet below the waterline before the boat was laded. These gunboats were flat-bottomed because they were designed for use on the Mississippi where there is much shallow water.

On the 12th we were ordered to proceed to Tennessee, as marauders were again on the loose. Twelve men from Company G and a similar number from Company I went out into the country some six or seven miles. A man whom we met said that some bushwhackers were eating in a house close by. We stole off as silently as we could, surrounded the house, and captured all of them (eight in number), as well as their horses, without firing a shot.

On the 13th we received pay for four months. We always had a backlog of eight months coming to us. On the 14th we fished two cannons out of the river that the rebels had sunk when they left the island. They were twelve-pounders (that is, designed to fire balls weighing twelve pounds). We cleaned and polished them until they looked really good; but as we did not have the right kind of balls we could not use them. Later they were sent to Vicksburg.

Now I was on the sicklist again and went to see the doctor every day; but after four days I had recovered sufficiently so I could resume my duties.

All was quiet the rest of the month.

[April, 1863]

In the early part of the month a great number of Negro families came here. There were about 400. They came from the neighborhood of Vicksburg and had fled when our troops had conquered the area and told them that they were free and could go wherever they wished. They came northward in droves so as not to be exposed to mistreatment by the Southerners. The island had been occupied by a farmer before the war. We found several buildings in the locality and about 30 or 40 acres of cultivated ground. Besides this there were some 100 acres which could be cleared. As Uncle Sam had to feed all these black folks, something had to be done. Therefore, a farmer was sent down from the North. He got the Negroes together—everyone from 16 years up to old cripples—and prepared a roster of their names. Some were put to work digging the dirt away from the roots of the large trees and clearing away the underbrush. Others were set to plowing the ground as it was cleared. We had an oversupply of mules, while plows and harrows were sent down from the North. Potatoes, corn, and all sorts of vegetables were planted. The foreman needed "bosses"—practically a boss for every Negro; we knew the Negroes from the time we had them working on the fortifications. Many of the soldiers became bosses, so the work went better than one might have expected. The things produced were useful for both the soldiers and others. A large tent was also set up that was to be used as a schoolhouse, and a teacher came down from Chicago to teach these colored people.

On the 8th it was a year since our company came to the island—94 men, strong and healthy. Now there were 76 of us—many weak and sick. Three had died on the island; the others had been sent north, either to their homes or to hospitals. Company G lost the same number of men. Today we were told that Charleston, South Carolina, had been taken, but later we learned that the report was false. Nothing further of importance happened during the month. On the 21st we were given four months' pay: $52.00 in paper money, each dollar worth $.65 in gold.

May 1863

After sickness had long made a weakling of me the doctor said it would be best for me to go home for a while. On the 8th I went by boat to Cairo, which cost me a dollar; from there I took the train to Chicago, which set me back $6.50; from there to Sparta cost me $5.40; and then I took the mail coach to Eau Claire, where I arrived on the 14th. This cost me another $5.00. There was no railway to Eau Claire at that time. I stayed at the Eau Claire Hotel overnight, and then went to see Doctor Galloway. He was the only doctor in town and I had to report to him. He gave me a flask of medicine which cost me a dollar—and did me no good whatsoever.

My home was eleven miles from town; but, fortunately, I met a farmer who had a yoke of oxen, and with him I got a ride for nine miles, leaving only two miles to walk. I arrived home late in the evening of the 15th. During the first four days at home I was attacked harder by ague than I had been down South. But it eased up, and I began to recover rapidly. I had weighed 200 pounds when I came to Madison in the fall of 1861, while now I weighed only 165 pounds. But it did not take long for me to improve; in a week's time I was able to visit friends in the neighborhood, and I also went to see the doctor in Eau Claire. I did not have much time left, as the sick-permit was only for thirty days—and now the end of May had already come.

June 1863

The doctor prolonged my leave and on the 15th he sent me to Madison where I was to remain until I became strong enough to rejoin my company. I arrived in Madison on the 18th—which cost me $9.75.

August 1863

I stayed in the hospital until the 4th. By then I was well enough to rejoin my company; and I came to camp on the 7th—at a cost of $10.75. I found everything on the island in about the same shape as when I had left for home.

September 1863

Now we received orders to rejoin our regiment, which was near Chattanooga, Tennessee. On the 6th companies G and I left the island, taking a steamer up the Mississippi to Cairo and then up the Ohio to Louisville, Kentucky, where we arrived on the 10th. We stayed there a couple of days and had an opportunity to meet Captain "Charlie"—a woman who had been captain of a cavalry company until she was wounded and sent to a hospital, where it was discovered that she was a woman. Then she resigned her commission and was given a post as accountant at Headquarters in Louisville. We left by train for Nashville on the 12th, arriving there the same day. Two days later we left for Chattanooga and reached there on the 19th. Between Nashville and Chattanooga we had to march long distances because many bridges had been burned and the railway destroyed. Our troops had driven the enemy away from this area a short while before and had not yet repaired the railroad.

When we arrived at Chattanooga on the 19th a great battle was being fought at Chickamauga, seven miles away. We were kept here in reserve in case the Confederates should drive our forces back. According to reports, our men had the advantage during the first day of battle. The fighting continued the next day and our forces drove the enemy back three miles; but then the rebels were reinforced by General [James] Longstreet with 20,000 Virginians. He managed to split our lines in two by rushing into an opening left when one of our divisions was moved to another part of the field. General [George Henry] Thomas, however, who commanded our left wing, held the enemy in check and thus saved the army. Because of this feat he was called "the Rock of Chickamauga." The 15th took part in this battle. Our troops fell back to the positions they had held the previous morning, where they had entrenchments. On the 21st we [companies G and I] marched out seven miles and found the army drawn up in line of battle, awaiting the enemy—but they did not come, so nothing developed except outpost skirmishes.

Our commanding general, Rosecrans, became frightened and fled to Chattanooga and sent a telegram to the government saying that his whole army was destroyed.

When we rejoined our regiment on the 21st there were not many men left—not a hundred. We numbered 156 men, so now there was a total of about 250 left out of almost 1,000. Our colonel, Heg, had been advanced to brigadier general, but he was mortally wounded in the battle and died two hours after he was brought to the hospital in Chattanooga. Our lieutenant colonel, Ole C. Johnson, was taken prisoner, while many other officers and privates were either killed or captured. The Union forces lost a total of 16,971 men in this battle.

General Thomas regarded our position as difficult to hold if the enemy should outflank either of our wings and reach Chattanooga, because then they would take all our provisions and ammunition, of which there were large stores. Therefore he decided to fall back to Chattanooga. In the evening of the 21st the retreat began and, since our corps brought up the rear, we did not enter Chattanooga until early morning. Then we began building breastworks by cutting down large trees and stacking them on top of each other to a height of three feet. Behind the breastworks we dug trenches six feet wide and piled the dirt against the wall of logs we had prepared.

Thus we had built breastworks from the Tennessee River along Lookout Mountain and over Lookout Valley as well as along the foot of Missionary Ridge to the Tennessee River above Chattanooga. Our lines were now seven miles long. A couple of days after our arrival, the Confederate army came and took up positions a short distance from us. Their general, Bragg, discovered that we had ensconced ourselves and dared not risk an assault against our positions; but then he got the notion that he would starve us out. It seemed as if he might do exactly that because he took Lookout Mountain and the railroad west of the ridge, thus cutting the lines of communication with our supply stations. Rosecrans had, however, built pontoon bridges across the Tennessee River; but this made it necessary to cross mountains and deep valleys in order to fetch provisions from Stevenson, Alabama, 70 miles away.

Before proceeding further, I want to say a bit about our way of life in those days.

A short distance outside our entrenchments there was a stream from which both we and the rebels fetched water. The pickets had agreed beforehand that no one who came for water should bring his rifle along. Soon we began trading coffee and to some extent salt for tobacco and finally we also exchanged newspapers. As a rule we had more coffee and salt than we needed and they seemed to have a superfluous amount of tobacco, so the trading became quite brisk at times. It did not take long, however, before this came to a stop. One day an officer and two privates from our brigade were taken captive. When they arrived at the stream, there was a Confederate soldier present; and while they were talking six armed rebels came out of the bushes and arrested them. Thereupon the trading ceased.

During this period lots of "teams" were sent after provisions. There were thirty wagons, each pulled by six mules. Of course a guard was to go along with this caravan, and the 15th Wisconsin was ordered to perform that duty. Now we had good days, because we found enough to eat. On the way out to Stevenson we rode in the empty wagons because they drove so fast that it was impossible for us to keep up with them on foot. In the forenoon of the first day out we stopped by a stream. Two or three of us went a little way upstream and found a lot of hogs there. Naturally, we killed a hundred-pounder and took him along. We had hardtack in the wagons; so now we made coffee, fried pork, and ate like kings. The owner of the hog came and demanded to be paid. We offered him a dollar bill of the new greenbacks, but he believed it was counterfeit and handed it back: he wanted silver coin, of which we did not have any. When it was time for us to leave, the man stood there looking at us without getting any pay for his hog.

The next day we reached Stevenson. It took us a couple of days to load up; and we came back to camp on October 8.

October [and November] 1863

By then hunger had already begun to announce itself among the soldiers. We had our bags full of hardtack and smoked pork, which we shared with our comrades as long as we had any. The next day provisions were doled out. A couple of days later, the caravan was to set off again; and again the 15th Wisconsin was sent along as guards. This time we had rain, so it took us longer than last time. An ammunition train that left Stevenson the day before we did was attacked by General [Nathan Bedford] Forrest's cavalry. The rebels drove the guards away, took with them what they could carry, and set fire to the rest. The cadavers of the horses were still smoldering when we arrived. This was at the foot of a hill and we could see some mounted men on the heights above us. Our force was divided—some men going in the lead and the rest bringing up the rear. We started up the hill; and when we were halfway, they began shooting at us; but they shot over us so not a single man was hurt. We returned fire and reloaded as we stormed up the hill. Then they took flight and we saw no more of them. We met no further resistance and reached Chattanooga in good shape.

The 15th did not accompany the next caravan to Stevenson. We were moved a little farther out toward the left. The entrenchments there were in poor condition, so we had to get busy improving them. We built a fort which we called Fort Wood, thus honoring the general of our division. Reinforcements were now arriving as General Sherman joined us with his corps and assumed a position on the left flank.

General [Joseph] Hooker with his corps—reinforced by both cavalry and artillery—took up a position to the west of Lookout Mountain. General Grant "himself" arrived and took command of our forces, which were now arranged as follows: General Sherman's corps on the left flank, then General Thomas's corps, then [James] McPherson's, and finally [John M.] Schofield's corps. The line of battle was seven miles long and we had about 80,000 men while the Confederates had about 60,000. On the 22nd General Hooker was ordered to attack. First he took the railway and then continued up the west slope of Lookout Mountain, reaching the top before sundown. General Schofield's corps hammered away at the rebels on the east slope of the mountain and succeeded in making good progress the first day. The advance guards along the whole line were dislodged during the first day of fighting. It was our brigade that drove the outposts back along our front and we stood guard there all night. The next morning the whole line of battle arrived and we were relieved and sent back to be held as reserves at the entrenchments. Our troops stormed the first barricades and also the second line of defense, but they were driven back at the third. The fighting there was hard. Our men rushed forward several times, but every time they had to fall back on the entrenchments that our forces had previously taken from the rebels. Here they had to rest for a while.

Then came our turn. We marched up, joined the line, and stormed up Missionary Ridge; we put the enemy troops between a double fire as we managed to get behind two entrenchments and captured both the men and the cannons. There were three cannons in each barricade and six men with each cannon. The rest of the men fled, so we caught no more prisoners. Many of our men fell in this encounter and many were wounded. I was wounded by a grenade splinter in the left hip, but not seriously enough to keep me from staying behind with the regiment. A comrade who was immediately behind me was wounded by the same splinter and was sent to the hospital, but he rejoined us in a couple of weeks.

By now the railway was again open so we received both provisions and ammunition—all we needed.

Then we learned that General [James] Longstreet with his corps was headed toward Knoxville to recapture this city, which General [Ambrose Everett] Burnside, one of our officers, had wrested from the Southern forces. Longstreet's objective was to take Knoxville, then continue up through Kentucky and enter Ohio. But General Thomas did not let him slip away as easily as that. After getting three days' rations in our bags we set off in pursuit under the command of General Thomas. A two days march brought us to Loudon, where we were supposed to cross the Tennessee, but the bridge was burned and the enemy was on the other side of the river. Consequently we had to march two or three miles downstream, where we found some boats and barges, and after a while we were across. The cavalry swam their horses through the river. Then upstream we went, but to our surprise the enemy had pulled out, so there was no fighting. We set off in pursuit and caught up with their forces the next day. A bit of a skirmish ensued with their rear guard, consisting of mounted men. Our cavalry soon put them to flight, but then we learned that this was merely a minor part of Longstreet's force—a detachment left there to prevent General Thomas from beating Longstreet to Knoxville. General Thomas, however, made a detour, thus bypassing this force and leaving it in peace. We marched both day and night, taking only short snatches of rest, and reached Knoxville on December 7th.

December 1863

We arrived just in time because Longstreet was there already, laying siege to the city. A fight ensued; but when Longstreet discovered that General Thomas had come with reinforcements, he withdrew toward the east. General Thomas followed in his tracks to keep him from heading north. The distance from Chattanooga to Knoxville is 130 miles.

Here I must remark that when Thomas set off in pursuit of Longstreet, our brigade and a cavalry company were sent back fifteen miles to a little town called Maryville because rebels were there tearing up the railway. The railway was in usable condition between Chattanooga and Knoxville except across the Tennessee River at Loudon, where goods had to be transported in boats or barges. Some Negroes wearing white pants were there building a bridge. Two locomotives and some freight cars were located in Knoxville when Burnside captured the city.

When we arrived at Maryville the rebels had already torn up some two or three miles of track. But when we came, they fled without offering any resistance. We pursued them about five miles, then returned and remained in Maryville a couple of days, then left for Knoxville. The cavalry corps remained to guard the railway.

At Knoxville provisions were scarce, as nothing came over the railroad and wagons did not get through either. Generally we had to provide for ourselves. There was no food in the city so the soldiers went hungry. Consequently we—our brigade, that is—decided to leave and struck out for Blain's Crossroad. From there an expedition consisting of two wagons was sent out to a prosperous farmer. These wagons were of the large government type, each pulled by six mules. The 15th Wisconsin went along as guards. You may well ask if our regiment always served as guards. Yes—because the 15th was always willing and never begged off. It was respected as a regiment that could always be depended on and could not be held back in thick or thin, as the phrase goes. Our destination lay some ten or twelve miles off the main highway. We bought two loads of corn and one load of syrup and smoke-cured pork. In payment the farmer was given a check drawn on the nearest quartermaster department, located at Chattanooga. Now we were ready for the return trip; but first the officers were going to have something to eat. It was a raw, cold day so some of us went into the kitchen while we were waiting. There was no chance of us getting anything to eat—there were too many of us, so we had to be content with gnawing away at some Indian corn. A fat colored woman was there baking biscuits for the officers. We were on guard here too. When the biscuits were about finished we opened the oven door and took them out. There was a crock in a corner which I thought contained buttermilk; so I filled my cup and went out and sat down. A fellow named Colby followed me; and after him came a string of others, all with their biscuits and brimming cups. But we discovered that it was not buttermilk—it was genuine cream; so at last we got ourselves a really good meal. When the cook came to take the biscuits out of the oven she naturally got a shock and, of course, had to bake more biscuits. Now one of the officers was given the job of guarding the kitchen. Our lieutenant came out and said we should feel ashamed of ourselves— which we did, as well as we could manage. Nevertheless it was a comfort for us to know that we now had the biscuits and the cream well taken care of.

The farmer had two barrels of syrup (sorghum) and a lot of hams left in his smokehouse—with the door securely locked. We pretended that we wanted to buy some of this stuff even though we had no money. But no, he could not sell any more. We insisted that we wanted some for ourselves, as the supplies in the wagons were intended for the army. He was adamant, however. Then we broke open the lock, went in and rolled out a barrel of syrup and filled our water canteens. Each one of us also spitted a ham on the end of his bayonet; and thus equipped, with rifles on shoulders, we sauntered off homeward.

At Blain's Crossroad we took command of a mill and ground our corn. So now we lived in great style on cornbread, syrup, and ham. As Christmas was approaching, I suppose we deserved to have something good to eat. On Christmas Day we received orders to break camp and be on the march—not a long one, however, merely five miles to Strawberry Plains on the Holston River where the bridge had been burned. Our regiment was given the job of building a new one because there were all sorts of craftsmen among us.

January 1864

On January 20th the bridge was completed and a locomotive crossed over, so everything was in good shape. The bridge at Loudon was also finished. Thus the railroad was in order from Chattanooga to a point twenty miles east of Strawberry Plains—where the larger part of General Thomas's corps was located. Now we were sent coffee, sugar, rice, and hardtack. Beef and pork we had to scrounge for ourselves. And this we did, because the area was full of cattle and swine. When we were on the march and evening came we always had a cow along for butchering or some sheep or a hog which we had killed and carried with us. We could never bring live hogs because they always wanted to take off in the wrong direction. There was usually a flock of hens and geese gathered together when we pitched camp in the evening.

On the 21st we left Strawberry Plains for Dandridge, where generals Thomas and Longstreet were in each others' hair. Longstreet learned that Thomas had received reinforcements from Knoxville—but it was only our little brigade that came to Thomas's assistance. Nevertheless, Longstreet left the field and struck out for Knoxville; but Thomas knew his plans very well because these two generals had been fighting each other more or less for two years. So we trekked back again along the railroad and crossed the bridge we had built, which we now burned, and made for Knoxville in quick march. Of course Longstreet was there, but on the other side of the Holston River. General Thomas crossed over and drove the enemy through Tennessee into Virginia. Leaving a part of the army behind, we started back toward Knoxville, where we arrived two days later.

Now the question arose whether the regiment would enlist for another three years. If we did, we would be granted a home leave of thirty days. All of us re-enlisted and on January 28 we started for home. The first day we reached Maryville (15 miles); the second day, Morgantown (18 miles); and on the third, Loudon (13 miles).

February 1864

While we were peacefully sleeping at Loudon during the night preceding Feb. 1st, we were aroused by orders to hurry back to a certain railway station where rebels were tearing up the tracks. Thus we were not free as yet to go home. Early in the morning we marched six miles to Lenoir station (the place in question) where some bushwhackers had burned a little bridge and torn up a piece of the track. We killed two of them and wounded four others. The rest managed to escape. We repaired the tracks and the bridge, and then a cavalry detachment came to guard the station.

On the 6th we left Lenoir for another station and the next day we proceeded to Maryville.

Our brigade and two other brigades of our division were now at Maryville, so Wood's whole force was assembled there. As we had no food left, we had to go in search of something to eat. A number of wagons were sent out and the 15th Wisconsin went along as guards. We proceeded some twenty miles from the railway and quite a distance from the main highway because there was nothing to be had near these much frequented thoroughfares. Many of the people had been forced to leave their homes for other places in order to get something to live on. We came, however, to areas where we could buy provisions, and the next day we began loading the wagons. As we could not get a full load from any single farmer we had to visit several places—all of which took us several days. We had nine wagons, three of which were for our brigade. Next we took control of a mill in Maryville that belonged to an old fellow; and now some men were set to unload the wagons and carry the corn into the mill, others had to do the shelling, while still others had to help the miller. Thus the grinding went on. These mills down South were much like the mills we had in the little streams in Norway.—Well, now we had food for a while.

Next we were given orders to march to Knoxville, where we arrived on February 16. We had been told that rebels were about to take the city, but we saw no enemies even though we went east, west, and north of the city. We had not seen any rebels since we were at Lenoir Station. On the 20th the paymaster arrived and gave us two months' pay. On the 24th we left Knoxville, marching sixteen miles that day and three miles the next— and so we were again at Strawberry Plains. We gave chase to a bunch of Bushwhackers who came from the east and tried to evade us and go north. We crossed the Holston River in boats and barges, not bothering to build a bridge this time. A march of nine miles took us to New Madrid from where we continued on to Morristown.[13] Then, at last, we caught up with the marauders, coming on them so suddenly that they were unable to form a line of battle. They jumped on their horses, and off they went with our cavalry in pursuit and we following them. But the rebels took an easterly course and disappeared among the mountains along the border between Tennessee and North Carolina.

March 1864

On March 2nd we arrived at the pass where the railroad enters North Carolina. Here the enemy made a stand, but we attacked them, killed several men, and bagged sixty-three prisoners. The rest took to the mountains. We then returned to Strawberry Plains, arriving on the 4th. Here a group of men were busy restoring the bridge over the Holston River a second time. We were now given clothing and shoes, which we sorely needed. Food was also distributed.

Our regiment was again given an opportunity to receive home leave on condition that we re-enlist for three more years. But it did not work this time. We had once been forty miles on our way homeward, only to be called back. We did not want any more of this. Only six men re-enrolled. A few recruits, however, arrived, as well as some veterans who had recovered from sickness. There were several from each company, the four following being from our company (I): Ole Rust, John Pederson, John Ramstad, and Olaf Andersen.

April 1864

On the 2nd of April several more men returned to the regiment, the following rejoining our company: Edvard Thoresen, Arne Knudson, Petter Lund, and Peter Harstad.

General Burnside evidently assumed that he could take care of things here without any assistance, as we learned that we were to return to Ringgold in Georgia and join General Sherman's forces.

But first I want to tell about our return march so people can see that we did not have it as easy as many seem to believe. After leaving Chattanooga we had not been at rest more than six days at one place and three days each two other times except when we built the bridge across the Holston River at Strawberry Plains, and then we worked every day.

Well, we were off on our march. The first day we managed 20 miles (two miles past Knoxville), the second day 8 miles, the third 13 miles to Lenoir Station, the fourth day 17 miles to Loudon. On the 11th of April we crossed the Tennessee River. On the 12th we rested. On the 13th we marched 12 miles, the fourteenth 13 miles, the fifteenth 14 miles, the sixteenth 18 miles. By then we were only two miles from Ringgold, where Sherman's army was located, and 5 miles east of Chattanooga.

The following day we covered the two remaining miles to where Sherman's army was encamped. Here they were busy drilling, reorganizing the army, handing out clothing, etc. We were paid up to May 1—and now we were ready to begin the campaign.

May 1864

Our brigade consisted of the 15th Wisconsin, 15th Ohio, 8th Kansas, and 32nd Indiana regiments. Our brigadier general was Augustus Willich, and we were in Wood's division of General Thomas's corps.

At this time Sherman had 100,000 troops and the opposing Southerners about 60,000. On May 3rd came orders to break camp and be on the go. That day we covered eight miles and ten miles the next, after which we lay quiet until the 7th. During the evenings we could hear music from the enemy camp and I assume they could hear ours. Now came orders to advance against the enemy. Our line of battle was eight miles long, and so was that of the enemy. Suddenly hell broke loose—first the roar of the cannons, then bomb after bomb fell and exploded near by. This went on for about two hours. Then the infantry was ordered to charge and the fighting became quite sharp. After advancing some distance we drew near the enemy breastworks, which we attacked, driving the rebels back four miles over Tunnel Hill. By then darkness had fallen, and we stayed there overnight. On May 8th we maneuvered a mile toward the right under constant advance-guard skirmishing. The following day we fought continuously and pushed the rebels back half a mile with heavy losses. On the 10th there was much skirmishing between the advance guards. We had now come to a high mountain called Rocky Face. We could see the rebels up on the mountainside behind large rocks. Their sharpshooters blazed away at us and they sent big boulders hurtling our way. It seemed quite impossible to do anything here so our main line drew back a quarter of a mile, but the 15th remained on outpost duty. Company I lost one man dead and two wounded.

Generals Sherman and Thomas conferred, planning how the mountain might be taken. As a frontal attack would mean a great loss of men, they opted for a flanking movement by way of Dalton [Georgia] with a part of their force. The rebels had large stores of provisions and ammunition in the little town of Dalton. In accordance with the plan, the army began maneuvering toward the rear of the enemy entrenchments; but one brigade from each division in the corps was left in place, our brigade being one of them. While these maneuverings were going on, the rebels also got busy sending forces to the rear with the aim of countering ours.

By the 13th the enemy had pulled back so far that only the outpost guards and the sharpshooters remained. Those of us who had been left watching the entrenchments at Rocky Face were now ordered to storm the heights and it seemed that the 15th Wisconsin were the best mountain climbers because we reached the top first, Sergeant John Wrolstad being our lead man; but many of us were right at his heels. I know that several of our men lost their lives—the rebel sharpshooters kept firing away while pulling farther and farther back—but I do not remember whether any members of Company I fell during this fighting. We kept advancing, and toward evening we made contact with the rest of our force. Then we pitched camp for the night.

On May 14th we went in pursuit of the enemy and after two hours' march we met stiff resistance. But the rebels gave up after a couple of hours and fell back some two miles to a place where they had entrenchments.

At daybreak on the 15th the battle here at Resaca [Georgia] began with tremendously heavy cannon and rifle fire. We were in a bad location because the enemy had their battlements up on a height, making an advance on our part seem impossible. Many of our men fell and many others were wounded. Nevertheless, in the afternoon we were ordered to launch an attack. We stormed the heights and pursued the enemy over a plain; but at the other edge of the plain the rebels had a second line of entrenchments and now we were forced to fall back on the entrenchments that we had just taken. In this battle our brigadier general, Willich, received a wound in the side; but he soon recovered and was able to rejoin us after three weeks. Søren Johnson of Company I fell and three others were wounded. The rest of the regiment lost quite a number of men and many were wounded.

In the afternoon we brought all our cannons forth and stationed them at the most advantageous places we could find. We also got the cartridge bags filled.

Our brigade was then ordered to pull back into the lowlands because we had been at the front fighting all day. But no sooner had we thrown ourselves down on the ground, rifles in arms, than a veritable thunder-crash broke loose from enemy cannons and rifles. The rifle shots sounded like a hailstorm. We jumped to our feet and rushed up the hill; but when we got there, everything was quiet, as the enemy had pulled away. It was not long, however, until the rebels renewed their attacks, but with the same results: they were again driven off. Early next morning they abandoned their positions and we pursued them to the Resaca River, where we took 15,000 prisoners. The rest had got across the stream. The prisoners were deprived of their weapons and then sent up north. We had a hard time getting over the river because the rebels had cut holes in the bottoms of the barges they used and then set them adrift.

We managed to catch some of these barges and repair them; and farther down the stream we found some boats. We then attempted a crossing, but this proved to be impossible because the rebels were on the opposite shore. In the meantime, however, our pontoons arrived and a bridge was constructed five miles farther down. By the third day the whole army had got across; but even this crossing was made in the face of fierce enemy rifle and cannon fire from positions on the other side of the river. The following day we continued our march past a little town called Calhoun [Georgia]. There we came to a halt in the hope that we might be able to secure some provisions, but we obtained very little. Anyway, our wagons had not yet arrived. So we continued our march and caught up with the enemy rear guard, which we drove on in front of us until darkness fell.

Then we halted until the wagons arrived with provisions and ammunition. The next morning the enemy had disappeared again. We set off in pursuit and passed a little town called Dorisville. By 4 o'clock we caught up with the enemy rear guard and a skirmish took place; but they soon fell back on a line of entrenchments where the rest of their army was

located. We left them in peace and pitched camp for the night. By daybreak the enemy were again gone, and again we were after them, passing
Kingston. Toward evening we had another little fight with the rebel rear
guard; but when darkness fell we went to rest.

The matter of securing food was now urgent. There was no chance of
securing supplies from the north because the bridges were burned and
the railway torn up. We remained here three days and managed to collect
some corn, pork, and syrup. Also we took control of a mill close by
where we ground raw corn. Thus we were supplied with cornmeal or
hog fodder for three days, and we also had smoked pork. From time to
time a wagon or two arrived with coffee and salt, so we were generally
stocked with these items.

After this halt we resumed our march, covering about ten miles.
General Hooker's corps got engaged in a tough fight that lasted two hours.
The following day a severe battle raged in which the 15th Wisconsin lost
92 men. This was the battle of New Hope Church. — We advanced in battle order over low-lying ground toward a ridge beyond which the rebels
were ensconced in a wooden area. They opened fire on us, to which we
replied; but as we were on open ground we had no cover. Neither could
we retreat without being shot down; so we threw ourselves on the ground,
loading and firing as best we could until darkness fell. But then the rebels
charged at full run and there was nothing for us to do but fall back as rapidly as we could, we being merely a brigade while the enemy apparently
had a whole corps. A great number of our men were taken prisoner while
numerous others were killed or wounded. The battle continued the next
day; but we now had barricades, so our losses were not severe. During the
night the enemy made three charges but were repulsed each time with
heavy losses. As far as we were able to determine, the enemy lost about
2,000 men while we lost 1,600. The battle went on another day and we
held our positions. After this, General Thomas received orders to take his
corps five miles toward the left; another corps took our place. Early the
next morning we attacked the enemy right flank and took a barricade they
had built of felled trees; but not far distant they had another entrenched
line, so we fell back on the barricade we had taken and held it.

June 1864

During the first days of June there was outpost skirmishing and bombarding, but things were quiet on the 5th. Some of our troops had managed

to get behind the enemy forces and by the morning of the 6th the rebels had left. We pursued them some five miles and pitched camp at a station called Acworth. There we stayed three days and were supplied with corn, pork, and other things. On the 10th we advanced four miles and had some outpost skirmishing from four o'clock until nightfall. The following day we went one mile ahead and one mile to the left. On Sunday the 12th we advanced two miles and came within range of the rebels, behind their entrenchments, with the result that some outpost skirmishing ensued despite very heavy rain. Skirmishing and cannonading continued all the next day—so did the rain. On the 14th there were two hours of hard fighting. We finally drove the rebels out of their entrenchments and pursued them until nightfall. Our brigade lost few men, the 15th Wisconsin suffering only two wounded. We took 260 prisoners and in the area where our regiment had advanced we found 30 dead bodies and many wounded men.

On the 15th we advanced two miles and caught up with the enemy on open ground. A tough fight ensued because we were about evenly matched. The battle lasted until three o'clock. Then we were reinforced by our artillery, and soon the enemy began retreating. Our division now joined the reserves in the rear, since we had been in the front lines several days.

"My gosh! Now we are out of food again. Let's go out to that-there house and see if we can find something. Do you want to go along, Jens?" "Sure"—and so, off we went. There were three or four hens left that the rebels evidently had been unable to catch. But Jens and I caught them. We also found some ears of corn which we took along. That's all we could find. The owners of the place had fled. Next we got the handmill out of the wagon, fastened it to a tree, ground our corn, plucked the hens, and baked our bread—"pone" as we called it, or rather as the Negroes called that kind of bread. On the 17th we again started after the enemy. We had covered only a mile when we caught up with their rear guard, which, without difficulty, we drove before us until late in the afternoon. Then, however, we met stiff resistance because the rebels had entrenched themselves. Consequently we fell back and also entrenched ourselves—and remained there a day.

On the 19th our brigade was ordered to proceed toward the left and find out if there were any rebels at the railroad station. We found some 200 or 300 of them engaged in unloading cornmeal and smoked pork from a railroad car. We came at them so unexpectedly that they could offer no resistance. Eighty of them were taken prisoner and we also seized 1,000 pounds of meal and 800 pounds of pork. The wagon was sent for and the loot taken to the camp—so now the brigade again had food for a while. On the 20th there was outpost fighting. The enemy charged our lines but were driven back with heavy losses. We, however, did not lose any men. The following afternoon we attacked the rebel entrenchments and took two cannons and 130 prisoners. Four members of our regiment were wounded.—Heavy rain that day.

On the 22nd there were outpost struggles and cannonading all day. On the 23rd we drove the enemy back after heavy fighting. The 15th Wisconsin lost four wounded and one killed. On the 24th—heavy outpost fighting all day. One man was killed, namely Daniel Pedersen of our company (I). A wagon arrived with shoes for us; it was high time because all of us were practically barefoot. The two following days there was more outpost fighting and one man was killed, Ivar Olson of Company I. Now a wagon with uniforms also arrived, so we cast the old rags aside and looked like new soldiers. General Sherman got the notion that he could fool the rebels into believing his new-clad soldiers were reinforcements just arrived. Orders were given for the whole line, six miles long, to storm the enemy entrenchments. But the new uniforms did not help. We had to fall back with heavy losses.

Our regiment was fortunate that day as we suffered only four wounded. But in this attack Sherman lost a total of 900 killed and 2,100 wounded. He now realized that it was impossible to take these positions by frontal attacks and therefore began to work his way around one of the flanks. After a few days he had managed to lead a part of his force so far to the rear of the rebels that they felt it was wisest to fall back. One of the Southern generals, Leonidas Polk, lost his life here.

July 1864

On July 2nd we moved a mile toward the left and the next day we were ordered to advance against the enemy. By now they had sent some of their troops away so their line was weaker than it was when we tried to storm their positions (in our new uniforms) and had to fall back. The rebels were forced to guard their right wing, which a part of Sherman's force was threatening with a flanking movement. We easily dislodged them from their entrenchments, pursued them, and took 90 prisoners. The pursuit continued the next day; we drove them some five miles and took 1,700 prisoners and four cannons. We continued pursuing them to the Chattahoochee River where we took 105 prisoners. But now the river was between us; the bridge was burned—and the river was both deep and wide. There was some cannonading, but this seemed to have no effect. Then some of our troops were sent ten miles down the river where there was a ferry. Pontoon bridges were constructed; and we managed to get across, but only in the face of rifle and artillery fire.

After the crossing—which took several days—we marched back up the river and found the rebels there, strongly entrenched. We attacked their positions and took 300 prisoners, at a cost of 237 men killed and wounded. The rebel losses in killed or wounded are not known. After this we rested a few days. A pontoon bridge was moved up to our position, near the railroad. The main highway also crossed the river at this place. Several wagons loaded with clothing, provisions, and ammunition arrived at this time so we got a variety of things as the need arose.

The following few days we were engaged in a flanking movement. Below is a record of our activities:

the 17th—outpost fighting; took five prisoners.
the 18th—marched four miles.
the 19th—marched two miles; heavy outpost fighting;
        took six prisoners.
the 20th—heavy outpost fighting; drove the enemy four miles.
the 21st—drove the enemy two miles; took 9 prisoners.
the 22nd—tough fighting, drove the enemy two miles;
        took six prisoners.

Thus our brigade was engaged during this flanking movement.

If the army as a whole, relatively speaking, took as many prisoners as our brigade did it would be quite a number, because there were 27 brigades.

Now we were so close that we could see the fortifications of the city of Atlanta, three miles away. Two officers and one corporal were severely wounded; they had dared to move too far forward. That night the rebels attacked our line and were near breaking through, but just in the nick of time a division came to our aid and drove them back. One of our best generals, McPherson, a corps commander, fell in this battle. Many others, both men and officers, were killed. There was also much strenuous fighting the next day (the 23rd). We managed to hold our ground, but lost many men. Whenever time permitted, we built entrenchments. On the 28th the enemy launched several attacks but were repulsed with heavy losses.

August 1864

We had rain on the 1st. The 25th Illinois regiment had completed its period of enlistment and left for home. On the 2nd, outpost skirmishing. On the 3rd the 32nd Indiana regiment had completed its term of service and left for home. It was the largest regiment in our brigade. On this day we had outpost fighting. We drove the enemy outposts up to the entrenchments but had to fall back when the enemy received reinforcements. Twenty-five men in our brigade fell, three of them from the 15th Wisconsin regiment.

Nothing happened during the entire month of August except a continual bombardment. There were many warehouses in Atlanta full of cotton that our bombs set afire. Many other buildings were also burned.

Sherman realized that it would be impossible to take Atlanta with a frontal attack and he did not have enough troops to besiege the city. Therefore he and Thomas decided to attack the enemy from the rear. Schofield's corps was sent back to protect the railway and keep the enemy within their fortifications. The cars were shipped back across the Chattahoochee. Both Thomas's and McPherson's corps (I do not know who was in command after McPherson fell) made a long flanking movement that took them twenty-five miles beyond Atlanta. During this maneuver around the city we tore up ten miles of the railroad leading to Memphis and burned two small bridges. Our cavalry was to the east of the city and tore up a railway leading in that direction. Three days later we reached the railway leading southward, and we began the job of destroying it toward Atlanta. Apparently the rebels were taking everything quietly. They had no reconnoitering parties out—at least not so far from the city. They evidently believed that the Yankees had fallen back, and they were willing to leave us in peace. According to rumor, when the rebels heard that Sherman's army was south of the city they threw a grand party, the officers becoming so soused that they could not stand on their feet. There were seven trainloads in Atlanta ready to leave with provisions, clothing, ammunition, bombs, cannons—in short, everything needed by an army. In the city were plants for manufacturing cannons, rifles, cannonballs, bombs, cartridges, etc. Now it was impossible for them to get these supplies shipped out, so they set fire to all of it rather than let it fall into the hands of the Yankees. We were only ten miles from Atlanta and could hear the thunder of the mighty explosions and feel the trembling of the earth.

When we entered the city two days later there was not a whole windowpane to be seen within six blocks of the station and there was a mass of iron on the railway. But then the rebels attacked and it was well that we had entrenched ourselves quite securely. They stormed our line and broke through, as they had their greatest strength at the main highway. We were stationed about 300 yards to the side so we did not encounter as heavy fighting as those on the right. The Confederate forces lost 2,000 dead and 1,500 captured, while we suffered 800 casualties.

September 1864

On the 4th we arrived at Atlanta—after a strenuous march and a hard battle—sore-footed and hungry. But now we were given rations for three days. Our forces had completed the railway to the Chattahoochee River so we had to haul our supplies by wagon just seven miles; and some laborers were building a bridge over the river. Gen. Thomas's corps was ordered to proceed four miles south of the city—and there we pitched camp.

On the 11th our brigade received orders to march out some five miles to capture a band of rebel soldiers who—it was said—were willing to surrender; but as we approached, we could not see any white flag. So we stopped and called to them, asking if they wanted to surrender. The answer was a volley of bullets. Fortunately, the area was wooded so we had lots of hiding places, and we got away as rapidly as possible.

Now things were quiet for a while. We were comfortable and merely did guard duty from time to time. Finally, on the 29th, the 15th Wisconsin regiment was ordered to proceed to Atlanta, where we stayed until the following morning. Then we boarded a freight train with 700 prisoners, whom we took to Chattanooga.

October 1864

The bridge across the Chattahoochee was now completed, so we covered the entire distance without getting off the train, arriving at Chattanooga in the late evening of Oct. 1st after a trip of 138 miles. The next morning we parted with the prisoners. We remained in Chattanooga until October 16th, doing guard duty. Very frequently we were sent to Nashville in charge of prisoners. On our first trip we had 1,100 captives, including those we had brought from Atlanta. On our return, 1,200 more prisoners had arrived—also from Atlanta. This meant another trip to Nashville for us. On the 16th we were sent to Whiteside Station, 15 miles west of Chattanooga, to keep watch over a railroad bridge. We remained there until February 10th, 1865. While there we did guard duty and also had to keep our entrenchments in good order as well as the blockhouses that guarded each approach to the bridge. We had lots of time there and all the food and clothing we needed.

Our time of service expired on December 20th, the date when we had entered Uncle Sam's service. But because a Confederate force under General [John Bell] Hood had arrived at Nashville, all available troops were needed. General Schofield's corps held him in check until General Thomas brought up his corps on November 30th. By December 15th Thomas was prepared to move. After hard fighting for two days he completely destroyed Hood's force and took 13,000 prisoners. Of these, 2,000 surrendered voluntarily. —It still took some time before the railroad was ready for traffic.

February 1865

On the 10th we marched up to Chattanooga, handed in our equipment, and received our discharge papers with a note stating how much money we had coming. We boarded the train that same day and arrived in Nashville the next morning at 10 o'clock. At 3 o'clock that afternoon we left for Louisville, where we arrived on the 12th; and there we received our pay. The same day we took the train for Chicago, arriving there in the morning of the 14th. The next day I left for Sparta, Wisconsin, where I arrived on the 16th. On the 17th I came to Eau Claire with the mail coach—three years and two months after we had left this town to enlist.

Below I will list the names of the members of our company (I) after we had been in the field one year and six months. At that time I was ordered to serve as corporal, and in this capacity I had to record the names of the men. I only wish I had a complete roster of the company as it was when we left Madison. Then there were 98 of us—now we were 53. Many had been sent up north to hospitals because of sickness. Some had passed away; others had been sick or wounded but had recovered sufficiently to guard prisoners in the North. Still others had been discharged before their term of service expired

Our captain, Gust. Gasman, had—after a short period of service—been sent home on sick-leave and was absent a long time. When we heard that he had resigned, we elected Lieutenant Wm. Montgomery to be our captain. No sooner was this done than Gasman returned and wanted to resume his position. But this we definitely opposed, as we had some complaints against him. He was then sent to that part of the regiment which was in active fighting and was later wounded at Chickamauga. Captain Montgomery stayed with us all the time and returned with us to Chicago. There we bought a cane with a gold head and presented it to him. In return he gave each one of us a six months' subscription to the Chicago *Tribune*. Lieutenant Finn Gasman also stayed with us through our whole period of service; but he remained at Whiteside Station. We were told that he had bought shares in a coal mine there, but we figured that he was afraid to come with us because he was not well liked.

Our second lieutenant, Martin Russell, was a Dane. He was wounded on Island No. 10 and was given a discharge. First Sergeant Christian Olson took his place as second lieutenant. He continued with us until he had completed his term of enlistment and returned home with us. We presented him with a beautiful watch and chain. He was well liked by everybody.

Sergeant Morten Nordre took Olson's place as first sergeant, but he became sick and was sent to a hospital.

Sergeant Hans Gunderson was captured at New Hope Church and died in Andersonville.

Sergeant John Wrolstad came home after completing his term of enlistment. Corporal Simon Pederson was taken captive at New Hope Church and died in Andersonville. Corporal Peter Harstad was wounded; he died later. Corporal Simon Myhre was captured at New Hope Church and died in Andersonville.

PRIVATES

O. P. Anderson: completed his term of enlistment; returned home.

James Anderson: ditto.

Olaf Andersen: wounded; returned to the regiment and came home with us.

Nils Bjørnson: captured at New Hope Church and died in Andersonville.

Andrew Erikson: re-enlisted for three years and was transferred to another Wisconsin regiment when we left for home.

Martin Figen: captured at New Hope Church and died at
Andersonville.

Halvor O. Haave: became sick and was given discharge.

Erik Johnson: fell at Resaca.

Christian Jacobson: was wounded but recovered and rejoined the
regiment while we were stationed at Knoxville.

K. L. Landrew: became sick and was sent to a hospital, later rejoined
the company and came home with us.

Peter Lang: sick and sent to hospital.

Peter Lund: wounded, returned to the regiment and came home
with us.

Hans Myhre: sick and was given discharge.

Ben (Bersvend) Nelson: completed his term of enlistment.[14]

Ivar Olson: fell at Atlanta.

Olaus Olson: sick and sent to hospital.

Knut Olson: sick and was discharged.

O. P. Westby: captured at New Hope Church and died
at Andersonville.

O. P. Rekrut: transferred to another company.

Daniel Pederson: fell at Kennesaw Mountain.

Elias Pederson: sick and sent to hospital.

John Pederson: completed his term of enlistment.

John Rambek: sick and sent to hospital.

O. Rambek: wounded.

P. N. Lund: completed his term of enlistment.

Arne Thorkelsen: ditto.

Ben (Bjørn) Thompson: ditto.

Torjus: wounded and sent to hospital.

O. E. Troyan: ditto.

Nils Sørensen: ditto.

Z. Williams: ditto.

M. Thompson: sick and sent to hospital.

T. Gilbertson: ditto.

Edvard Thoresen: completed his term of enlistment.

Arne Knudson: ditto.

Martin Jensen: ditto.

Ole Nustad: ditto.

M. G. Heier: I do not know what became of him.

J. W. Daae: sick and was given discharge.

Samuel Pederson: completed his term of enlistment.

Nils Starkson: was wounded, rejoined the company, and was
  dismissed at the end of his term of enlistment.

Herman Andersen: completed his term of enlistment.

Casper Hanson: returned home before we did.

Hans Hansen: was wounded at Kennesaw Mountain. I do not remember whether he returned to the regiment; but he recovered
  and returned home because I met him in Eau Claire after the war
  and filed an affidavit for him regarding his pension.

NOTES

1. Ole Rasmussen Dahl came to Wisconsin from Norway in 1854. He had studied to-
   pography and surveying at a military academy in Trondheim. He gained considerable recognition as a topographer while serving with the 15th Wisconsin regiment.

2. This was presumably the noted pioneer pastor Herman Amberg Preus, who served
   a congregation at Spring Prairie, Wisconsin, from 1851 to 1894.

3. The flag was donated by the Scandinavian club Nora. It was made of silk, carried
   the American and Norwegian national emblems, and the device: "For Gud og vort
   Land" (For God and our Country).

4. Island no. 10 was located at the bottom loop of a hairpin curve in the Mississippi
   River. It covered about 200 acres and several batteries were emplaced there, but
   heavier fortifications were located on the Tennessee shore opposite the island. The
   island has been carried away by erosion.

5. This evidently refers to Commander Henry Walke's exploit aboard the ironclad
   Carondelet during the night of April 4, 1862.

6. A more realistic figure seems to be 7,000.

7. Dr. S. J. Hansen from Koshkonong, Wisconsin, was the first doctor to serve the
   15th Wisconsin regiment. In January, 1862, Dr. Stephen O. Himoe (Hoimo) became
   chief doctor and Hansen served as his assistant.

8. Bushwhackers were Confederate soldiers who engaged in guerrilla warfare.

9. "Velling" is a Norwegian dish made of milk and rice.

10. The chaplain at the time was the famous pioneer pastor Claus Lauritz Clausen.

11. General Forrest was one of the most daring and dashing cavalry officers in the
    Confederate forces.

12. The rumor was greatly exaggerated. Ager says that about 500 men from the 15th
    Wisconsin took part in the battle of Murfreesboro. Buslett says that the regiment
    suffered the following losses: 15 killed, 70 wounded, 34 missing. The total Union

force of 56,649 engaged in the battle suffered the following losses: 1,730 killed, 7,802 wounded, 3,717 missing.

13. New Madrid, which is in Missouri, is a careless mistake for New Market, which is in Tennessee, where the 15th was then fighting.

14. Ben Nelson was sent home on sick leave during the months May–August, 1863. On September 16 companies *G* and *I* were ordered to leave Island no. 10 and rejoin the rest of the regiment. This took place on September 21, immediately after the bloody battle of Chickamauga where Colonel Heg was mortally wounded and his regiment almost decimated. Ben Nelson and a large number of his comrades from the 15th Wisconsin were mustered out in February, 1865.

The Norwegian Regiment at Chickamauga

Waldemar Ager

On the boundary line between the states of Tennessee and Georgia lies a city named Chattanooga. It was an important place during the American Civil War because it was a railroad center and it blocked the way for Federal troops' further penetration into enemy territory. Chattanooga is encircled by a range of hills, and to the south of it looms a mighty peak 3,000 feet high that, at a distance, looks like the butt of a giant musket. This crag—"Lookout Mountain"—extends southward as a double chain called Missionary Ridge. Parallel with these heights is another range of hills farther to the east; and between them lies a plateau about five miles wide through which a stream winds, quietly and peacefully, with many twists and turns. This steam bears the queer Indian name of Chicka-mauga, which is said to mean the waters of death. Perhaps Indians of long ago also fought a bloody battle here to give the beautiful little river such a terrifying name. But if such is the case, then the Muse of History has forgotten what once she knew. Chickamauga is really an idyllic stream as it slowly carries its water northward to join the much larger Tennessee River. On September 18, 1863, it was merely a tiny unknown river in a remote Georgia valley; on the 19th it was known to thousands; on the 20th to tens of thousands, and later to millions. Every American schoolchild has since then been forced to test his or her spelling skill on this sinister word that is now inscribed with blood on the pages of history.

The great American Civil War had reached a critical turning point. At last the fortunes of war had favored the Federal forces. The surrender of Vicksburg and the victory at Gettysburg had inspired the Union soldiers with courage and the entire North was breathing more freely. Never-theless, the Southern states remained defiantly firm. The Boys in Blue were to them an enemy from the North who had pushed into their land in order to suppress and subdue them. What right did the stronger Northern states have to decide for them, be it slavery or any other question? The

Constitution gave them the right to rule themselves. This was the right for which they fought—and they fought with the courage of despair. Their coasts were blockaded, their mess kits nearly always empty, and their uniforms in tatters. Now they had mustered for a major battle, and they wanted to win. This battle was to compensate for Vicksburg and Gettysburg. Volunteers would again rally round the flag and fill the thinning ranks decimated by bullets, sickness, and desertion.

The men of the North knew that a victory here would open a way to the heart of enemy territory. Victory would mean that the Stars and Stripes would again wave over a united people—and, moreover, a people that had cleansed itself of the stigma of slavery.

But could they conquer an equal number of desperate rebel soldiers whose feeling that they fought for hearth and home inspired them with indomitable courage? That was the question.

On the 17th of September the two great armies faced each other from opposite sides of the little stream. On the west side stood 60,000 Federal soldiers and on the east side a similar number of Confederate troops. The former had blue and the latter had gray uniforms. Most of the Confederate soldiers wore hats. And instead of knapsacks they had their belongings wrapped in a piece of tentcloth, which they carried like a sling over one shoulder. Night came dismal and gloomy, making it impossible to distinguish between the Blue and the Gray. Dead tired from their marches and countermarches the soldiers now rest on their weapons. Silence broods over the breathing of thousands of men among many other sounds: the changing of guards, a mounted orderly on duty, or the whinny of a horse in the darkness.

The rest is not for long. Even before the break of day the camp is astir and vigilant. The commanding general is uncertain as to the enemy plans. More marching over the muddy roads and the wet grass, new positions taken. It is rumored that the enemy has sent a brigade across the stream. Again, new positions and new problems to solve. A thousand questions surge through the commander's brain.

And not through his alone. There are thousands of men under arms. They are prepared to fight unto death. Only a short while ago they were citizens of the same land under the same flag. Only last night they sang the same songs around their campfires. Those who prayed did so to the same God. Many had kinfolk on the opposite side. There were brothers against brothers and fathers against sons. All had homes where someone would feverishly scan the casualty lists. Here were men newly immigrated, still ignorant of the country's language, ready to fire at those who had possessed the land through generations. Was there no other way of freeing America from the curse of slavery? Why must we kill each other?

By noontime the whole Federal army is drawn up in line of battle two and a half miles long. It has the shape of an immense, clumsy question mark extending from the north to the south. The dot under the mark is formed by [Philip Henry] Sheridan's large division. Next to him, constituting the right flank of the army, are located the divisions led by Wood and Davis—the latter where the question mark makes its smallest swing inward. At this point two roads converge, one being the broad highway toward Chattanooga.

In Davis's division stood the Heg brigade commanded by the Norwegian Hans C. Heg. It consisted of four regiments, of which the 15th Wisconsin volunteers was the smallest. The brigade had been stationed at the dangerous post by the highway. The line of battle was formed by three regiments, with one in reserve. The 15th, the Norwegian regiment, formed the right wing.

Long hours under arms. It felt good to lie down even though the ground was wet, and to get that heavy Dresden rifle off the sore shoulder. The Norwegian soldiers had taken part in many battles and by now considered themselves veterans. Furthermore, the regiment had been honorably mentioned on several occasions in reports from field commanders. Hence they could view the situation with proper calm. They heard the muffled roll of artillery as it shifted position. Orderlies galloped by on the road. They knew but little of what was happening elsewhere. The division chief rides by with his staff, and the men greet him with "hurrahs". "An important position, boys. Do not yield." More hurrahs.

The minutes were long. The lively Vossings, too ready with their jokes and laughs, were in form now too; and the genial dalesmen chuckled quietly. "I guess we will get soup now." "Yes, now Old 'Rosy' will prepare us a fine dish." "Yeah, and probably he will cook soup on our bones." "You mean the rebels, of course." "Not by a ___." General Rosecrans, who was in chief command, had stopped in front of the 15th during a review—he wished to get a closer look at the already well-known regiment. "What is it that makes these men so short of stature?" he asked Colonel Heg. The Colonel could give no answer. "You do not give them

enough soup" explained the General. "Soldiers must have lots of soup."
The 15th did not like his remark about them being so small—if he had
merely said "young." And while lying there awaiting orders, they had
a good opportunity to recall the many "soups" they had been in. But
many remained silent. Here amidst the forests and mountains they probably thought of the dear ones at home, whom they might never see again.
Only a year and a half ago they had left for the front with banners flying
and bands playing—800 men strong. In Chicago a great fuss was made
over them and there they received their Norwegian flag. Now there were
only 176 left of them. Two companies remained on guard duty at Island
No. 10 where they had won their first laurels. Memories—memories of
past campaigns: Knob Gap, where they took their first cannon in a bayonet charge; Perryville—but especially the bloody battle of Stone's River,
which ushered in the new year, and where Captain Ingemundsen fell
together with so many other boys of the 15th. At that time, also, they
were stationed in the very front line of battle and on a highway where
they took the first thrust. Always the 15th was placed well toward the
front in a dangerous position where they caught the first fire. Was it because they were Norwegians? Now there were merely a handful left of
them. Whenever there was hard work to be done, such as felling trees
and floating logs for bridge building, it was so convenient to call out the
15th. Thoughts also wandered off to hospitals, like the large one in Nashville, where so many were lying in pain who once had stood by their side
in the ranks. Bullets were bad but sickness was worse. It was a comfort
that their colonel was now a brigadier general. He knew what he was
doing when he placed them in that position. He had something in mind,
certainly.

Long waiting. A prankster pretends to be asleep—and snores. "Shut
your gap!" "Hey Nils! Poke your head into his maw and see what's wrong
with his belly." "Get up Ole, Louise is here by your bed with morning coffee." "Quit that snoring at once! The Rebels will think that artillery is
rolling up here." "Hush" says someone else, "if the Rebels come we will
retreat into that gap of Ole's." "And then we will be in Valdris," adds
another with a yawn that reveals a gap every bit as large as Ole's.

While this takes place on the extreme right of the curved battle line,
the enemy are making their preparations. Like two big irritated animals
the rival forces watch each other's movements. The rebels were massed
in two great forces. Confronting the large outward curve of the Union

"question mark" we find General Leonidas Polk. Against the smaller bend of the line on the right flank are stationed, ready for attack, the valorous Virginia troops under the famed General Longstreet.

But there are many questions to be answered. No one seemed to have any definite plan. When and where shall the firing begin? The enemy commander has an objective in view, however: he wants to reconquer Chattanooga and the road runs directly where Heg's brigade is posted. Some feelers there had to be. Attacks were made here and there—but they were, in fact, merely preliminary feints made by the two combatants as they attempted to find a vulnerable point. They hammered and probed along the enemy lines. With every blow, brigades or divisions were sent forth to deadly encounters that, nevertheless, proved to be of little significance. Historians have primarily been occupied with the main battle, which came the following day. But it was one of the preliminary attacks which proved so be fateful for the Norwegian regiment.

"Fall in!" An instant, and the men are in arms. Shots have been fired at the front. The brigade is soon in motion and advances in rapid strides.

At Chickamauga, as practically everywhere during the first years of the war, soldiers did not like to use axe or spade. Almost always they fought in open fields unless there just happened to be some chance cover. And an attack was usually met by a counterattack with a stone fence or some other cover as objective.

There was a feeling in the air—a premonition—that the fight would be a hot one, because the decks of cards were taken out of the pockets and thrown away. That was a rule in the Norwegian Regiment when the soldier went to battle. The cards were fine as a pastime, and they got new ones when the fighting was ended; but they would not risk dying with a deck of cards in their pocket or knapsack.

Forward!

The brigade storms forward in good order over a hillock, the 15th far toward the front. Anders Urnæs carries the banner. Just as they reach the crest of the hill the rifles again begin crackling. The minié bullets sing their waspish song over the soldiers' heads, but they pay no heed now. Only an occasional raw recruit involuntarily ducks his head. They push farther on and the enemy advance guard is driven back; but now they are met by a terrible rifle salvo just as a battery opens fire on their left wing. The brigade seems to melt away and large holes are torn in the ranks as men topple over each other and remain lying there. The Kansas Regiment that forms the center of the brigade hesitates, wavers, and falls back in disorder. The Fifteenth is now without cover on either flank—still it remains firm and fires ten or twelve rounds. The position becomes impossible. "Fix Bayonets! Storm the front line"—such is the command. The boys answer with a "hurrah" but do not get far in the face of the crossfire. Then they are ordered to retreat, which they do in good order while holding the enemy off and taking the wounded with them. Just then another brigade (Carlin's) arrives as reinforcement, which grants them a little breathing space. But within minutes it is also driven back; and Heg's brigade again takes on the struggle alone, but is still pushed back by the superior numbers, over a field where they find cover at the edge of a forest.

Among those left on the field was the brave Bergensian Captain John M. Johnson, who was shot through the heart. Now the reserve is sent forward. Colonel Heg is busy everywhere holding his forces together. Then an attempt is made to recover the lost ground, but the numerical superiority of the enemy is too great. The brigade is thrown back into the woods with a great hubbub. Then rifle fire announces that a new column—the third brigade of Sheridan's division—is being sent against the enemy. Now is the chance for still another attempt. Captain Hans Hanson from Sogn had his sword broken by a bullet and showed the stub to Colonel Heg, saying in his good-natured way: "There will be hot work today". But there is no time for jokes. The Colonel swings his hat. Now for the test! "Forward!" For the fourth or fifth time he leads his little brigade against the enemy. With fixed bayonets they again cross the bloody field that is already covered with corpses. Captain [Hans] Hanson falls, mortally wounded. Sergeant Niels Johnson takes command of a company that has lost its officers. Colonel Heg is pierced by a bullet and a private, Lars Larsen, rushes over to help him off his horse in the shower of bullets—gets him to safety, but is himself badly wounded. The brigade halts, wavers, advances anew and must again fall back, still fighting. Young Urnæs, the standard bearer, has ventured too far forward and is shot in the chest. The rebel soldiers press on with a "hurrah." Then Private Hans Hansen rushes forward, rescues the standard, and the enemy advance is stayed for a moment. The powerful Torger Larson sees a badly wounded officer in danger of falling into enemy hands, rushes forward, and carries him to safety, but is himself badly wounded. Corporal

Jacob Overson took charge of Company C when Captain Hanson fell; but he, also, was wounded and then Corporal Emmonson took his place. Major Wilson and Captain Gasman are wounded. Captain Henrik Hauff has fallen. Lieutenant [Christian] Tandberg is wounded.

But now the boys take a position on the field itself. They lie flat on the ground and keep up the fight. Suddenly the area in front of them is filled with fleeing soldiers: the attacking column, mentioned above, is in full retreat. But Heg's men do not join the flight. They have retreated enough today. Again soldiers swarm over them. Will they be swept along this time? No—they have retreated enough. The fleeing soldiers are an Illinois regiment that had formed the Brigade's own reserve. It had been sent forward and had heroically stood firm a long time. The commander says that he will reassemble his regiment in the rear of the 15th, but he does not succeed. They continue their disorderly rout and fall back through a new column that is being readied for attack. Heg's soldiers keep the fight going in the now rough and bloody cornfield. The balls plow up the soil around them and between them. A sergeant is talking with a comrade at his side. Suddenly the companion's leg makes a quick jerk. "What's wrong, young fellow?" But there is no reply A minié bullet has pierced his head.

Behind them they hear powerful "hurrahs." It is the assault column pressing forward. The commander and his men were unaware of any Union troops so far toward the front. They take them to be enemies and open fire. The 15th was thus caught in a crossfire; then they broke and ran. This had never happened to them before—being fired at from the rear. Now they fled towards the woods in wild disorder. But there were no deserters. Behind a barricade of windfallen trees that they dragged together, they reassembled and from this improvised fortification Heg's Brigade made its last attack of the day. They took the field again and also captured some artillery, after which they settled down behind a barricade in the woods and held it until darkness fell.

Seven of the officers and more than a third of the privates had either fallen or been captured or badly wounded. Lieutenant Colonel Johnson mustered the remainder of the regiment, after which he went to see Colonel Heg, who was still alive. He asked him to greet the regiment. The colonel was very happy because they had done their duty to the last. He, also, had performed his duty to the last—and died soon thereafter.

The state of Wisconsin has placed a beautiful and costly memorial where he fell.

Again a bitterly cold and foggy night.

When the morning sun burst forth, the Federal battle line still formed a giant blue question mark on the plateau, except that it had been drawn closer together and somewhat farther back. The Davis and Wood divisions were still located in the smaller, inward-bending swing of the question mark. The two great armies were still prepared to meet in a mighty death grapple. But still they hesitated. There was so much at stake.

Marches and countermarches. Brigades are shifted back and forth. After such marches, many find that they are again placed exactly in their original positions.

The Heg brigade, now led by Colonel Martin, still forms a part of the Davis division; and here is found what is left of the Norwegian Regiment.

Now and then is heard the rumbling of cannon, and shells begin exploding. Rifle shots start crackling with the now familiar metallic sound—like hail on a tin roof.

The brigade formerly commanded by Heg is now held in reserve for Carlin's brigade. General Rosecrans has all the time expected a major attack on his left wing. A position there is threatened. He therefore orders Wood's division moved toward the left, and its place in the line of battle is to be filled by the greatly weakened Heg brigade which, after the previous day's losses, scarcely numbered 600 men.

This was the fatal maneuver at Chickamauga. General Longstreet, trained in Lee's and Stonewall Jackson's school, became aware of this opening in the Union line and immediately directed a furious attack against it.

The Gray ranks came hurtling on in mass formation. "Yah—hei—ei—ei—ei," the frightful Rebel yell had as by spontaneous impulse burst forth from thousands of throats at the battle of Bull Run. The Virginia troops, probably the world's best infantry, poured into the opening and drove everything before them. The Norwegian Regiment held a barricaded position for a while, but nothing could withstand this onslaught. Lieutenant Oliver Thompson was killed by a bullet; Lieutenant Colonel Johnson and Captain Gustafson were taken prisoner. The remnants of the regiment saved themselves through hasty flight.

General Longstreet clipped the huge question mark in two. One part was chased in wild disorder toward certain mountain passes. But the other part—the large curve of the question mark—fell back on a ridge of hills formed like a horseshoe and took up a strong position there. Time after time Longstreet and Polk led their brave but weary troops against this formidable position only to see them mowed down. Then darkness fell, and General Thomas was able to pull back toward Chattanooga.

The South had won, but it was not a decisive battle. The war was to continue a long time yet—there was not much to point at as compensation for the 28,290 men dead or maimed who remained on the field.

The battle still stands as a great question mark in history.

The Norwegian Regiment was reassembled at Chattanooga. There were 75 men left of the 176 who went into battle. But now they were reinforced by the two companies from Island No. 10. Convalescents also arrived; and a month later the Regiment could again take its place with the storm columns that drove the enemy away from Missionary Ridge and took part in Sherman's famed campaign against Atlanta.

Letters Written at the Front

(Nils J. Gilbert, Sergeant Co. F; later Lieutenant Co. A, 15th Wis. Reg.)[1]

Hickman, 1 April 1862

Dear Brother,

We have now paid the rebels a brief visit and we had a hard march. We left Hickman, Ky., at ten o'clock Sunday and came within four miles of the enemy camp (at Union City) where we spent the night. As soon as it was light in the morning we had to be at it again and marched with full equipment. About eight o'clock we reached the place. The force consisted of our regiment, some cavalry and artillery, and the 25th Illinois Regiment. As we were on the left flank we arrived last at the scene. The cavalry and the artillery were in the lead. We came out of the woods and directly to their camp—pitched on a little field—the force consisting of three regiments. As soon as our cavalry arrived and made contact with theirs, the rebels fled and our artillery fired at their infantry while it was attempting to form a battle line. They had not eaten breakfast yet, and when they saw that we were forming lines on both sides of the field they fled in fright as if there were fire in the seats of their pants. They took to the woods, each man for himself. Our cavalry set off in pursuit but because of the forest we caught only ten prisoners. Some of the enemy were killed, however. We lost one dead and one wounded. We set fire to the camp and burned everything we did not take with us. We captured about 100 horses and mules, some wagons and ammunition, and various other things. I stole away from the company and went over to the camp accompanied by Christian Lie. There I got hold of a large sword and many little items, but most things had been burned. Everything was over by ten o'clock a.m. and then we went back in quick march. Those who were not used to walking were given the job of driving the horses and mules or allowed to ride. By 3 o'clock p.m. we were all aboard a boat again in Hickman, quite sore-footed and tired but still much pleased with the

63

results—and all of us were unharmed. But everyone regretted that we did not even get a shot at the rebels. The infernal rascals did not dare fight the Norwegians even though they outnumbered us two to one. Perhaps they will dare to face us next time. God willing, we are going to win.

Island No. 10, 29 April 1862

Dear Brother,

I hope you have got full information about our activity in Union City through the newspapers. We have noticed that *Emigranten* reported quite accurately about this event. Therefore I will say something about the taking of Island No. 10.

Several days after we returned from Union City our company was ordered to mount outpost duty. That was the 6th inst. We went directly down to Island No. 10 and were stationed as guards along the riverbank on the Missouri side. The following night a terrible rainstorm struck our company and that same night one of our gunboats ran the blockade. The enemy opened fire at it from four batteries on the island. The bullets flew thick and fast, whistling about the ears of the guards, but without doing damage to either the men or the boat. The vessel passed by and puffed away without giving an inkling as to whether it sank or floated. When it was beyond range of the batteries, however, it signaled that it had gotten through, something that undoubtedly riled the enemy. The next day we returned to our camp, but came back in the evening. Very tired after the strenuous duties of the previous night, we went to bed and slept soundly. At 2 o'clock in the night, however, we got orders to pack our tents; and off we went. Taking along all our equipment, we boarded the steamer *Graham*, which always followed us. At 5 o'clock in the morning we were aboard, ready to depart without knowing where we might be going.

In half an hour's time, to our surprise, we noticed that our boat lay to at Island No. 10, directly under the same batteries from which we had received so many shrieking bullets the previous night. I went back and forth on deck, keeping an eye both on my brother, who was lying there sick, and on the island. The first thing I noticed was a regiment that had landed half an hour before our arrival. They had rounded up a mass of gray-hatted men like a flock of sheep, around whom they stood guard with lowered bayonets. Our men had undoubtedly taken the weapons from those fellows in gray, who looked very dejected while the ones in blue were jubilant because of their captured sheep.

We were not put ashore on the island that day because the other regiment had taken possession of it. But our regiment was put ashore on the Tennessee side, directly opposite the island, where the enemy also had batteries; but they had been deserted by everybody except the sick. Our company (F) was the first to land, our captain being an impetuous fellow, and we took the lead as we went down the shore gathering up prisoners and goods. I was sent to guard a hospital boat that lay close to shore, having ten men with me. This proved to be both a difficult and a dangerous post because those who were well enough to move about had got hold of one or more whiskey containers when the officers left the boat. Now they were drunk; so we had many fierce fights to get the weapons away from them and put them under guard. At one time, Anders Thompson and I were attempting to enter a little room to fetch some weapons and liquor that were stored there. But then a daring devil met us at the door armed with a great dagger. He feared that we were going to take his whiskey. I put my rifle to his cheek and told him he had to drop the dagger, otherwise I would shoot him dead. At that he surrendered willingly everything in his possession; and finally another man came whom Colonel Heg had sent to help me get the boat underway. We got steam up and brought the boat to our landing place.

I guarded the boat until the next day. Then it was sent up the river and we were rid of the nasty graycoats from the South. The reason they abandoned their batteries so hastily was that when the aforementioned steamer ran the blockade, General [John] Pope had landed downstream on the opposite side and begun marching up the Tennessee shore to attack their rear. It was this that scared the life out of them. But flight was of no avail because Pope cut their line of retreat and took 15,000 captives. This did not cost us a single life.

On the 12th of this month five companies (A, F, H, I, K) went over to the island while the rest remained on the Tennessee shore to gather up everything left by the rebels. Our company is now busy putting up barricades for a battery on the island. We are in a hurry because cannons are being brought to fortify the island on this side in case any intrusions should be attempted.

(Now we must don our uniforms as we are to receive our pay and be inspected by the general.)

Island No. 10, 20 May 1862

Dear Brother,

. . .We are still at peace on Island No. 10. Only three of our companies are left here, while formerly there were five. Two left yesterday for the other side to reinforce the guard there because a couple of times the enemy S[outh] C[arolina] cavalry has been seen; by now most of the work on the fortification of the island has been completed and our company is being trained to man the cannons. Because of this I hope that we will remain here a while. The island already has more than 30 cannons in its defenses and we expect that more will be emplaced. I reckon that the island is about one and a quarter miles long and three-fourths of a mile wide. Every day there is much guard duty and drilling. We must say, however, that all is well as long as we have our health—that's much to be happy about. There are not many who can report that they have not been sick for a while.

I also want to tell you that we had a 17th of May celebration here in memory of Norway's liberation; a very gay affair it was. We sent to Cairo, Ill. for beer. Our company got one and a half barrels, and the other companies also got some. The first thing in the morning, just as the sun came up, we fired a salute of 13 cannon shots in honor of the day. Later, we had a parade; and on our return we drank both much and freely. In the evening, at sundown, we were also to fire a salute as in the morning. But this did not redound to the honor of Old Norway because when we reached the battery two or three were a bit tipsy and got into a quarrel, which caused trouble between the guards.

When we returned from the battery the other companies had been called out, rifles in hand, and they marched around Company A so the men could not go anywhere. A bit later the men of Company A were ordered to fall in line with their rifles and were marched to the highest officer on the island, Major Riise, at headquarters. There they had to give up their guns, and six or eight of them were put under guard in the guardhouse. It is rumored today that they will be shot, but this will possibly not happen to all of them. Report has it that Corporal Nils Brown will get the most severe sentence. The lieutenant, O. Thompson, has also been arrested and put under guard. He will be tried or court-martialed.[2]

It has rained incessantly since yesterday morning so the poor fellows who are on guard have had a difficult time these days.

Camp near Murfreesboro [Tennessee], 2 Sept. 1862

Dear Mother,

We came here yesterday after dark and are to be off again tomorrow. We have been on the move more than a week; but during this time I have not walked more than three days, having been somewhat sickly. Now I am quite well, however, which makes me happy.

We left the camp at Iuka [Mississippi] for Eastport on the Tennessee river, following it up to Florence and thence to Columbia. They said then that we were going to Nashville; but when we got a bit farther north, we headed east for Murfreesboro. A whole army corps is here at present. Tomorrow we will be on the go again—toward the southeast; but we do not know how far. We have had a very tough march and God knows where we are going next. Every day we have expected to meet the rebel army, but so far in vain. One night they made contact with our outposts, but they did not dare advance any farther. We were waiting anxiously because we knew of their movements, and lay ready with rifle at hand.

(Later): This letter was put aside until the 9th. We have now moved to the northern boundary of Nashville, arriving here yesterday evening. There are more than 100,000 of us, but what we are to do or where we are to go is beyond me. The rebels do not dare come north and meet us because they have nothing to live on. It is also rumored that a great mass of rebels have bypassed us and crossed into Kentucky—probably some of us will be sent there.

As I am not feeling very well I will close with a sincere greeting to all of you. Tosten [his brother] is as well as can be. Christen I. Larsen is quite sick but improving somewhat.

Louisville, Ky. 1 Oct. 1862

Dear Mother, brother, and sisters,

Yesterday evening I received several letters from you bearing different dates. It made me very happy to hear that you are all alive. I notice that you have tasted both sickness and health, which seems to be the fate of man at all times and in all places. As long as our tribulations do not overcome us we ought to be of good cheer. No matter how it goes, we will have to keep our courage up and put our trust in the Almighty. We are, God be praised, in good health and have stood the march well It was a tramp of 500 miles, and now toward fall we have come way up north while during the hottest part of summer we trudged farther south. God knows that it has not all been child's play. And we have accomplished nothing. We have been within sight of the Confederate General Bragg and his army, but we were not permitted to launch an attack. If we had been, we would have given him a beating and sent him to his just reward. We were ready to do this, but nothing came of it. And we can thank the great General Buell for this: he has always held us back.

We have been here three days, living like rich people. Now, however, the orders are for us to be on the march again; but where to—that I do not know. The Confederate army is beginning to tire more and more. They had hopes of crashing their way into Louisville, but this proved to be a disappointment for them. We have so many soldiers here that we could crush the whole South. An area of some eight or nine miles surrounding the city is completely covered with encampments, and within the city soldiers mill around like ants. We are located near the center of town but today we have orders to leave.

A curious affair occurred yesterday between generals [Don Carlos] Buell and Nelson. They met in the Ladies Parlor and General Buell saluted General Nelson. The latter did not return the salute, however, but said: "I do not want to have anything to do with you, you dog." Nelson said this because he was angry that Buell would not permit him to fight Bragg at the Green River when we were there. Then Buell whipped out his pistol and shot Nelson through the breast. He collapsed right there. A tremendous hubbub broke loose in town and many threatened to shoot Buell, who is now in prison.[3]

There are those who claim that our captain is a mean rascal; but that is a plain lie. He has a lot of sympathy for us; and among us he is held to be one of the best captains in the regiment. This is also Colonel Heg's opinion. When he joined a brigade he was given certain orders, the same as we were. But some believed that he had cooked up these rules, which were not to our liking. —As time is running out I will close for this time with sincere greetings.

16 Oct. 1862

Dear Mother, brother and sisters,

I have neither heard from you nor written anything to you since I was in Louisville. We are now about 100 miles southeast of that city; and as both of us are in good health I can report that we are well satisfied. We took part in the battle of Perryville and came out of it in good condition. On the 7th of this month, a couple of hours past noon, we heard cannonading at the front and had to take off at double-quick time. Shortly before sundown we were drawn up in line of battle over a plain and some hilly terrain; and there we lay behind a fence all night. We did not have anything to eat in the morning; but we found a flock of sheep and there was not much left of it after the Norwegians had eaten their breakfast.

After breakfast we were ordered back to the road, where we lay until after midday listening to the thundering of the cannons. Then we received orders to prepare hurriedly for an advance. Our brigade proceeded at once. It consisted of four regiments and a battery. We advanced about a mile, whereupon we heard great tumult of battle to the left. Then we were drawn up in line of battle on the right, directly facing the town, which was about a mile away. The battery took up a position on the left flank of our brigade and fired several shots. We lay quietly behind a fence; the rebels had sought shelter in a cornfield. Shortly, our regiment and the 21st Illinois regiment, the oldest in the brigade, were ordered to advance in line and the battery followed on our right. The rebel line drew back before we spied them and the battery opened fire. We crossed over the cornfield and got up on a hill where we caught our first sight of the enemy down in a valley. Then the worst pandemonium ever broke loose! As already mentioned, our regiment and the Illinois one were advancing in line of battle; and when we detected the enemy every man shrieked as with one voice and charged toward them. But the rebels kept quiet and crept back as rapidly as they could—with us following them for about half a mile, clear to the edge of town. Here the enemy had a battery that began returning the fire from our cannons. In half an hour's time dusk fell, and as nothing more could be done that evening we withdrew about a quarter of a mile to encamp for the night. We did not hear anything about the other two regiments in our brigade until the next morning. They had been sent out to the left and got clear to the other side of town where they took several prisoners and the rebel ammunition train consisting of 15 cars. That morning we entered the town but by then the rebels had skipped away. On the left the battle had been very bloody with thousands killed and wounded. After the fight we pursued the enemy and fragmented Bragg's army.

Time does not permit me to write any more, since we have to be off again, so I will close with a farewell for now.

Bowling Green [Kentucky] 2 Nov. 1862

Dear Mother, brother, and sisters,

As I have not heard from you for some time I will write and let you know that we are still alive and on our way south again—toward Nashville, Tennessee, it is said, where there has been much turmoil lately. Otherwise I have nothing of importance to relate. You have probably not received my last letter because it was sent with our quartermaster who was captured by a guerilla band near Bardstown while on his way to Louisville to get a supply of clothes. On the 25th of last month we were encamped near Lebanon and that night some snow fell. Our company had a tough time of it as it was on guard duty and many of the men were not equipped for winter. How long we are to keep marching like this I do not know. We have now marched between 600 and 700 miles. But all is well as long as we feel well. I have no more time to write as we are to be on patrol duty. So for this time—my best wishes.

Camp ten miles from Nashville
13 Nov. 1862

Dear Brother,

As we have little time, I will merely send you a few words to let you know that I am in good health and well satisfied for the present. But we have had a busy summer, having marched more than 800 miles since July. We arrived at our present camp on the 7th of this month. Since then we have been lying quiet except for one day when we were out looking for a guerilla band. We went more than 20 miles and returned without finding anyone.

We must also drill three hours daily while lying in camp and mount guard every fourth or fifth day. Our provisions are better now than when we were on the march, except for the fact that our coffee rations are cut in half because the railroad bridges are burned, making transportation very costly. I still think, though, that we live tolerably well, so you can tell mother that we are doing fine and have no reason for complaint. I have heard that some of the discharged soldiers are home now and have shocked people with their tales about the poor food we are getting. Presumably they did not do anything but lie around and think about eating. But when people are as busy as we have been lately they do not think of anything beyond keeping body and soul together. I am as vigorous as I ever was and that is also true of my brother and the others who are in good health. I must report that Ole Ramberg died at the hospital in Louisville on the 7th of this month. He died of consumption.

Furthermore, I can report that we evidently are going to stay here in winter quarters. You do not need to join the army unless you are drafted. Possibly you can avoid this also if you petition the sergeant at arms in Madison and explain to him that you have two brothers in the service.

As I have no more to write about I will close for this time with a sincere greeting to mother and you.

In a hospital near Murfreesboro
4 Jan. 1863

Dear Brother,

I must now, with both sorrow and joy, tell you that I survived the great battle of Murfreesboro. I was wounded, but thank God my condition is such that I hope to regain my health. A bullet struck my left thigh, with about seven inches between where it entered and where it left. This happened in the morning of December 31, and had it not been for my anger and exasperation I would surely have had to surrender to the rebels because our men were forced to retreat more than a mile; I ran so fast that God alone knows how I could have got away with such speed. Now I could not cover a mile even if my life depended on it. But, the Lord be praised, the chances of recovery do not look bad.

As regards the battle—we began advance-guard skirmishing on December 27, the same day we left Nashville. Our brigade was in the lead that day and we drove the enemy from encampment to encampment. At one time they offered resistance, putting up a battery on a high hill to bar our way. Our battery returned fire and our brigade charged the enemy position. Our regiment stormed the hill and drove the rebels away, capturing a cannon that they did not have time to take along. We did not lose a man either killed or wounded; but one of our regiments lost thirty men in this fight.

On the 27th another brigade was sent ahead to a different place, where they remained for about half an hour. The following night, and during the day, it rained as if the heavens had opened up. Finally, after the enemy had been driven away, we got a bit of rest and got a fire going. On the 28th, a Sunday, we lay quiet; and we drew rations for three days. On the 29th we set off in the morning and marched all day without meeting any opposition. By evening we neared the main force, and there we lay all night in rain and slush without fire or tents. On the 30th we advanced to be drawn up in line facing the batteries that were all through the woods. In the afternoon an exchange took place between the outposts; and about 3 o'clock, through bombardments, our battery discovered that several cannons were planted in front of our brigade. Advance detachments were immediately sent out by our regiment and the 21st Ill. They advanced in skirmish line and very soon Captain Ingemundsen of Company E, who was in command of them, was shot and several in the company were wounded. Before long it was discovered where the battery was located— on a little hill on the opposite side of a stream. Our regiment and the 21st Ill. rushed on at double-quick time to take the battery. We came within a rod of it; then the enemy opened such fire that you might think all Hell had been poured over us. Colonel Heg, however, shouted "Onward!" But the other regiment fell back and we had to do the same. We retreated about twenty rods and took up a position behind a fence. Our company lost one dead and five wounded. The man who was killed came from Iowa. We remained at ease until night fell, merely firing at the enemy as the notion struck us. They did likewise, without doing us any harm. The loss to our regiment was about fifteen killed and wounded.

During the night we fell back half a mile while the other half of the brigade advanced to take our place. In the morning of the 31st we arose before dawn and had a cup of coffee and some food. The cannonading and rifle fire now grew fierce on our left and every minute drew closer to our right flank, where we were stationed. Soon, we were ordered to draw back to the battery some rods away. Now the rebels charged our brigade, hitting the right flank of the battery with such force that it had to fall back in order to avoid being swamped. The enemy opened a terrific fire; and they nearly maneuvered around our right flank. Our regiment and the 21st Illinois were close to the battery and the left flank of our brigade withstood the fire as long as it could and was then driven back in disorder to where we had our position along a fence. We were lying quietly and planned to let the enemy come close enough so we could make an effective rally. Suddenly one of our captains shouted: "Fire away, boys!" And immediately we blazed away with full force. But then the enemy covered us with a fierce barrage that I am unable to describe—we were caught in a terrific crossfire. After half an hour's stiff resistance we received orders to retreat. As soon as we got up, some began to run. This threw us into confusion, which was true of the whole division. I did not have my gun loaded when we left the fence; so I snatched a cartridge, got the powder into the barrel and the bullet into the muzzle of the gun; but just then I was shot and had to jump along on one leg as best I could through a cornfield across which everyone was running. Soon I became so tired that I had to lie down; but when I saw the rebels coming I set off again and finally got into a wagon that took me away from the field; thus ended my participation in the battle. The rest of it I had to leave to the others.[4]

I could not see any way of escape from the firing as the loss of blood made me incapable of movement. After a while, however, I regained sufficient control of myself so I could get up; and being between the two lines I jumped on one foot toward my companions. As soon as they saw me they came to my aid. I fainted and was put into an ambulance with others who were wounded. We were taken about a mile behind the lines and placed on the ground. But almost immediately came orders saying that the wounded had to be moved because our right wing had been outflanked and was falling back. I heard the order and jumped on one foot toward a wagon but when I was near it I fainted again. This happened about 10 o'clock a.m., and until after dark that evening I was like a dead man. They moved me some three or four miles and placed me in a barn. There I recovered consciousness when a man stepped on my chest in the dark. I realized then that my right leg and side were frozen to my clothes, which were drenched with blood and rain. It rained and snowed all night, and as I lay close to the door the sleet blew in on me. A member of the 25th Illinois regiment, who knew me, heard my moaning and rolled me up in a blanket and dragged me into a corner and left me there with my pain. I can not describe the tortures of that night. Gradually, however, my clothes and limbs thawed a bit and when day broke the wounded were brought to a building on the Nashville-Murfreesboro highway called the White House Hospital. The third day we were given some hardtack, which tasted good after going three days without anything to eat or drink But my digestive organs were so weak that for several days I could not retain any food. I must end my writing. God only knows if I can stand it. I do not live—merely exist. Farewell!

The hospital near Murfreesboro
Jan. 1863

Dear Brother,

When in my sorry condition I received your letter of December 19 I was greatly cheered. Time passes very slowly. This is a poor hospital; it is impossible for those who are badly wounded to be healed here. But God be praised—I am not so ill but that I can take care of myself. As to the way in which I was wounded, you were informed about that in my last letter. I do not believe the bullet damaged the bone; and, with God's help, I hope I will soon be sent from here to Nashville where we can get good care. Ole Christensen is here with me and is of great help to me. He was wounded in the right arm.

. . . Our army is now stationed on the other side of Murfreesboro and is awaiting another battle, since the rebel army is nearby.

The hospital at Murfreesboro
4 Feb. 1863

Dear Mother, brother, and sisters,

Despite the fact that I have not heard from home for two months, and do not expect to hear from you as long as I am in this miserable condition, I will write to you. Possibly you have not received the letters I wrote you since I was wounded, because this hospital is the worst den of thieves I have struck since I joined up. Our doctor and our steward are of the worst types imaginable. We hope to be sent to Nashville—or anywhere; but I do not believe there will be much moving until I can move myself. I am at present so well that I can get around without a cane. Now that I am feeling better, I am doing quite nicely; and I have bought food from someone I have become acquainted with.

It is said that the forces are at each other again; but we know nothing about the outcome. The army has received marching orders for tomorrow. Ole Christensen left me and went back to the regiment three days ago. He had not fully recovered but was much improved.

Camp near Murfreesboro
26 Feb. 1863

Dear Brother,

Yesterday I received your very welcome letter of January 6, which gave me great joy. I notice that there has been a great rumpus about the draft. My suspicion is that those who remained at home may not have had much respect for soldiers, and now it is so decreed that they shall get a taste of what the latter have endured. The greatest disgrace is that the proudest and best men in the neighborhood have proved themselves cowards and because of it have fled.

By way of news I can tell you that I returned to the regiment and the company yesterday, and thus escaped from the tiresome hospital. I am practically all well again, but probably not strong enough for marching. However, I am finally back with the company and am taking care of myself.

When on that rainy day I returned to the company, the boys received me with great rejoicing—and the officers too. Furthermore, they came with an offer to make me "orderly sergeant"—to which the whole company gave its approval. But as I am not very strong yet, I thanked them for the offer and said that I could not accept it until I had recovered fully. Everyone has given me help and encouragement—first and foremost my brother and Ole Haldorsen. Votes have been cast to pick those who showed most bravery in the battle. They are to get horses and serve as cavalry and be free of guard duty. There are to be five privates, a corporal, and a sergeant. I was chosen sergeant by our company and Ole W. Olson corporal.

Our captain has asked for discharge papers and expects to leave us and return home. He has been in poor health. Lieutenant Thor Simonsen will undoubtedly become captain, but it is uncertain who will become lieutenant.

It began raining yesterday and has continued without letup. As a result my letter is so poor because there is hardly a dry place to sit. I will therefore close with a friendly greeting to all of you.

Murfreesboro, March 1863

Dear Brother,

. . . I also want to relate that I am again in good health but not able to take part in the marches because my wounded hip continues to be weak.

Three or four days ago practically all the troops were readied for battle with the rebels. Our division was stationed out front, two miles from the main encampment. We were back in our camp again when suddenly one night at 12 o'clock orders came to leave in a hurry and get inside the fortifications. We felt certain that there would be a fight. Naturally we obeyed orders and took everything with us. In the morning we heard cannonading and all of us believed that a battle would take place. But nothing further happened. The next day our division returned to the place where we had been stationed, and there was no fighting. The rebels had discovered that they could not do anything and went back the same way they had come. At present we are encamped a mile and a half from town. The prospects for a battle are very slight because rumors have it that the enemy is beginning to tire.

I want to mention that a man named Svend Borgarson, who was wounded at Murfreesboro, has had one of his legs amputated above the knee.

Near Murfreesboro
21 May 1863

Dear Brother,

. . . I am in good health and am living well. The same can be said of my brother and all our acquaintances. We have been on outpost duty for four days and we may continue a few days more. Yesterday our regiment paid the rebels a visit; and our young little major was in command. There were none but the 15th and a few cavalrymen. We crossed the advance line and then made our way through a dense cedar forest, over a mountain, and across a clover field. We chose this roundabout way so as to avoid the main highway. After an hour's march we came to some fine farms where we trudged over well-seeded and planted fields and tore down all the fences in our way.

After a while Lieutenant Colonel Johnson learned from a Negro where the rebels had their outpost. Preparations were then made to capture the whole group. Company A was left directly facing the sentry. The rest of the regiment made a detour, and at the proper moment the company was to attack the post. The rebels manning the fort would then have to fall back toward the main force and would thus be trapped. Everything was carefully planned and was easy to execute. If the lieutenants in Company A had not started arguing about the command and thus given the alarm too early, the whole thing would have gone well. Even so, our company and another had come so near to surrounding them that when the rebels fled they were within range of our rifles, as we were at their rear. We gave them a salvo, killing two and wounding several. But then we had to withdraw because we were far forward and our line of retreat could easily have been cut.

Our regiment has a good reputation hereabouts, but as a result we have to be both hounds and hares and are sent hither and yon like the cavalry. It is said that we are to be on the go again in the morning; but I hope this is not true. The other regiments have done nothing, so it must be another's turn—but then, of course, we are not being forgotten either.

Camp near Murfreesboro, Tennessee
7 June 1863

Dear and precious Brother,

Your very welcome letter of May 23 reached me a couple of days ago while we were out reconnoitering, so I could not answer it earlier. First I will tell you that I am in fairly good health. But I am not well satisfied with our march because we returned yesterday evening both tired and wet. On the fourth of this month we received orders to pack up rations for seven days and be prepared to march at any time—and to carry all of it. That meant having three days' rations in the bag and four days' rations in the knapsack. We got ready because when the order comes to "go," it's futile to say "no." Soon we were in full march and before long we heard cannonading directly ahead of us. We advanced almost to our outpost and lay there in line of battle a couple of hours; then forward again to the outpost—and another halt. But we did not listen very long to the cannons before we made an attempt to capture those rebel guns. In this we failed, however, because the rebels took to their heels. When darkness fell we returned to the outpost, where we spent the night and were pelted by a severe rainstorm. On the 6th we returned to our old camp and today several members of our company served as sentinels. Tomorrow the whole regiment will be sent on outpost duty for ten days. I am not feeling well at present. If I am no better tomorrow, I will not go with them.

The heat grows more intense every day.

The worst thing is that we lost our doctor who had been with us since the battle of Murfreesboro. He was the best one we have had, and we have had five since we left Wisconsin. The last one became ill. The others grew tired and got themselves discharged because the soldiers complained about them. God knows what we will get now.

Camp near Manchester [Tenn.], 30 June 1863

Dear Brother,

. . . We left Murfreesboro on the 24th and came to our present camp, thirty miles southeast, on the 28th at 12 o'clock midnight. These thirty miles were the toughest we have ever experienced. It started raining the moment we left and has kept on almost continuously since. Furthermore, the road was so blocked by rebels that we had to fight them practically all the way and drive them off whenever they showed up. But forward we had to go, often in mud almost to the knees. We took some prisoners and three little towns, Manchester, Shelbyville, and Tullahoma.

Today we were on review so I have reports to write—therefore this very short letter. It is said that we will be on the go again tomorrow, down toward Chattanooga—to take the city. That will be a great fight if the rebels decide to offer resistance. But "Rosy" [General Rosecrans] is the man to crush those devils. They call him a dog, but they are as afraid of him as hens are of a hound.

> Old Rosy is the man;
> By him we all will stand.
> Rosecrans we all stand by
> And fight the rebels 'till we die.
> The glorious Union we will restore,
> The Negroes we do not care anything for.[5]

Adieu and farewell for now—they are yelling and shouting "Nils" all around me because they are to draw rations, write letters, and such things.

(The rest of the letters for 1863 are lost.)

Strawberry Plains [Tenn.], 18 March 1864

Dear, precious Mother,

Now while I have a bit of spare time I will take the opportunity to tell you, dear mother, that I am in good health and that I am pleased to be back with my regiment. I arrived at our present station on the 9th of this month. We are located sixteen miles from Knoxville, by a Virginia Rail-road bridge over the Tennessee River. The regiment returned from the front the evening I came. At present we are doing guard duty at the bridge and working on the fortifications nearby. Some say that we will be staying here, while others are expecting marching orders.

I was well received by the boys. All of them had been anxiously awaiting my return because there had been much disorder in the company during my absence. I was very glad to find that all the men in the company were in good spirits despite the fact that they had endured terrible hardships, fighting and doing outpost duties. They had lived on half- and at times quarter-rations and were out in severe weather with poor clothing, since they were too far from the railroad to secure supplies. Now, however, we are fully equipped with both clothing and rations. The army has advanced more than twenty miles; but it is said that Longstreet has pulled back, so there is no fighting going on.

I must not forget to mention that the whole regiment had agreed to reenlist and was already on the way home; but when they had gone some thirty miles they had to do about-face because the rebels were advancing and our brigadier general, Willich, did not want to meet them unless the 15th was in the brigade. He praises our regiment very highly and said to General Wood that he could take his Norwegian regiment, the 15th, and his German regiment, the 32nd Indiana, and lick Wood's whole division. He is the best general we have had because he always sees to it that we have enough to eat.

I do not hear any more talk of reenlisting; and in our company they say not a single man will do so if I decide against it. I have been offered the rank of first lieutenant if I will stay on; but I have no such desire, and Tosten goes crazy when they talk about reenlisting, so you need not fear that he will join again. Those who refused to reenlist the first time they were to have furlough were sent to other regiments in the brigade. Thus, Andrew Thompson was transferred to the 68th Indiana regiment; and it is uncertain whether those men will come back to the 15th.

The things I brought with me came through in good shape, and you are thanked ever so much for the cheese I took along for Lieutenant [Thor] Simonsen. Tosten and I have eaten the butter but, of course, we shared it with certain acquaintances. Tosten also sends his thanks.

Strawberry Plains, 1 April 1864

Dear Brother,

. . . There is no more talk in our company of reenlisting. Those who had signed up have taken their names off again. There possibly are some forty or fifty who have agreed to continue, but none from our company. It is not certain when they will be going home.

The regiment received twenty-nine recruits two days ago, but no one joined our company. Andrew Thompson has returned to the regiment. We are busy with guard duty and work on the fortifications; but we have full rations and live very well all the time. Lieutenant Simonsen will probably go home on furlough.

I can not write a real letter but merely scribble a bit in the hope of hearing from you again.

McDonald Station, 25 April 1864

Dear Brother,

. . . I am in good health as before, and so are Tosten and all your acquaintances in the company. We are now encamped about twenty-five miles east of Chattanooga. We came here on the 19th of this month and pitched camp in a cornfield on very high, level ground. This makes things very unpleasant because of the severe wind which practically rips up both rocks and soil. We have had company, regimental, and brigade drills; but we mount guard only once a week. Our corps is now commanded by General Howard, who previously led the eleventh corps. I believe our division is at present located in this area, so presumably we will soon be advancing. Rumors have it that the rebels are pulling their forces away from here toward Virginia for the defense of Richmond. Today most of the company is on guard duty with Lieutenant Simonsen, thus leaving me some time for writing while they are away.

Yesterday was Sunday and I was out in the neighborhood visiting farmers. But the girls are not easy to get along with. They always want to discuss the secession question—and there is this about all the girls in Tennessee that they both smoke and chew tobacco. You know that I am very moderate in the use of those articles; and I can't stand women who use tobacco.

McDonald Station, 1 May 1864

Dear Brother,

I received your letter a few days ago, but I have been so busy copying muster rolls, payrolls, and monthly reports that I did not have time to write earlier. I am still in good health; so are also our brother and others whom you know. Yesterday we had review and expect to be paid soon, unless we get marching orders before that happens. I am afraid that we will have to be off in a day or two. It is certain that we are to advance against the rebels at Dalton. I hope we will beat them easily because we are strong enough and old General Bragg's army is afraid of us. Of course, we have also put some fear into Longstreet's army and the other rebel forces which came here last fall to teach us how to fight, so they said. Our army has been strengthened with numerous recruits and everything is in such good order that we hope to give them the death blow. A march of about two days will bring us to the firing line near the fortifications at Dalton—and then the outcome rests with fortune.

Just now orders came to pack up everything which is not absolutely needed on the march and to fall in line with light equipment, because the roll of the drum may sound at any time. It will very soon be heard; the tents will take wing, and masses of bayonets like forests will suddenly appear moving along the roads. There will be the crash of thunder again and the shrill signals of trumpets.

We now have a strong brigade, and yesterday we got our old German Brigadier General Willich back. He has been home on furlough. He reviewed the brigade yesterday and was greeted with jubilant hurrahs, after which he delivered a speech. He gave a special talk to us in which he said: "Now, Fifteenth, we will soon be off to flail the rebels; and by God, we will make it hot for them and thrash them so they will not trouble us any more—those mongrels. And you can be happy," he continued, "because you are 'the bully boys' of the brigade together with my own regiment, the 32nd Indiana."

Thanks for the stamps you sent me.

Battlefield near Kingston [Georgia], 20 May 1864

Dear Brother,

I have not heard from home for a long time. But I can report that recently we have endured many terrible struggles and battles. On the third of this month we broke camp at Cleveland, Tennessee, and set off on the campaign through Georgia. On the seventh we arrived near Tunnel Hill, eight miles from Dalton, where we first became aware of the now familiar music of cannons and rifles. The place was soon attacked by another division, so our corps did not take part in the fighting. In the afternoon, however, we advanced, but soon had to halt because the rebels had mounted batteries on a high mountain half a mile away and were ready to receive us behind their strong entrenchments. In the evening our regiment advanced in order toward that mountain. We could hear the rebels all night, but there was no firing. In the morning came orders for our regiment to assume advance-guard duty. We made ourselves ready; but before we got off, new orders came for "the 15th" to storm the heights immediately. So away we went, but with heavy hearts because we would sooner have tried to storm a fortress: this mountain is so steep that a man can hardly climb it.

Onward and upward we went, however; and it did not take long before the familiar "pop-pop-pop" sounded, followed by the whine of the rifle bullets as they whistled by. Nevertheless, we went steadily on—"like bold lions," said General Willich. Fortune was with us this time: when we began climbing one side of the mountain our men had also arrived at the other side, and one regiment started to climb. So we were fortunate enough to reach the top without losing a single man. But the whole ridge was not captured at the time, as it is many miles long. Later in the afternoon we were relieved and went back to our brigade. There we found practically the whole army drawn up in battle array; and the roar of cannons became more and more pronounced along the whole line. In the morning a certain regiment (35th Illinois) of our brigade was to storm another part of the same mountain. But there the climbing was even worse and the rebels were prepared to meet them. The brave regiment, however, steadily forced its way upward against the rifle fire. But when our men came very close and the rebels saw them pressing on to take the heights, they began rolling stones on our troops while others kept up the fire. It was horrible to listen to this and, of course, much worse to take part in it. The regiment was forced to pull back. General Willich was displeased with this development and immediately planned an attack with the whole brigade. This was denied him, however, as the chief of our corps, General Howard, forbade such an attack

The day passed without our brigade engaging in any fighting beyond some outpost skirmishing along the mountain. But the next day the whole line was in motion again. Our regiment assumed outpost duty along a part of the mountainside where covering for us had been prepared during the night. There we lay all day; and in the evening, when we were relieved, our company E lost a man whom the sharpshooters hit in the head. Until after noon on the 11th we lay listening to shooting on our left; then we were suddenly ordered toward the left flank on the run. We arrived there at the fixed time just as the alarm was sounded that the rebels were intending to outflank our position. We threw up entrenchments and were ready to receive them. Everyone itched to get into a fight with the rebels so that we could make use of our breastworks—an opportunity we seldom enjoy but which the rebels always have. We waited until sundown; however, nothing was heard from them.

At night we were again on outpost duty and in the morning we were ordered back to our right flank. We had barely got underway when orders came for us to march to Dalton. The rebels had bypassed our men on the right, who were thus in danger of being surrounded. We marched through Dalton and ten miles beyond, but did not become aware of the enemy except for some skirmishes with their rear guard.

During the morning of the 14th we advanced several miles and made contact with the rebels at a point where they had taken up positions behind barricades that they had thrown up. Skirmishing soon began and before long three of our corps—the 4th, 14th, and 20th—were in battle order. Then the fight broke out in earnest with cannonading and uproar as if all the elements were let loose. Our regiment got involved after a part of the enemy entrenchments had been taken and there was a threatened shortage of ammunition. We went at it briskly and got into a very hot spot: the rebels tried several times to dislodge us and reconquer the lost positions. The rain of bullets was terrible, but the breastworks helped us very much, otherwise we would all have been wiped out. A couple of hours passed before we were relieved.

On the morning of the 15th we were sent in again with 60 rounds of ammunition. In the night our advance guard had been moved forward and trenches had been dug so near the enemy strongholds that from the position our regiment occupied that day we fired right into their fortifications. The rebels could not get near their cannons because we kept close watch and picked them off as quickly as they came out from their shelter. Finally they became so scared that they did not dare show themselves or even fire at us. You can take it from me that "the 15th" kept an eye on them. The following night the rebels tried to storm our lines in the dark, but they failed miserably. In the morning they left their positions and continued the retreat. We have pursued them and are now forty miles from Atlanta. Today we are resting; but tomorrow there will be fighting again. I believe the rebels will soon get enough of the Yankees.—During the day we fought at the above-mentioned entrenchments. Our company, which now numbers only twenty men, fired 3,000 shells.

General Willich is wounded, leaving our brigade to be led by a colonel.

Battlefield near Dalton, 1 June 1864

Dear Brother,

I have delayed writing to you day after day, hoping to see an end to this battle, but as yet God alone knows what the outcome will be. The present battle began the 25th of last month and is still raging. We are within rifle range of the enemy and have thrown up quite good breastworks. Skirmishes occur both day and night. Every now and then we make a sally, and in other places they attack us. On the 27th our division was pulled out of the line and sent toward the left. Soon we attacked and the fighting grew more severe. Before long we came clear up to their entrenchments and were ordered to storm them. Both sides opened fire so the ground shook and everything trembled. Six Union lines, consisting of two brigades from our division, were driven back with heavy losses. Our regiment was part of the third line, and as usual it stood its ground too long. Finally, a counterattack after dark by the rebels drove the rest back. As far as I can determine, our regiment lost half of its men in dead and wounded, besides a few prisoners whom the rebels took after nightfall. Our company, thank God, was quite fortunate as we lost only Lieutenant Simonsen and three men: two killed and one wounded.

Every night the rebels have launched a foolish attack against us and have been driven back from our trenches with great losses. Yesterday our division took up a new position nearer the rebel fortifications. We advanced during the night and dug trenches until daybreak. Then some fellows began chopping a bit with their axes. The rebels immediately became aware of our presence, and for four hours they launched charges against us. But because of our work that night they were given a glorious reception, despite the fact that we had had no sleep. The rifle fire crackled like a severe hailstorm. Tonight our regiment was on duty in the line; and as usual the rebels attacked at one o'clock, but we sent them packing with heavy losses.

Today there is continuous fighting, with terrific cannonading. We have put several cannons in place and are still working on our trenches to enable us to keep the enemy off with fewer men. Our plan is to attack their flank. This battle will likely be the greatest one in the western area; and God knows when and where the end will come because there are fortifications and breastworks extending fifteen or twenty miles in length. The enemy rests one of his flanks on a river and the other on a mountain so he will not be easy to outflank. But I believe he will soon get enough, unless fortune forsakes us. Now the uproar is growing stronger everywhere; I believe we are going to launch a flank attack against them.

I am in good health and so is my brother. All of us are in good spirits and feel assured of victory, unless the officers drive us pell-mell straight into the enemy entrenchments to be slaughtered, as happened on the 27th when we lost 1,500 men. Our brigade lost twice as many as any other brigade in the division.

Battlefield near Atlanta, 4 August 1864

Dear Brother,

. . . At present we are in our entrenchments about two miles from Atlanta. We have been lying here ten days without any engagements except for outpost skirmishing, which goes on both day and night. Yesterday a fight of some importance took place on the right flank, but as yet we do not know what the results were. We have almost worked our way around Atlanta and every effort is being made to get control of the railroad. When the road is wrecked, it will not take long to conquer the place. It may, of course, take several days. Our batteries exchange bombs with the rebel fortifications every day, and at times bombs are also fired into this beautiful city. On July 20th and 22nd we were engaged in some fierce fighting. During the first of those days the 4th and the 20th corps were on the right flank and on the second day the 15th, 16th, and 17th corps were engaged. These corps were led by General McPherson, who fell in battle. The outcome of the two fights was that the rebels were badly beaten. I must tell you that after the battle our troops, who remained in control of the field, had to bury the dead and take care of the wounded. Among the dead we found a girl in rebel uniform. She was shot through the breast. Another girl was found among the wounded. One of her legs was shot off. She was taken to the hospital.

Several days ago an expedition was sent south to Macon, Georgia, for the purpose of relieving some prisoners. The distance is about one hundred miles and it will take many days. I hope the expedition succeeds in freeing the captives from their tough position. Yesterday I got news of Lieutenant Simonsen—he is alive, a prisoner. He is at the prison camp toward which the expedition was sent. We have been on outpost duty every other day, but of late our company has not lost a single man. Two men in company I were wounded some days ago; and yesterday company H lost a man. We engaged in a line attack by rushing forward against the rebel fortifications. Our brigade lost many men.

Camp near Atlanta, 18 August 1864

Dear Brother,

I will again report that I am still in good health and spirits. We have been lying here almost a month and there is little change. Our entrenchments are so strong by now that it is impossible for the enemy to sally forth against us. It is rumored that we are to be moved so as to change the direction of the battle line. Our corps, which is on the left flank, will be sent to the Chattahoochee River to protect our lines of communication. At the same time the right flank is to circle around to the south of the city in order to cut the Atlanta & Macon railway, which forms the rebel line of communication toward the south. We have done quite well here except for the continual outpost skirmishing. At times we go on raids to bring in such things as corn for cooking, peaches, apples, etc. It is warm here, but not as extremely so as last year.

Camp near Atlanta, 19 September 1864

Dear Sister,

. . . We are lying quietly in camp and expect to be here a while—until we are paid. And probably we will not be sent out again as there are only two months left of our military service. I am also sending you a heart made of a shell as a souvenir of Atlanta, where we won our great victory over the rebels.

We are to have a good supper as Tosten is cooking dried apples and frying meat. What are you having to eat today? Let me know how my dear old mother is getting along, Sigrid,—if sorrow is with her still.

Camp near Atlanta, 20 September 1864

Dear Brother,

We are now encamped about four miles from Atlanta, and here we have been since the eighth of this month when we returned from south of the city. I wrote on the 10th and told about our movements. Nevertheless, I can not refrain from rehashing some of it while we are lying quietly waiting for the paymaster, who is coming to pay us off. Possibly we will escape going out again. Anyway, we are well satisfied, as I believe we have done our duty in this war.

The regiment is out foraging today and I am in the camp; but I am very busy drawing up the company papers. The pressure is on to get everything in shape before we are discharged; and our commander, Lieutenant [Ole] Olson, is a poor writer—as are most of the lieutenants. It is beyond my comprehension how they can obtain their positions without being able to write well enough to prepare their own reports. I am ashamed to mention it, but that's the way they have all been in company F except Lieutenant [Svend] Samuelson.—They get the pay while others do the work. I am a poor marcher because of my wounded hip.

What kind of work shall we undertake when I get home? I have never thought of my homecoming until recently. But now it does not look too unpromising, after the numerous tough fights we have gone through. It is odd to think of the many bullets which have whistled by one's head without doing any harm. God's blessings on you.

Your brother
Nils J. Gilbert

NOTES

1. First Lieutenant Nils J. Gilbert from Manitowoc, Wisconsin, enlisted 12 December 1861. The next day he was appointed sergeant of Co. F. By order of General Rosecrans he was placed on the Roll of Honor because one night he, with three companions, crept through enemy lines to rescue a wounded soldier who had been left behind on the field of battle. He was badly wounded at Stone's River . . . He was born, 1842, in Østre Slidre, Valdres. Resides (1916) in Eleva, Wisconsin. [Ager's note]

2. Corporal Nils Brown later escaped and disappeared. Lieutenant Thompson marched with the company until he fell at Chickamauga. [Ager's note]

3. It was General Jefferson C. Davis, not Buell, who killed General Nelson. He was court-martialed, but the matter was hushed up. Davis later commanded the division in which the 15ᵗʰ Wisconsin regiment served. [Ager's note]

4. The rest of the letter is missing, but it can be supplemented by a letter he wrote to Mr. O. Torrison, which is found in Buslett's *15ᵗʰ Wis. Reg. Historie.* [Ager's note]

5. These lines, evidently a popular song, appear in the text in English.

Letters from Lars and Knud Olsen Dokken[1]

Camp Lyon, Bird's Point [Missouri], 8 March 1862

Dear Parents,

As we have arrived here safely we must send you, dear parents, a few words to let you know how we fared during the trip. We left Madison on March 2 and arrived in Chicago at 7 o'clock that evening. We were greeted by the people there with hurrahs and great applause as we marched through the city. We came to a halt not far from the station where we were to board the train again, and there we were given a flag that the Norwegian women in Chicago had made for us. As soon as we were quartered on the train we were treated to coffee and cakes. We left Chicago about 11 o'clock that night and arrived at Alton on the Mississippi the following evening. There we boarded a steamer that brought us to St. Louis Tuesday morning. We remained there until early Wednesday and then continued by steamer, arriving here—a few miles from Cairo—Thursday morning. The trip from St. Louis was pretty chilly, as we had to sleep on deck. Lars is sick—presumably with a cold. He has been in bed now for four days, but of course we hope that he will soon be well again. He is in the hospital and has good care as regards food, doctor's help, and medicine. Otherwise conditions are pretty fair in this camp, since we have good houses or barracks to live in. Besides our regiment, there are a couple of other infantry units stationed here and an artillery detachment.

There is no enemy force in the immediate neighborhood, but our outposts did pick up three rebel soldiers yesterday. We do not believe, however, that we will get into any battles very soon—probably never, because the South must be almost on its last legs. Furthermore, there are so many

Left: Lars Olsen Dokken   1839–1863.
Right: Knud Olsen Dokken   1843–1862.
Courtesy of Della Kittleson Catuna.

troops who have been in training longer that we have. They will naturally be sent into action before us.

Your devoted sons, Knud and Lars Olsen

18 March 1862

My precious parents,

I must write a few words now to tell you that I am in good health and
am feeling well. We left Bird's Point on the 14th and went down the
Mississippi aboard a steamer. My brother Lars remained behind, however, as he was sick. But I hope he will follow in a few days because he
was improving when we left. It is now three days since we arrived here.
We are only three miles distant from the enemy. Our gunboats are firing
at them every day—and they at us, so there is no safety at any time. We
believe we will attack them when our whole force gets here. We do not
know how strong the enemy is, but there are quite a number of them.
They are located on an island and are surrounded by our troops. Five of
our men have been killed and four wounded. But we infantrymen have
not fired a shot as yet.

There is nothing else to write about. I hope that all is well with you. Whether we shall ever see each other again rests in the hands of the Almighty, since he rules our ways.

Knud Olsen Dokken

Camp Lyon, Bird's Point, 26 March 1862

Dear precious parents,

Since I have the opportunity I will send you a few lines and tell you how I am getting along. Since I came here I have been sick much of the time, but at present—thank God—I am improving somewhat and I hope that in a short while I will be well again. Our regiment got orders to leave here on the 13th for New Madrid, which is situated some forty miles farther down the Mississippi. All who were well packed up and left, among them my brother Knud. Those who were sick, besides a few other members of the regiment, remained here at Bird's Point. I believe there are about a hundred of us here—several from each company. Some of the men who are in the best physical condition have been set to guard the railroad that runs through this place. Thus, the regiment is divided into three parts and we do not know when we will join the others. It may be a long time before we are reassembled. I do not believe there is any danger from the enemy as long as we are here. Very many got sick as soon as we arrived, due—I believe—to the unfamiliar climate and the filthy Mississippi water that we have to drink.

New Madrid was evacuated by the enemy the day our regiment arrived. Thus our men did not take part in any battle. They are still quartered in the boat that took them down the river. It is said that they find the nights pretty cold and dismal. There is an island in the Mississippi called Island Number Ten that is strongly fortified by the rebels. The northern forces have tried to take it with their gunboats, but it is so well protected that they have not succeeded yet. The island is located some distance below New Madrid. As land forces can not be used against it, our regiment has not seen any action there.

I do not have anything more to write about this time, so I will end my simple scribbling with a sincere greeting to all of you from your devoted son.

Lars Olsen Dokken

April 1862

Dear parents,

I was very sick for a while. But now I am in fairly good shape again. I am thankful to God for having given me back my health and strength. Furthermore, I can report that I rejoined the regiment on April 2 and met my brother Knud, who is hale and hearty in every respect.

I will now tell you a bit about an engagement we had on March 31. About 500 men of our regiment took part in this fight as well as seven companies of the 27th Illinois, a cavalry company, and an artillery detachment—probably some 1,400 men, all told. We left camp on the 30th and advanced some distance. Then all of us bedded down for the night in a cornfield. But we were up bright and early in the morning, arriving at the rebel camp when they were about to have breakfast. Then the artillery and the cavalry began firing at them. They became so frightened that they took to flight like bewildered sheep, leaving everything behind: guns, clothing, and many other things. The enemy force was quite large—probably some 3,000 or 4,000 men. Very few were killed, but we took 15 prisoners.

Now Island No. 10 has also been taken. We caught between 5,000 and 6,000 captives. This happened on the 6th of April. There was no fighting because many of our troops managed to get behind the enemy, who then surrendered quickly. Our regiment arrived at the island on the 8th of this month. The gunboats had been lying here for three weeks, firing at the batteries without doing them any harm. There are now five companies on the island and five on the other bank of the Mississippi, namely companies C, D, G, E, and B. They keep guard and do various types of work, cleaning up after the rebels. The companies on the island are similarly engaged. We are now setting up batteries on the other shore in case the rebels should attempt a breakthrough in the future.

There are lots of cannon hereabouts, both on the island and on the other shore, and all sorts of ammunition that they had to leave. The general has said that we have had too little drilling to get engaged yet in battles, and we must therefore do guard duty some place or another. I do not know anything in particular about the war. I believe you learn much more about it than we do, except what happens in our immediate surroundings, because you receive *Emigranten* earlier than we do. The last issue we have seen of the paper is no. 14. I have no more to write about this time.

I must tell you that the woods are in full leaf and the fields and meadows are covered with flowers. The weather is already quite warm so we are afraid that it will be very hot here when summer comes. Please write to us as soon as possible and let us hear about happenings in the neighborhood.

Lars Olsen Dokken

Island No. 10, Tenn., 4 May 1862

Dear parents, brothers, and sisters,

We received your welcome letter of April 10 on the 20th, and we thank you very much. We have read it with much pleasure. Brother Knud has been ill for a while with typhoid fever and has stayed in bed for about a week. Fortunately, I am well at present, for which I must thank the Lord. Many members of our regiment are suffering from typhoid fever; and several have died, among them Christian Røstø and one by the name of Ole Evensen Dal. I do not know the names of the two others who died. Ole Evensen has a brother near Perry or Primrose. May God strengthen all who are sick or sorrowing, both those at home and those in the land of the enemy. . .

We are continuing the work on the fortifications but have not completed much more than the trench. It is six feet deep along one side and ten or twelve along the other, and is filled with dirt. On the inner side of the battery a board fence is raised six feet high to keep the dirt from caving in on the cannons that are to be stationed there. We have emplaced four cannons so far, but there are to be fifty all told. The fortifications stretch clear across the island; and this will be the best place for setting up a blockade on the Mississippi. Every boat that comes up the river must give a signal; otherwise we fire at it with one of our newly emplaced cannons.—As regards the war, I have nothing to relate. But we have heard that New Orleans has been taken. Best wishes.

Your sons, Lars and Knud Olsen Dokken

Island No. 10, 4 June 1862

Dearest parents, brothers, and sisters,

. . . Many men of the regiment are sick and confined to the hospital. Five members of our company have died since we came to the island and six are at present in the hospital. Furthermore, about a hundred others are unable to work. Our company and company K have been moved from the island and are now encamped on the opposite shore, about a mile from the other five companies that were stationed here earlier. We are now located within a fort, which is surrounded entirely by deep trenches, so we are unable to get out or in. There is a gate at a bridge where guards are posted day and night. We must have a pass from our captain for either exit or entry. Each side of the fort measures about twenty rods in length. Since coming here we have had to mount guard every other day. There are so many guard posts that those of us who are well have enough to do. It is pretty difficult, because we do not get as much sleep as nature craves. We can, of course, rest during our free day; but then we have to clean our guns and do other jobs. In the morning when we are to mount guard, we are inspected by our captain. We have just gotten a new captain by the name of George Wilson from Madison. He is a very kind fellow. Our former captain (Knud Sime) was discharged for incompetence and has now returned home. Our colonel, Hans Heg, came back this evening. He has been home in Madison for a brief visit, as you probably know.

And I must tell you that on May 26 we were issued new uniforms which are very dressy. Our hats are black, decorated with a bugle and an eagle and a black feather stuck on one side. We were also given a black coat and pants to match, a white woolen undershirt, and a pair of shoes. But we have not received our pay, nor do we know when we will get it.

Next I must say something about the 17th of May, which our officers managed to make a free day for us so the regiment could celebrate and have some fun. Our company got beer shipped in from Cairo. But some men in company A got drunk, started to fight, and were then shut up in the guardhouse. Other members of the company, however, went to the guardhouse, drove the guards away, and freed the captives. Our captain, who was officer for the day, appeared and tried to restore order among the men. But one of them struck him a blow, and the whole company went wild. Then the other companies were given commands to restore law and order. "Fall in! fall in!" shouted the officers, and we fell in line as quickly as possible. We were told to load our guns at once and were marched to the guardhouse, where we lined up. Company A was mustered by itself and we surrounded them. The major then put the group on trial and the whole company had to hand over their rifles to him. Six of them were put under arrest—so also their lieutenant—and there they are still sitting; but sentence has not been pronounced yet so we do not know what will happen to them. Most likely the punishment will be severe. A member of our company is also under arrest for falling asleep at his post. His name is Ole Olson Nedrejordet.[2] He has not come to trial yet but I know the judgment will be severe because there is a death penalty for those who fall asleep while on guard. Yesterday a fellow was punished because he refused to tidy up his tent. He was hanged up by the hands for a short while—as long as they thought he could stand it. So we either obey our officers' commands—or else!

We do not know how long we will be staying here. The 7th Wisconsin artillery has arrived and a cavalry company from Illinois. They are stationed here for picket duty. They roam about in the country and capture rebels wherever they can find them.

As regards my brother's death—I suppose you have received the last letter I wrote you. He fell asleep on May 7. His mind was clear until the last breath. It was very sad for me—that it should happen so suddenly, here in a hostile land. But the Lord does all for our good. He knew what was best for him—to escape further strife in this evil world. I hope he is better off now than we, poor sinners, who are left. May God help and direct us along the right paths. . .

I must now end my brief and simple message. You are greeted most sincerely from all your neighbors here. Ole Iversen is poorly and so is Arne Helgesen; but the others are feeling quite well.

God's blessings be with you
Lars Olsen Dokken

Island No. 10, 11 June 1862

Dearest parents, brothers, and sisters,

I want to thank you most heartily for your letter of May 25. I see that you have received the information about my brother's death, which, of course, was a great sorrow for all of you. But we must be patient and let the will of God rule in all matters. You ask me to tell some more about his death. He was well reconciled to his fate, except that he had a desire to talk with you again. But it was not God's will that he should come home. He prayed much for himself, asking the Lord to show him his mercy. I read frequently for him, which gave him much consolation. His last days were passed in peace and quiet. He was resigned to the will of God and wished that all of us could be gathered together again with our Lord and Savior.

I have packed his clothes and delivered them to the captain. The bundle is addressed as follows: "To Mr. Kittel Larsen Dokken, Madison, Wis. Deceased Soldier's Clothes." I do not know when the bundle will arrive, since it has not been sent yet.

We have received orders to proceed up river by boat to Kentucky. We do not know exactly where we are going, but as soon as we come to a halt I will write to you again.

And now I will end my poor scribbling by telling you that many in our company are sick: Arne Helgesen, Ole Iversen, Svend Olson Larsgaard, and many others who will be left here in the hospital.

Union City, Tenn., 18 June 1862

Dearest parents, brothers, and sisters,

Since there is an opportunity, I will take pen in hand to write you a few lines and let you know that I am in good health—for which God be praised.

We left Island Number 10 in the evening of June 11 and arrived at Hickman [Kentucky] the next morning at 7 o'clock, where we stayed until about noon. Then we marched some twelve miles, and slept in a field overnight. The next morning we were off again, reaching Union City at 11 o'clock. There we pitched camp and set up our tents. We have been guarding the railroad and have repaired the bridge that the rebels had burned. There is a railway crossing here that is in utter disrepair. No trains have run since the rebels were driven away last spring when we were here and burned their camp and tents. Practically all the people have fled the town and the houses hereabouts are standing vacant.

I can report that the 12th and 13th Wisconsin regiments are here; also a regiment from Kansas and one from Missouri, as well as the 7th and 8th artillery companies from Wisconsin, besides contingents of artillery and cavalry that are stationed in this area. We have been transferred to Mitchell's brigade so we are now under the orders of our general. All the Norwegians in the 12th Wisconsin regiment are in good health. They were here and visited us several days ago. They have not been in any battles either, but they have had tough marching here in the South. However, they are living well and are in good spirits. We have received orders to leave here at 5 o'clock tomorrow morning. We are to follow the railway and put it in working order. I believe all the regiments I mentioned above will be kept together because we are under the same general. But I do not know how far we are to proceed on our march. Two companies of our regiment were left on the island as well as many individuals who were in the hospital. I am to greet you most sincerely from Nils Levorsen Slaaten and tell you that he is in good health and that he hopes you are the same.

Humboldt, Tennessee, 3 July 1862

Dear parents, brothers, and sister,

... We broke camp on June 20th and marched five days, then we came to Trenton, a town eleven miles from here. There we got our mail. I received letters from Helge and Anders, and one from you. From Trenton we marched to Humboldt, where we are stationed now. We have our camp in an apple orchard, which is very pleasant. A lot of troops are stationed here, so the rebels can find us on every path in the state. Much property is destroyed when the union troops press forward—especially if they can find a rebel-owned farm. Lots of rebels come to town and swear loyalty to the union because now they dare not do otherwise. All who refuse to take the oath are put under arrest. The other night I stood guard by a house where we had six such people locked up, and I saw one whose hands were bound. Our troops scout the countryside and pick up such people and bring them in to town where they are cross-examined by the officers.

I do not know how long we will be staying here. We have not been paid yet, nor do we know when this will happen. We have not been paid for four months, and I know that you are waiting for money from me. I notice in your letter that you have talked with a member of our regiment who was back for a brief visit and that you wish I could also take a trip home. But that is impossible now when we have no money for travel. I also believe that those who are well will be refused furlough. This will be granted only to those who are sick.

The health condition of our regiment is getting better and better because we are getting more used to the food. We know nothing about those who were left on Island Number 10 or whether they will rejoin us.

Camp Iuka, Mississippi, 18 August 1862

Dear parents, brothers, and sisters,

. . . I can inform you that we have moved again since I last wrote. That was in Camp Erickson. I have now written six letters since we left Island Number 10 and have received no reply; but I hope every day to hear from you. Our last move was some 15 or 18 miles to a little town called Iuka, located on the railway which runs from Corinth down through Alabama. We are not far from the state line. I have heard that we are soon to move farther toward the southeast, but we do not know exactly where we are headed.

We have not seen any of the rebel troops; but it is said that they flee farther south as rapidly as they are able. I saw in *Emigranten* that a member of our regiment named Anderson has written about our trip from Island Number 10, so you have evidently read about our whole journey. I will tell you about an order that was given while we were on dress parade the other day. We were to roam around in the area and find all the Negroes, and we should appoint one Negro for every eight soldiers to clean up in camp and around the tents. We have not secured any yet; but there already are many in our regiment who cook for the officers—also in other companies. We forage about in the neighborhood and find corn and apples—as much as we want every day; also hens and other things that the soldiers like. Lots of farmers have left the area. The farmers in many districts are unhappy because if the soldiers discover that the owners are in the rebel forces they will lose practically everything they have. And, of course, they will lose all their Negroes, because they are to be free. The Negroes are now working in the regiments for a salary running from eight to ten dollars per month.

Greet Engebret Paulson and P. Paulson from Syver Larsen and tell them that he is well. In conclusion I will ask you to write me as soon as possible.

Nashville, Tennessee, 5 September 1862

Dearest parents, brothers, and sisters,

I will now take pen in hand and let you know that we left our former campground, at Iuka, on August 21. Since that day we have covered, in our marches, about 180 miles. We went to a little town called Eastport on the Tennessee River. The first and second brigades crossed the river there, so we did not get through until the afternoon of the 23rd. On the 24th we arrived at Florence, a town in Alabama, where we remained quiet the next day. On the 26th we marched about 18 miles and on the 27th we came to Lawrenceburg, Tennessee. On the 28th we arrived at a little town, Mt. Pleasant, and on the 29th we reached Columbia. The following day we marched about 25 miles and spent the night in a forest. On the 31st we passed through the town of Franklin. On the 1st of September we went to Murfreesboro and the next day we lay quiet near that town. Then we stood guard until the morning of the 3rd. In the evening we set out toward Nashville and were on the march until midnight. There we lay until early morning when we were off for another march of some 15 miles. Now we are about 3 miles from the city and the whole army is gathered here. As regards our food—it is very poor, because we get nothing but pork and crackers while on the march. At times we get a little coffee, other times not. It is difficult to feel like a red-blooded man on such food during such marching. We hardly ever see milk. It may happen in places along the march that we can get our canteen—which holds a quart—filled at a price of 15 or 20 cents. It is difficult to get out to the farms because guards are posted when we pitch camp. Guard is kept at nearby farms even when the owners are serving in the Confederate army. Such methods of warfare I have never seen. If we do not behave differently, the war will never end. The rebels are reported to have advanced far into Tennessee and Kentucky, so it seems that this war is going no better than when it started. I have also heard that we will be pulling back again.

I am in good health, but we are footsore from all these marches.

Louisville, Kentucky, 28 September 1862

Dearest parents,

We are in good health and vigor, for which I thank the Lord. But we are quite exhausted from these long marches. Since August 21, when we left Iuka, we have marched about 400 miles. On the way to Louisville we ran into the rebels, who were stationed at the Green River. A battle took place on September 4 where the Confederates took about 4,000 of our troops prisoner. For two days we lay quiet about 12 miles from the enemy; and while we were lying there, they had time enough to escape.

Before the rebels left, they burned a railroad bridge and cut our communications with Louisville. Consequently we have received no mail nor have we sent any home. Ever since we left Iuka we have been right at the heels of the enemy. When the rebels were about 15 miles form Louisville they had to change their route in order to avoid our troops. I do not know how many men have participated in our march; but I should judge it is about four divisions. As for food, it has been pretty poor.

Perryville, Kentucky, 10 October 1862

Dearest parents,

. . . We did not stay long in Louisville. On October 1st we were again ready to break up and follow the rebels. They took a stand about 6 miles from Perryville, which is located some 60 or 70 miles southeast of Louisville. We marched through the towns of Mount Washington, Bardstown, and Springfield, and then to the little village where we engaged in battle. It began in the afternoon of October 7, and there was quite heavy fighting the rest of the day and on into the night. In the morning it broke loose again as early as possible. Our division and many of our troops were still held back as reserves, but about 3 o'clock in the afternoon our brigade and division rushed forward—then the fighting was very sharp. We were advancing on the right flank just as the 2nd Minnesota battery opened fire on the enemy, who replied immediately. Then we were ordered to lie down in a little ravine. While we were there, both the rebels and our own forces fired over us, the bullets whistling in the air. This went on for about an hour. But then the rebels beat a hasty retreat—and we after them on the run. We managed to take about 150 prisoners as well as eleven ammunition wagons loaded with powder and cannonballs. This happened on the right flank. In the center and on the left flank the fighting was quite intense that day. But finally our troops drove the rebels back and they began fleeing as fast as they were able. As soon as night fell, everything became still. At 3 o'clock in the morning we were again drawn up in line of battle and marched forward, but we could see nothing of the enemy. When we realized that they had fled, we marched back to the camp, which is located near the rebel hospitals where there are numerous dead and wounded. It is also said that there are many corpses lying about in the woods—a terrible thing to see. I do not know what it looks like where our troops were stationed, but a great number fell on both sides. We have not heard, as yet, how many of ours were killed or wounded. It is horrible to see so many dead and maimed. I must thank God for holding his hand over us and saving us from the bullets.

According to reports, the enemy is not far from here—only some ten miles; so we must be prepared any minute to pursue them. I have not more to report about this at present, but I will say that our regiment is now very small. In our company there are only 39 men, so many are sick and have been left in various places—some in every town we have passed through.

Crab Orchard [Kentucky], 19 October 1862

Dearest parents, brothers, and sisters,

. . . And now I will let you know that we left the battlefield at Perry-ville on October 11th and started searching for the enemy. We criss-crossed through some woods hunting for them. Then we marched to a little town called Danville and from there to another called Lancaster. There we got in touch with the rebels, which resulted in some skirmish-ing between the advance guards. But when we began firing at them, they fled in a great hurry. Then we pitched camp in a little gorge where we lay until the next morning when we were again ready to pursue the rebels. But we saw neither hide nor hair of them. Then the whole division fell in line and marched through the town, only pausing a while to hoist the Union flag. We finally learned where the enemy had gone, and then we went on toward the little village—about a mile from here—where we have been encamped since October 16. Our regiment received orders to enter the town and post guards there and in the surrounding area. Yesterday our company was on duty and I was stationed beside a large decrepit building that was once a tavern but is now deserted except for a few old people. There are many such places that we must watch. We also have about 100 rebel prisoners whom we are guarding. The enemy is said to be some twenty miles from here and we are expecting orders to set out for Cumberland Gap. I do not know how soon we will be leav-ing, but we must be prepared to move at any time. I have no more news to relate this time, but I should love to see my home again, if only for a short while. It is now getting colder and colder at night to sleep under the open sky—as we must do, and have done, since we left Iuka. We have had no tents to sleep in, and that is pretty miserable when the weather is rainy and chilly, which it has been at times during our marches. Neither have we any clothes besides what we have on every day, except for a woolen blanket that we carry with us. The rest of our clothes and knap-sacks are said to have arrived in Louisville, but we have no idea when they will catch up with us.

Bowling Green, Kentucky, 3 November 1862

Dearest parents,

I take this occasion to write you a few simple lines and let you know that we have now returned to the town we left on September 17. We left Crab Orchard on October 20 and marched back to Lancaster and thence to Danville, after which we stayed a couple of days near a little town called Lebanon. During the night of October 25–26 about four inches of snow fell and it stayed on the ground more than a day. That made it pretty cold for us as we were without tents several days. But we built ourselves huts out of bushes and branches in which we stayed during the night. The next day (27th) we left for Bowling Green. On October 31 we were mustered in for two more months; but we have received no pay, so now we have four months' wages due us, which we expect to get soon. . . . We have now recovered our clothes and knapsacks that were left here when we set out for Louisville. Also many men have left the hospitals and rejoined the regiment. Among them are Arne Helgesen, Julius Haaverud, and others whom I do not know.

Camp near Nashville, 10 November 1862

Dear parents, brothers, and sisters,

I received your welcome letters of August 1 and 22 yesterday for which you are dearly thanked. At present I am in good health except that my feet have been quite sore at times during the lengthy marches we have been engaged in of late. I only hope that we can now stay here for a while and get matters in order again. I also want to thank you for the ten three-cent stamps. It is so difficult to secure such things here.

We left Bowling Green on November 4th and marched to Nashville where we arrived on the 7th. Our camp is located about ten miles from the city and I believe we will be here for a while. We cannot proceed farther south, as we lack provisions. The railroad between Nashville and Bowling

Green is in disrepair so our supplies from there are transported in wagons pulled by three span of horses. The roads are very poor, so the going is tough. Lots of troops are encamped everywhere hereabouts.

Camp near Nashville, 12 December 1862

Dearest parents,

. . . I will inform you that we have changed camp sites and are now located about five miles south of Nashville. How many Union troops are lodged here I do not know, but there is said to be a strong rebel force not far distant. We expect to be attacked, because the rebels are anxious to recapture Nashville, according to reports.

A pound of butter now costs $.75 and a pound of tobacco $1.50. A skein of black linen thread costs $.25. A one-and-a-half-pint bottle of whiskey costs $2.00.

I can also tell you that Colonel Heg returned to the regiment on December 7th, bringing along a whole case full of items for company C—such as socks, boots, shoes sent them from home. He says that he has some recruits in Madison who will soon join us.

Hospital near Murfreesboro, 10 January 1863

Dearest parents, brothers, and sisters,

Despite my miserable condition I will attempt to take pen in hand and send you a few lines to let you know how I am getting along. I will first relate that we left Nashville the day after Christmas to drive the rebels away from Murfreesboro. We had a hard march all day in rain and mud way up our legs. In the evening we met some opposition and had a sharp little engagement where we took a cannon and five prisoners. The rest fled from us. Then we rested for the night, but the next day we were off again in rain and slush. We met no opposition until December 30th. That day we got into a fight where some men of our regiment were killed or wounded. One was killed and two wounded in our company. Then all was quiet until the following morning, when we were all ready again and the battle opened with a terrible exchange in which the rebels got the upper hand so we had to retreat. At that time a bullet struck the upper parts of my thighs. It went through one thigh and was taken out of the other, so both were wounded. But I must thank God for delivering me from sudden death, which became the lot of so many of our men on that field.

I was left lying on the field and the rebels swarmed around me from all directions. One of them swore and shouted: "Here is a damned Yankee." I lay still, but, of course, they had to take something from me, so they stole my blanket, my canteen, and a red leather wallet where I kept all the letters I had received from you. They also took a packet containing needles, thread, and such things. And, finally, they took the explanation of the catechism from me, which I regret the most. I, of course, expected that we would be taken prisoner, but two days later our troops drove the rebels back several miles, which cheered us greatly. I do not know how many men our regiment lost; but many are wounded and many were killed, one of them being our lieutenant-colonel.

As regards the pain—it is tolerable, and with God's help I hope to re- cover. I will soon be sent to a regular hospital in Nashville. I can think of nothing else to tell you at present, but I will write as often as possible.

Hospital in Nashville, 20 January 1863

Dearest parents, brothers, and sisters,

Today I will try to write you a few simple lines. I am now in the General Hospital at Nashville, having arrived here on the 12th of January. To begin with, I can tell you that I sent you a letter on the 10th which was written with a lead pencil. In it I told you that I had been wounded on the 31st of December. I assume you have already heard about the battle of Murfreesboro, which took place during the days around New Year's. It began on December 30, and the next day I was wounded in both thighs. The bullet pierced the left and was extracted from the right. The pain has been severe at times; and as yet I can not walk at all, but must stay in bed. With God's help, however, I hope to improve; but how soon this will occur is difficult for me to say. We can only hope that in time we will meet again, if that is the Lord's intent. Whatever happens, may His will be done.

Hospital in Nashville, 5 February 1863

Dearest parents,

I will take my pen and attempt to send you a few lines and let you know that I am in about the same condition as I was when I sent my last letter, which was dated January 20. Regarding my wounds, they have not improved any as yet. I hope, however, that I will recover, but it will

take a long time before my wounds begin to heal because I sometimes
suffer quite severe pain. It is worst at night, as I am unable to get much
sleep—and the hours seem so long.

But I have my hymnbook from which I read as often as I can—when
the pain and the aching of my wounds are not too severe. I hope that
God will give me health and strength again. He helps all those who suffer and are in need; so I hope he will also help me.

"I am poor and full of trouble
O merciful Jesus, come
And let my weak heart taste
Your sweet gospel,
That I even here in life
Must rich and blessed be."[3]

And I hope the time will come when we can meet again, but how soon
that will be is difficult to say. With this I will have to end my brief and
humble letter for now. Greet all my friends; but first and last you are
greeted from your devoted son.

May God's blessings be with you. This is my wish.

Nashville, 26 February 1863

Dearest parents,

I will try to take pen in hand to send you a few simple lines and let
you know that I have been feeling very bad lately, so it has been impossible for me to write to you earlier. At present I am a little better, but my
wounds are as open as before and drain night and day. The pain, however, is not as severe now, for which I must be happy and praise God. I
notice you have heard that the service in the hospitals here is supposed to
be poor. It may not be so great but I have not suffered want of anything.
I have not been in any condition to eat very much anyway. But I have
had some milk at times, and that has done me the most good, and I have
bought a few other things also that I am able to digest. But prices here
are so high; and now I have no more money, so there must be an end to
my buying because we have not received our pay yet.

And you ask whether I have any information as to when I can come
home. At present it is difficult for me to answer specifically. I will not
be able to leave for a long time, however, because I am still unable to get

out of bed. They must lift me into another bed whenever mine is to be made. But with God's help I hope to improve from now on—a hope that cheers me.

I did not lack anything in particular when I was wounded and lay out all night, because the rebels built a fire for me. So I was warm during both the day and the night. I had some food myself—but for me the hours seemed awfully long. I must ask you to greet Halvor Milesten and Hans Volstad and tell them that I do not know anything about Ole Milesten. There are more than twenty hospitals here, and I am unable to go anywhere to look for him. I am the only one from our regiment at this hospital.

When we are paid, I will try to get some money sent home to you. I notice that you have received the $20.00 I sent some time ago. Excuse my poor writing. I am forced to lie on my back while writing, and that makes it very difficult.

Nashville, 16 March 1863

Dearest parents,

I will now let you know that I have received your welcome letter of February 27—for which I thank you with all my heart. I notice that all of you are in good health. I was glad to get this report from you—thanks be to God! In return, I can inform you that I am beginning to improve slightly. My wounds are healing a bit as time goes by; so with God's help I hope to be well again. But it will undoubtedly take a long time because I am still unable to help myself—I will have to stay in bed quite a while yet. It is tough to be confined as long as I have been; but I must be patient, and God will assuredly help me. He will not place greater burdens on me that I can patiently bear. As regards my wounds, the bone in the right thigh has been hurt somewhat, but not sufficiently to injure me permanently. The doctor extracted some bone splinters several days ago.

The service has been fairly good up to now; but I long so greatly for milk and dairy products, which I am unable to obtain. As long as I had money I got others to buy me some every day. Now, however, I have no more cash and will not get any until we receive our pay. I do not know when that will happen. At present I have six months' pay coming to me. The price of milk was ten cents per pint, so it was expensive.

Our food consists of beef, pork, potatoes, stewed apples at time, and coffee or tea. At first we received a little butter, but that has come to an end. We do receive wheat bread, but I cannot eat much of it because it is so dry.

Oh, if I only were at home again with you! But God alone knows when I will be able to go. Of course, it is difficult to say whether I will be granted home-leave even if I do recover sufficiently.

There is no one in this hospital whom I know—only Yankees and Irishmen. A great number of wounded soldiers are here but also others who suffer from various ailments. About 100 men are confined in the ward where I am, as it is a very large room. The other wounded members of our regiment are in other hospitals here in Nashville. Some of them, who are well enough to go about and visit their friends, have come to see me.

Heartfelt greetings to my beloved parents, from their devoted son.

Lars Olsen Dokken[4]

NOTES

1. Lars and Knud Dokken were from Perry, Wisconsin, and enlisted with Captain Ingemundsen 2 Oct. 1861. They were from Valdres. Lars was 23 and Knud 18 years old at the time of enlistment. [Ager's note]

2. Ole Nedrejordet was later punished for being absent without leave and deserted on 31 March 1863. [Ager's note]

3. Here he quotes a Norwegian hymn.

4. Lars Olsen Dokken died 1 April 1863 at Hospital no. 8 in Nashville and was buried there. [Ager's note]

Letters from John Olson Wrolstad
Sergeant 15th Wisconsin Regiment[1]

Strawberry Plains [Tennessee], 28 February 1864

Dear Mother,

As time permits, I will write several lines to you so you can see that I am still alive. We have had a hard time, as we have been plagued by both hunger and frost. Now the weather is beginning to warm up. So we will not be plagued by the cold. The other affliction—hunger—becomes worse every day. Yesterday evening we received five small crackers that are to last us for two days. A man can easily eat all five of them in one meal and still not be satisfied—that's all there is to them. We have been marching back and forth around Knoxville all winter. Sometimes we have had to flee from the rebels; and sometimes they have had to run from us. Now we are after them again at full steam; and I believe there will be *no more retreat*. At present we are sixteen miles from Knoxville, at a railway bridge we built last winter and burned to the ground as soon as it was finished. Now we must build another bridge before we can get at Mr. Longstreet and his forces. We have become so strong that we will thrash him wherever we may meet him.

Rumors are afloat that the war will soon end; but I do not believe it will be over until several more tough battles have been fought. I have no greater wish than that the war will end so we can escape this eternal hunger. If food could only be had for money, all would be well. But that is not the case.

I must end for now, as we have received orders to pack up. And so hurrah—after Longstreet!

A warm greeting to you all! Write soon, please.

Your devoted son,
John O. Wrolstad

Strawberry Plains, 2 April 1864

Dear Mother,

Your letter of March 10 has been received. I see that all of you are in good health, which is cheering news. I can report that I, too, am well and in fine spirits. For several days I was quite sick, but now the kid is all right again. There is no news—everything is quiet and peaceful here. But the discipline is very strict. We must be either on picket duty or at work. Nevertheless, we must say that these are pleasant days since we are being served full rations. The railway has been completed and railroad cars pass every day. Those that go toward the front are loaded with troops, mostly recruits or "three-hundred men" as we call them.[2] Coming back, the cars are loaded with women and children who can not subsist any longer *in the sunny South* because of hunger.

We have had terribly bad weather—rain and snow every day for a long time.

There has been an awful commotion in our regiment of late. Our offi-cers want us to enroll again for three years. They try to tell us that the war will not last more than six months, and during that period we could earn from $400.00 to $600.00—so they say. Quite a few have enrolled, and I was on the point of doing the same. But this came over me just as I was to eat dinner: "No," I reasoned "if I am to eat crackers for three more years, my teeth will be so ground down that I will have to lick mush the rest of my days." I have decided to serve my time, then one of my friends can have my place. They said it was only fools and good-for-nothings who went to war, became they could not earn a living by honest means. I am glad that they have begun to draft people, and I hope it will catch those of my friends who are so very virtuous.

Johan Rambek and several other recruits have come here. They look so well that it's a joy to see them. That Rambek fellow is in fine fettle, and it may be needed, because three years is a long time. I will end this poor excuse for a letter with a hearty greeting to all of you and with a hope to see you again next fall—God willing.

Camp near Big Shanty, Georgia, 2 July 1864

Dear Mother,

Your letter of June 7 has been received, and I see there that you peo-ple have been sickly and that times are hard. It pains me to hear this. As for me, I am—thank God—hale and hearty and in good spirits.

A great many in our company are ill. We are at present seventeen miles from Atlanta. Driving the rebels back is slow business because here they have thrown up one breastwork after the other; and they are equally well supplied with artillery and cannons.

We have had lots of rain for a long time, and we have suffered greatly. One day when we were on picket duty it rained all the time. We were sta-tioned in a long ditch or rifle pit, as they call it. The water stood over our shoes, and we had to lie on our knees lest the rebels should blow our heads off.

Please write again as soon as you can.

Chattahoochee River, 15 July 1864

Dear Mother,

I have received your letter of June 27 and learned that you people are still sickly and that there is such a bad drought and such heat up your way that people must quit working. Well, that's hard, to be sure. But you must not give up hope. There is no guarantee that things will always go according to our wishes.

I am in good health and feel fine. But we have had a hard time, and the end is not yet. We are on the march daily and build barricades even though it is so hot that I have never known it worse. When we are on the march there are hundreds who must give up and lie down by the road-side. We are now so close to Atlanta that we can see it from some nearby heights. They say it is a distance of five miles to the city and that these five miles are covered with nothing but forts and entrenchments and all the deviltry that the mind can conceive. Atlanta will be a tough nut to crack. But since the times are such that nothing is impossible, we are living in the hope that we shall soon see the Promised City. We have chased the rebels more than 100 miles, over mountains and rivers where they believed that the Northern armies never could penetrate. But, by golly, Mister Johnny had to get moving even though he had dug himself clear into the earth.

We had quite a bit of fun for several days when our army was lying on one side of the river and the rebel force on the other. The outposts were stationed on opposite banks of the stream, and both groups agreed not to fire at each other. Then we strolled along the river and chatted like the best of friends. Some of our men and some of the rebels even went out into the river and swam together. They traded tobacco for coffee and had the best of fun.

Our regiment is at present miserably small. We have no more than seventy men who are well enough to bear arms. It seems as if they are bent on destroying the Norwegian regiment. Our company has lost twenty-three men—dead, wounded, or captured.

Write soon, please, and let me know how uncle is getting along. I have sent several letters to him, but never received any answer. And here I will conclude with a hearty greeting to all of you.

Your devoted son,
John O. Wrolsrad

NOTES

1. John Wrolstad was born in Tørdal (Drangedal parish), Telemark, in 1839 and came to America with his parents in 1843. He enlisted in November 1861 and was made sergeant in Company I on 1 February 1862. Wrolstad and two others were the first to reach the summit of Rocky Face Mountain when it was stormed by Willich's brigade. Wrolstad died in 1907 in Scandinavia, Wisconsin. [Ager's note]

2. "three-hundred men" may refer to the bounty paid to recruits in the latter part of the war.

Letter from Lieutenant Thor P. Sloan[1]

Murfreesboro, Tenn., 12 January 1863

Dear friend,[2]

It is a long time now since I heard from you or sent you a letter. First I must tell you that I am, thank God, hale and hearty as of this date. Quite some time ago I heard that you had returned home and that you are in poor shape as to health. This is very deplorable; but you can thank your lucky stars for having escaped the situation we are in. What a life—what an existence! And what miserable times and fierce struggles we have had to endure in storms and rough weather, both night and day. And on top of this, the rations and supplies have generally been poor. I can honestly say that I would care for neither gain nor anything else if I could only be out of the service, free and unfettered. But there is no use talking. A man must do his duty.

Briefly I also want to tell you that we have had a rather miserable Christmas, even though I, thank goodness, am in good health and ought to be satisfied. But we have again endured much and seen many a human being mangled and in misery—all merely because of the politicians.

During the period from December 26 until January 4 I can say that we were lying with rifle in hand without any fire and at times with poor rations. We took part in the battle at Knob Gap near Nolensville and later at Murfreesboro. At Knob Gap we were very lucky as we did not lose a single man dead or wounded. But what a fix we were in at Murfreesboro where the enemy rushed at us by the thousands and showered us with bullets like a hailstorm. It is a God's wonder that not everyone of us was shot down or taken prisoner, because we generally—when either the rebels or our force attacked—were bullheaded enough to stay to the very end. On the last day of the fighting General Rosecrans said to our Brigadier General Carlin: "If the troops in front of your brigade should fall back, then you must post your men and hold the enemy in check." Carlin answered: "I have only 800 men left of 2,000 and I fear that my men have lost courage and will do little now since they have always been in the front ranks." To which Rosecrans replied: "For the sake of the country, and for our own sake, you must do your best because your troops are now the only ones we can depend on."

At the time it did not matter because the rebels made no more attempts to pierce our line. Our captain was killed and our lieutenant wounded. Eleven men of my company were wounded. Captain [Mons] Grinager was wounded, as was Captain Gustafson. Lieutenant Fandberg and Captain Wilson were also wounded and Lieutenant Colonel McKee was killed. All told we lost fifteen men killed, seventy wounded, and thirty-four missing—a total of 119 men. Some of the wounded have later died. There is fear of a renewed attack.

A sincere greeting to you and your parents as well as all my other acquaintances. Best wishes to you. If you are able to write, I hope you will send me a few words in return.

Thor P. Sloan

NOTES

1. Thor P. Sloan was a farmer from Coon Valley, Wisconsin, when he enlisted with Captain Ingemundsen at the age of 28. He first served as sergeant and later as a clerk at army headquarters. In April 1864 he was made first lieutenant. . . . Lieutenant Sloan was killed at the battle of Kennesaw Mountain. Lieutenant Gilbert reports that during a rest period he, Captain Gustafson, Lieutenant Simonsen, and Lieutenant Sloan were making coffee. An enemy bomb fell directly into their campfire and Lieutenant Sloan was struck in the head by a grenade fragment. [Ager's note]

2. The friend to whom the letter was written was Østen Rulland.

Letters from John Johnson Thoe
Company K, 15th Wisconsin Regiment[1]

Island No. 10, 21 April 1862

Dear friend Levor Levorsen and family,

Long have I waited for letters from you, but in vain. Most of the men in the regiment receive letters very often; but I neither see nor hear anything from anybody. I am therefore writing in the hope that if these lines reach you, you will then without delay write to me because I am very anxious to hear from home.

As for me, I am—thank goodness—in good health at present. Some time ago I was in poor shape; but I recovered, so I should not complain.

We arrived here the 17th of this month. There are now five companies on the island, namely K, A, C, F, and H. The other five are stationed on the Tennessee bank of the river. This island is said to be about 400 acres in size. There used to be a fine farm here with a beautiful orchard of large apple trees. If we stay here until the apples ripen I am sure we will sample them. We are to begin building batteries on the island; then we will have to work practically every day. But we will receive twenty-five cents extra per day—over and above the regular pay—which will then total seventy-five cents.

Johs. Johnson Thoe

Dear friend Levor Levorsen and family,

. . . I learned from the letter to Theodor Knutsen Heimby that you are doing well. I am glad to hear this; and the Lord deserves to be praised for His goodness. I also understand that you feel hurt because you have not received any letters from me. I cannot understand why the letters do not reach you, seeing that I have the right address. Every member of the regiment receives letters except me, which has often made me wonder.

I can tell you that we are at present constructing a big entrenchment and must work ten hours per day. As regards the war, we have nothing to say because it is seldom that we get an opportunity to see newspapers.

Island No. 10, 6 June 1862

Dear friend L.L. and family,

I have received your letter of May 10 and it pleased me very much to learn that you were in good health—for which the Almighty be thanked. I can also, praise God, give you the cheering news that I am in fairly good health and am feeling quite well. There are many sick men in the regiment. I believe there are about sixty in the hospital and many have died. We carry on with the work as before, when we are not on guard duty. We are still building entrenchments and emplacing cannons. The weather is very warm and we have had little rain.

I can also report that we have been issued new clothes which are rather attractive. They are black. We received a pair of pants, under-pants, a pair of socks, a military coat, and a hat. Our pay, however, we have not received, but it is rumored that we will be paid on July 1st.

As regards the war, I know nothing except that Corinth is said to have been taken and that the rebels have left. So goes the rumor, but I do not know whether it is true.

I can greet you from your brother Nils and tell you that he is in good health and is feeling fine. The same is true of Theodor Knudsen.

Humboldt [Tennessee], 30 June 1862

My dear friend L.L. and family,

First I must tell you that we left the island on June 12th. We went by boat up the Mississippi to a town in Kentucky by the name of Hick-man. There we went ashore and marched to a town called Union City [Tennessee], fifteen miles distant. This was a pretty tough stint because we had to carry a full pack and the road was so dry that dust swirled about us continually; and as we were sweating unusually much, we could hardly see. We reached Union City the next day about ten o'clock and pitched our tents near the town. We remained there about eight days. Then we received orders to march to Trenton [Kentucky] some fifty or more miles away with full pack—a hard job in the severe heat. We arrived there four days later, pitched our tents, and remained over night. Then came orders to head for Humboldt, eleven miles distant, which took us a day. At present we are encamped in an orchard about half a mile from town. This is a beautiful campground as there are numerous apple trees loaded with fruit, so we can eat apples practically the whole day. But as they are not ripe yet, we do not dare eat too many of them. Most of the townspeople here have been rebels, but now they are Union people because they are afraid to raise opposition against the Union troops. A large number come in every day and swear loyalty to the Union. Those who do not do this voluntarily are arrested. During the march we found many who were good Unionists.

As for the nature of the land here in Tennessee, it is—generally speaking—covered with heavy forest and it seems that the farmers must have had a struggle in clearing their fields. Not much wheat is raised here but primarily corn and potatoes. They also, however, have beautiful orchards full of fruit trees.

I know nothing as to the outcome of the war. But I hope it will come to a speedy end so we can go home. With God's help I hope this may happen soon.

As I have nothing else to write about I will conclude with a sincere greeting from your ever devoted friend.

Corinth, 8 July 1862

Dear friend L.L. and family,

. . . We left Humboldt on July 4th and went by rail about 60 miles to Corinth in the state of Mississippi. Our camp is located about five miles from the city. It is a fine camp on high ground, and we have pretty good water since there is a spring close by. I do not know how long we will remain in here. A great number of our troops are encamped in this area.

Louisville, Ky., 29 Sept. 1862

Dear friend L.L. and family,

. . . We left Iuka on August 21st and have been on the go ever since until our arrival here. We had to march about 20 miles per day—sometimes more—either night or day in order to meet the enemy at Green River. But when we got within six miles of them, the rebels skipped away. According to reports they were 60,000 men strong. We then had to chase after them toward Louisville; but where they are now I cannot say, as we see nothing of them. However, they are reported to be not far away from here.

You must not imagine that we had an easy time during this long march. We were given only half-rations because we were not able to take any more along. And the roads were unusually dusty so it was difficult for us to see. But God be praised for good health. I shall not complain as long as I can retain health and vigor, which I have done every since I entered the service except for a brief spell of sickness at Bird's Point. Since then, with God's help, I have been well.

At present we are encamped close to the city, on the north bank of the Ohio River. There is a great mass of Union troops here, but I do not know how many.

Camp near Nashville, 1 Nov. 1862

Dear friend L.L. and family,

. . . I can tell you that we have had occasion to meet the enemy since last I wrote to you. We left Louisville October 1st and followed the rebels until October 7th and 8th. By that time we had arrived near a little town in Kentucky called Perryville. There the rebels made a stand. The battle began on the 7th but since our brigade brought up the rear we did not get into action until the afternoon of the 8th. At 4 o'clock we were drawn up in line of battle with artillery next to us. We drove the rebels about two miles—clear to the town, where they took a stand: the cannons began thundering and the bullets whistled right above our heads. They kept this up until nightfall when it became too dark to carry on. No one in our regiment was wounded, for which we ought to thank God. We fell back some distance; but the next morning we were again drawn up in battle order and marched toward the town. The enemy fired only a few shots, and we did not reply because the rebels had retreated early in the morning so we did not catch sight of them. We set off in pursuit and in the evening had a skirmish with them near a town. But the next morning they were missing again. We trailed along to a town named Crab Orchard, where we were given orders to remain a couple of days. Then back to Nashville we went—where we are at present. I could have written more about the battle of Perryville, but I assume you have read about it in the papers. From your letter I learn that the Indians in northwestern Minnesota and Iowa are restless, which is bad news.

Murfreesboro, 8 March 1863

Dear friend,

. . . It was exceedingly pleasant to receive the letter from Norway. It is so long since I have heard from them. I intend to write to them as I see that they long to hear from us. I see also that they have no particular desire to come to America. In this connection I will give no advice either pro or con but let them follow their own discretion. This I believe is wisest because then there will be no one to blame.

We are now encamped near Murfreesboro, where we guard the camp and do outpost duty, and at times we are out on short scouting trips—so we have enough to do. But when a man is in good health, he should not complain.

Murfreesboro, 9 May 1863

Dear friend Levor Levorsen,

. . . We are still lying quiet and it is uncertain how long we will be staying. We have been moved to the third brigade but we are in the same division as formerly. We are presently faring tolerably well, as provisions are plentiful so we do not suffer any want. We must do outpost service and other types of guard duty, and we drill from time to time. I hope we will not be forced to do such strenuous marching as we did last summer. Concerning the war, I have nothing to tell you because I suppose you read about it in the papers.

Winchester [Tennessee], 30 July 1863

Dear sister Margit,

I will send you a few words to let you know that we have left Murfreesboro. We had a hard march because the roads were bad. Our present location is 55 miles from Murfreesboro. We are taking things easy and conditions are fairly good. Even though we do much guard and outpost duty this life is as nothing in comparison with the long marches, and judging by the look of things I believe we will stay here a while. But, of course, we cannot say anything definite about it. I assume you have heard that Vicksburg has been taken and that the Mississippi is now open. In many other areas also our troops have done quite well of late; so we may dare hope that this war will not drag on too long, since things look much better now than they did some time ago. With God's help I hope we will be victorious. Without His aid we can accomplish nothing. But when we put all our trust in Him there is no danger.

Winchester, 12 Aug. 1863

My oft-remembered sister Margit Johnson Thoe,

. . . I can bring you the happy news that I am in good health at present, for which God deserves great praise. I want to thank you so much for the stamps you sent me. They came in very handy as stamps cannot always be obtained here. There is very little news to write about. We are lying quiet in camp near this town, but we do not know how long we will stay. There is talk to the effect that we will soon be given marching orders. It is uncertain, however, if anything will come of this. It has been pretty hot down here.

I must also tell you something about the rations we receive here. We are given pork, beef, hard bread which is called "crackers," peas, and grits; but never butter or milk. This we must buy if we want any—and even for money it cannot always be had. Butter costs fifty cents per pound and milk twenty-five or thirty cents per quart—so things are not cheap. We do, however, have excellent water, and there is no shortage of it, as we have both river and spring water in this area.

Chattanooga, 15 Nov. 1863

Dear friend Levor Levorsen,

. . . As regards the battle of Chickamauga on Saturday and Sunday, September 19 and 20, I assume that you have long since read in the papers how it turned out, so it is not worth my while to tell you about it. Yes, dear friend, it was a hard battle while it lasted. I have thus far taken part in three big battles, and this was about the worst one. But God be praised and thanked. He held his protecting hand over me, as He has always done, so I got out of it unharmed. Unless God holds His hand over us we are as nothing, because we cannot accomplish anything by ourselves. One bullet ripped through my pants below the knee but without hurting me. Yes, it is the great mercy of God who saves us in such dark hours when the bullets rain about us as in a hailstorm and we have a mighty host to fight against.

We are presently lying quiet in camp at Chattanooga, and I believe we will remain here a while. It is quite peaceful except for a few bombs tossed our way now and then without doing any damage.

Our provisions have been rather slim for some time because they must be transported a great distance and the roads are miserable. We have had to get along on three-fourths rations, which is rather skimpy; but it is claimed that we will soon receive full rations again.

Camp near Knoxville, 13 Dec. 1863

Oft-remembered friend and family,

. . . I will let you know that I am well at present, for which God be praised; and it would please me greatly to hear the same from you. There is no great news to report this time either, as I assume that you have heard or read about the battle of Chattanooga, which took place some time ago. The battle lasted three days and it was hard fighting throughout. But we won a great victory there over the rebels so they had to flee and abandon their entrenchments in great disorder. We took numerous captives and a great number of cannons from them. Whether Bragg went with his army I do not know; but he had to leave, and in a great hurry. I took part in the battle but got out of it unharmed, for which I must thank the Almighty God who delivered us again. Right after the battle we were given orders to march to Knoxville, which is located more than 100 miles from Chattanooga. A considerable rebel force was lying in the area and we were to strengthen our army there. But when the rebels learned that we were coming they took off, so now there are no enemy forces in the neighborhood. We are encamped here awaiting marching orders.

Newmarket, Tenn., 7 March 1864

Dear and unforgettable friend,

I received a letter from you some time ago, but I have not had any opportunity to write earlier, since we have been on the march from one place to the other and have hardly ever been at rest all winter. I can tell you that I am hale and hearty at present—God be thanked and praised.

As regards the rebels, they have pulled away from here but no one knows exactly how far. Personally, I do not believe they are far away. The winter has been fairly nice with rather little snow; but it was quite cold at times. We have not received full rations as it has been impossible to supply them fast enough, the transportation route being so long. We will have to be satisfied with what we get and hope that matters will improve in time. Neither should we grumble; one cannot expect everything to be so fine during times of war.

Yes, my dear friend! With God's help I hope this war will be brought to an end next year.

Strawberry Plains, 30 March 1864

Dear friend,

. . . At present we are lying quiet at Strawberry Plains and conditions are fairly good. We must work on the fortifications and do outpost duty—which occurs frequently. But this is as nothing compared with marching. That is much tougher. We are now given full rations, so we do not suffer any want. Earlier in the winter, however, things were rather bad as regards both rations and marching. But we are through with that for a time. We have been here about three weeks. The rebels are encamped some distance away, but I do not know how far. Neither do I know how long we will stay here. Well, my dear friend! Next winter, if God grants me life and health, I will be seeing the North again; by then I will have done my stint and be free from military service. However, God alone knows what may happen. We know nothing, but must place everything in His hands, because He turns everything to the best.

Camp 20 miles from Chattanooga, 17 April 1864

Dear sister Margit Johnson,

. . . We left Strawberry Plains on the 7th and arrived here yesterday evening. Today we have been lying quiet; whether we are going on to Chattanooga, I do not know. We have marched more than 100 miles, but we have fared pretty well because the weather was pleasant and the marching not too strenuous. . .

Camp near Kingston, Ga., 22 May 1864

Dear friend L.L.,

. . . As for news, I can relate that the army is now in motion and the campaign has begun. On the 7ᵗʰ of this month we approached Tunnel Hill, where the rebels were lying with a considerable force, and a rather sharp encounter took place. They held a very strong position on a mountain called Rocky Face. There we fought them for several days, but at last they discovered that it was best for them to withdraw, since otherwise we might outflank them and get to their rear. Consequently they had to leave their entrenchments—they had entrenched themselves rather well, but all in vain. We followed right at their heels until we were far past Dalton; then we came to a river where they had to stop. We pressed them so hard that they were forced to fight; and a hard battle ensued. The fighting went on quite fiercely for two days—and again they had to retreat. They withdrew at night and early next morning we took after them, following right on their heels. Skirmishing went on daily, clear until we arrived at our present location some days ago. We have been lying here quietly. Now we are to be off again, however—but whither? That I do not know. I believe the rebels will continue their retreat. Possibly I should have written more about this campaign, but I assume you have read about it in the papers. I hope, with God's help, that the outcome will be favorable.

I must also let you know that in this battle I was struck in one of my shoulders by an enemy bullet, but it did not harm me seriously. I am almost well again, thanks be to God.

As I have no more to write about, I will end these lines with a sincere greeting from your always devoted friend

Johs. Johnson Thoe

NOTES

1. John Johnson Thoe was a farmer from Worth county, Iowa, and enlisted with Pastor Clausen in December 1861. He was born in Telemark in 1837 and fell at New Hope Church 27 May 1864. [Ager's note]

Letter from Østen Rulland[1]

Madrid Bend [Missouri], 5 May 1862

Dear Parents,

As I have not had any mail from you lately, I will again take pen in hand and write a few lines to let you know that I am still among the living. I should like to get another letter so I could find out if you have received the money I sent and also learn whether or not you are alive.

I have been sickly since I came here but am now improving. Ole Olsen is quite ill and has been in the hospital since April 11, and there are no signs of improvement. Two men of our Company died last week.

Now I must close with sincere greetings to you all.

Østen Rulland
Company E, 15th Wisconsin Regiment

NOTES

1. Østen Rulland was from Portland, Monroe county, Wisconsin, and enlisted with Captain Ingemundsen. He became ill at Island No. 10 and was later moved to the hospital at Farmington. Because of illness he was discharged early as unfit for combat duty. [Ager's note]

Letter from Ole Tollefsen[1]

New Madrid, Mo., 7 April 1863

Oft-remembered friend, Ole Aanensen,

I can no longer delay taking my pen in hand and sending you a few lines to let you know how the world is treating me these days. First I will inform you that I am a soldier in Uncle Sam's army in the same regiment as your brother Kittel, and that I am well pleased with my condition. I have been in the army more than seven months and have never been sick, so I cannot sufficiently thank the Almighty for the mercy He has shown me—and your brother Kittel has also been well.

I must tell you what induced me to write to you. I read a letter which Kittel had received from you, and that brought back memories of the many enjoyable days we have spent together. I understand that Asbjørn and Thom also enlisted and that they were taken prisoner but were lucky enough to escape, which was good news for me because the devil himself could not mistreat people worse than they do the captives down here.

Let me tell you one thing, Ole: I have resolved that if this war soon comes to an end and I get out of it unharmed, then I will visit you and your brothers—granting that all of us are fortunate enough to survive. But I surmise that if we should happen to meet, we would not recognize each other. I suppose you are just as big as I am, and I am not one of the small ones.

I have been very sick twice since I came to Iowa—with pneumonia. I stayed in bed a month each time and spat blood for about a week both times so I hardly had any hope of getting well again. But with the help of God and the doctor I am now in very good health, and I hope that these rambling lines will find you and yours in the same condition. I should like so much to see you again. And thus I will conclude my artless letter with a cordial greeting from your sincere friend

Ole Tollefsen

NOTES

1. No Ole Tollefsen is found on the rolls, but the Kittel Aanensen mentioned in the letter was in Company B. Ole Tollefsen must have been in Company G or I. There was a Tollef Olson in Company I who was attacked by consumption and was declared unfit for military service. [Ager's note]

Letters from Thomas Emerson[1]

Bird's Point, Mo., 8 April 1862

Dear Brother,

. . . I do not have much news to tell you except that our troops took possession of Union City a few days ago. They did not need to fight for it, either, because the rebels took to flight before the 15th Wisconsin regiment. We have had rain for several days. I am in better condition now than I was a week ago. Albert went up to Cairo, otherwise he would have written. Bird's Point is a slave owner's plantation. The 10th Iowa regiment put him in the guardhouse—and there he sits.

I must end my writing with a sincere greeting to you from your brother

Thomas Emerson

Island No. 10, 25 May 1862

Dear Brother,

. . . We have received new uniforms which are much more attractive than the ones we had before.

I have not had much time to write because the rebels left so much property behind them. This gave us lots of work to do—I can't enumerate the half of it. We meet lots of rebels here, but they call themselves Unionists. All the Negroes run away from their masters and come to our camp where they can feel safe and are beyond the reach of the cat-o'-nine-tails. They are very happy because we came to free them from their cruel slavery.

Please send me the ballot list so I can see who were elected officials in the township. The weather is very hot here and we have had much rain; but now it has cleared up.

Thomas Emerson

NOTES

1. Thomas Emerson, Company C, died in Stevenson, Alabama, 20 October 1863. He was a younger brother of Sergeant Albert Emerson. [Ager's note] Albert, in his letter of 12 November, gives the date as 5 October.

Letters from Sergeant Albert Emerson

Camp Randall, 22 Jan. 1862

Dear Brother,

I received your letter last Saturday and was very glad to hear from you; but I have not been able to write sooner. If I have a little extra time, there is always some commotion of one sort or another. Some of the boys play cards, which I believe is the worst thing they can do in the camp. So you see, a person cannot do any writing even if he has the necessary time. And then there are the drills. In the forenoon we receive instructions from the army "Manual" and are put through the exercises. In the afternoon we are out on "Dress Parade"—and thus it goes.

I am in pretty good health, except for a cold accompanied by a bad cough. Our rations have at times been rather restricted in variety, but we get enough of what is served. We live primarily on bread and meat; we receive no butter. I can go to town as often as I wish, and yesterday evening I went to the City Hall and saw the noted Professor Anderson give a lecture. There is much sickness in the quarters of the 16th Wisconsin Regiment. Four or five of its men died during the space of a few days. There are also quite a number of sick men in our regiment, but mostly they are troubled by bad colds. There have been no deaths in our regiment.

In the papers I see that the Union troops have won a great victory in Kentucky, and many say that the war will be over in a month; but I do not believe everything I hear.

New Madrid [Missouri], 30 April 1862

. . . I am still in good health, and so are all the boys from Norway [Wisconsin]. We are on the Tennessee shore, directly facing Island No. 10. I presume you have heard how the island was taken. It has rained a lot lately and the river is high. When we took the island we also captured a number of large cannons and lots of ammunition. Numerous Negroes come here every day. At times their masters come to fetch them, but they are rebuffed . . .

Camp near Nashville, 3 Dec. 1862

. . . From this letter you will see that we are encamped near Nashville, the capital of Tennessee—exactly where we were two and a half months ago. In the meantime we have been through Kentucky to the Ohio River and almost up to the Cumberland Gap—and are now back again at Nashville. So you see that the distances back and forth were of the same length. But I do not think we will do any more retreating after getting rid of old General Buell. General Rosecrans is now in command and he is a man who wants to advance and not retreat—that's my opinion. I believe we will be equally busy, and see more fighting this winter than we have had before. All of us wish to go forward and sweep the rebels away—I hope we will get the opportunity.

You mention in your letter that it makes you sad to consider that all of us brothers may get into the war. But, brother—even though it is hard, you must remember that our country needs all the help we can give and that it is our duty to join. We must trust in God and hope that all of us will return home. Won't we be much happier than if we had not gone? All the boys in our company are well except one, and he is improving. [Brother] Thom is in good health. He, Ole Svandsen, and I drive ambulance wagons. These are equipped with springs for carrying those who are sick . . . .

Camp near Nashville, 23 Dec. 1862

. . . Our camp is now located six or seven miles from Nashville between the main highways to Murfreesboro and Franklin. We have a very fine camping place with good water and enough firewood. We have had the opportunity to secure all the clothing we need and are doing well. The rebels are only two or three miles from here and at times we have had little skirmishes with them. None can say when we are really going after them. Some say we will have to wait until the Cumberland River rises so we can transport our provisions upstream. Everything now comes by rail, but a great number of troops are needed to guard it.

I believe we are able to whip the rebels with ease now. If we are to wait until the river rises, we may have to wait a long time . . . .

Camp near Murfreesboro, 21 Feb. 1863

. . . We are still encamped two miles south of Murfreesboro, and have been here ever since the battle. It has rained practically all the time. If the weather clears up a while then the rain immediately sets in again and continues falling twice as long.

The captain and the boys in our regiment are all in good health. Knud Hansen and Jacob Jordahl, who were wounded in the battle, have been granted furlough to go home. When you write you must let me know whether they have arrived. How long we are to stay here I can not say. I do not believe the rebels are far away, but General Rosecrans wants to wait until he is ready. Then, believe me, the rebels will catch it unless they run away from us. There is talk to the effect that our regiment will be detailed for garrison duty, but we do not know anything definite.

Camp near Murfreesboro, 18 May 1863

. . . It is very urgent, dear brother, that you make use of the golden opportunity to learn something now while it comes easiest for you. You are now at the age when people acquire habits for the rest of their lives, be they good or bad. Therefore, I want to urge you to make use of your time to develop your capabilities. Besides, I must remind you that you now have three brothers in the army, and that you alone are left with our dear sister, which is a great responsibility. You must bear in mind that war is a very risky business and you do not know when you may be left alone. We can merely hope for the best.

I have no news to report this time. The only change which has occurred is that our regiment has been moved from the second to the third brigade; the reason is that Colonel Heg has been put in command of the latter brigade. I believe this came as a result of orders from General Rosecrans. Be this as it may, it would not surprise me if Colonel Heg is made a brigadier general. He is in command of our brigade now. The large tents have been taken from us, and it is quite warm; but we have built roofs over our pup tents, so we stand the heat quite well. We are fully stocked with all sorts of food supplies. It is said that the rebels are to our front in considerable strength; but as yet they have not attacked us—nor do I believe they will. The work on the fortifications is in progress still. Our regiment had a turn at this work day before yesterday. I do not believe the whole rebel force could drive us out of this place.

We hear lots of confusing rumors about General Hooker's movements in Virginia, and it seems as if his campaign has ended in failure. It is altogether too bad that they are always defeated over there.

Camp Erickson [Mississippi], 1 Aug. 1863

Dear Brother,

I was glad to receive your letter and learn that both of you are in good health. The same happy news can be reported as far as I am concerned. I have never in all my life felt better than I do now. Thomas is also feeling well. He acts as teamster for the company. You want to know whether he is any good at the job. I can tell you that he drives four mules hitched to a wagon.

We are now located farther south—some fifteen miles from Corinth and about two miles from a little town in Mississippi called Jacinto. The weather has been quite warm, but we have managed rather well thus far. We are on outpost duty every fourth or fifth day about nine miles from the camp and are stationed in platoons of 6 to 12 men at various places along the road leading from the camp. Our company is doing guard duty today. We have not seen any rebel soldiers hereabouts. People come with rotten apples and push things that they want to sell. However, they will not accept as payment anything but silver. When they refuse our paper money, we take their goods without giving them a penny . . . .

15th Wisconsin Regiment
Camp at Chattanooga, 12 Nov. 1863

Dear Brother,

I should have written earlier but have not had the time. Our regiment has been to Stevenson, Alabama, with a supply train. We were away almost a month because of the poor roads, and since our return we have been busy setting up sheds and shanties for living quarters. We have moved camp twice since we came back, so I have not had much time to write.

I have very sad news for you this time. Our brother Thomas is dead. He died in the hospital at Stevenson, Alabama, the 5th of October. He did not take part in the battle at Chickamauga because he was working as a teamster. The last time I saw him was about two weeks before the great battle. He was quite sick then and said that he likely would have to go to the hospital. That's what happened, and he did not get out again. A couple of days after the battle I received a letter from him, saying that he was improving and hoped to leave the hospital in about ten days. I wrote to him and sent him your last letter, but they arrived too late. He did not live long enough to receive them. I expected to find him well when we went to Stevenson with the train. You can imagine my emotion when I found that he had died.

This is hard to take, dear brother, but there is nothing we can do about it. God's will must prevail and we must put our trust in Him.

I assume you have heard that our oldest brother Charles fell at Vicksburg. This is all I have heard about him. I have written the regiment for fuller information about his death, but I have received no reply.

Just now we have heard that Captain Hanson, who was wounded the first day at Chickamauga, died of his wounds in Atlanta. The rebels had brought him there as a prisoner. This is very sad because he was such a good and brave man. The whole company mourns his untimely death.

I can tell you, brother, that it was a tough battle we fought on September 19 and 20. You cannot possibly imagine the thousands of bullets that whistled past my ears, but I escaped unharmed. We are still at the front near Chattanooga, and the work on the fortifications is progressing as rapidly as possible. The rebels are directly ahead of us and we can see their encampments very clearly. I believe, however, that we will soon be able to drive them away. We are not receiving full rations at present but hope that we soon will.

Camp of 15th Wis. Regiment, fifteen miles from Knoxville,
22 Dec. 1863

Dear Brother,

We have had rather difficult days since last I wrote. During November 23, 24, and 25 we fought the rebels and drove them from Chattanooga. Our regiment was fortunate in these fights: we did not lose a single man, and only a few were wounded. I presume you have heard lots about the battle at Missionary Ridge. I will merely mention that after three days of fighting we were ordered to march to Knoxville, and we set off two days after the battle. The distance is about 150 miles—which we covered in nine days. We were given no rations during this trip but lived off what we could forage along the way. At times we were well supplied with victuals, but at other times they were skimpy. We arrived at Knoxville on December 8th and left on the 16th, when we moved to our present location. I do not believe Longstreet has left eastern Tennessee yet. Consequently we will remain here and help Burnside either to drive the rebels away or to capture them. When this has been accomplished, I suppose we will return to Chattanooga.

You wrote about enlisting. I will advise you against doing so. You know how it has gone with two of our brothers. It requires robust health to be a soldier. I am sure that I will always bear marks because of what I have endured in the army. However, I will place no obstacles in the way of anyone who wants to enlist, provided he is vigorous and old enough to perform the duties of a soldier. But it is foolish for one as young as you to join up. Not a thousand dollars would tempt me to enroll in the army. I enlisted because our country had need of each and every one of us; and that is the reason why I serve . . . .

Strawberry Plains, 18 March 1864

Dear Brother,

. . . We have been on the go all the time and have had to keep watch at a bridge where the railway running from Chattanooga to Richmond crosses the Holston River. It is a very important bridge. There are two other regiments besides the 15th Wisconsin. How long we are to remain here depends entirely on how well our armies at the front can hold their positions. I heard today that our troops have fallen back fourteen miles, from Morristown to Moose Creek. Whether or not they intend to hold this place, I can not say. Luck has not been with us in this sector. We need a Burnside, a Rosecrans, or a Hooker if we are to defeat old Longstreet. He seems to be entirely too smart for the generals we have at present.

I still have the hope that I will see you again, and that this evil war will have a triumphant ending for us. General Grant has been appointed lieutenant general and is in command of all the Union armies. If he retains this position, I do not believe it will take long before the rebellion comes to an end. I hope you have attended school this winter. You will discover as you grow older that the more you learn the better it will be. I have been offered good positions but did not dare accept them because I was afraid that I could not fulfill my obligations. . . .

On the battlefield, 28 Aug. 1864

Dear Brother,

. . . We have had pretty tough hiking the last five days. In the evening of the 25th we left our breastworks two miles north of Atlanta and marched all night and the next two days. During the first night and day we marched in a westerly direction while yesterday we went south, so we must be west of Atlanta. Before we moved, our troops were lined up east to west, facing south. Now I believe the line stretches from south to north, facing east. The purpose of this movement is presumably to get around the flank of the enemy and thus drive him out of Atlanta. Last night it was so cold that we had to wrap heavy wool blankets around ourselves in order to sleep. . . .

                                                            12 Sept. 1864
Dear Sister,
    . . . During the night before August 26 General Sherman put the whole army in motion except the twentieth army corps, which was assigned to guard the communications, and got around Atlanta. In five days he had led the troops up to the Macon railway, which is the only line by which the rebels obtain provisions; and, of course, it was heavily guarded. When Sherman left his entrenchments facing Atlanta General Hood—who now commands the rebel army—believed that a great maneuver was afoot. He therefore left General [Alexander] Stewart with a corps and the Georgia state militia to guard Atlanta, while he himself took two corps—Hardee's and Loring's—and set off for Jonesboro to whip the Yankees. But here Hood miscalculated, because instead of whipping the Yankees it was they who whipped him, and he had to pull back. When General Stewart realized that we had come between him and Hood—and that we had defeated the latter—he hurried to evacuate the city. They destroyed five locomotives and 200 railway cars full of ammunition and weapons of all sorts. The next day the 20th army corps entered the city. A great number of houses in the city are laid in ruins . . . .

                                        Whiteside, Tenn. 21 Oct. 1864
Dear Sister,
    I will now write you again and let you know that I am still in the land of the living. From the heading you will see that we are back again in Tennessee.
    After lying in camp from September 8 to 28, we were given orders to leave for Chattanooga, where we did guard duty until October 6. Then 70 men from our regiment were sent to Nashville with 300 prisoners. They returned on the 11th and we continued our guard duty until the 18th when our regiment was ordered to go to Whiteside. This place is located 14 miles north of Chattanooga on the Nashville-Chattanooga

Railway. Here the railway crosses a deep ravine on a wooden bridge. The bridge is about 100 feet high and quite long, so you will realize that it is important. A cavalry regiment and an artillery battery are also stationed here. I do not know how long we will be staying. Our company has only a month and eleven days left to serve, so you can begin looking for us around the 1st of December.

The rebels have undertaken daring raids. Some time after we left Atlanta, the Confederate generals Forrest and [Joseph] Wheeler were sent out to cut the railway between Chattanooga and Nashville; but they were defeated and driven back. A bit later General Hood launched at attack, with practically his whole army, against our lines south of Atlanta and took some outposts; but I do not believe it will mean very much. Old man Sherman has driven them away and it is said that the rebels are now surrounded so they will hardly attempt another attack.

With best wishes from your brother,
Albert Emerson

Letter from Nils L. Slaaten[1]

Island No. 10, 21 April 1862

Dear Brother,

As there is such a good opportunity, I will send you a few lines about how I live at present. I have, thank God, been well ever since I left home. And now I must greet you, my old and gentle mother, and ask you to forgive me for what I have done against you, namely that I went down here without your consent and knowledge. Furthermore, I wish to greet all of you most sincerely—you, my old mother, my brother with his family, and in general all my friends and acquaintances back home. I am getting along well and hope that with God's help we shall see each other again.

NOTES

1. Slaaten, from St. Ansgar, Iowa, died in the hospital at Nashville, 14 February 1863. [Ager's note]

Letters of Army Surgeon Stephen O. Himoe[1]

Camp Randall, 25 February 1862.

. . . I have arrived here in good health. The colonel with his family boarded the train at Waukesha and came along as far as Eagle yesterday. On Friday we shall leave via the Beloit, Galena and Chicago Railway and arrive at Chicago in the evening, where we are to be presented with a flag by the Scandinavians. We will eat supper at Tremont, and at 9 or 10 o'clock that evening we will continue our journey via the Chicago, Alton and St. Louis Railway. Ole (Heg) will leave a day ahead of us to prepare for our reception in St. Louis.

Major [Charles M.] Riis was also on the train. He was returning from Chicago where he had seen the Norwegian prisoners.[2] There are about 30 of them and they are all determined to enlist in our regiment. But we cannot get them except through a lengthy red-tape procedure on the part of the War Department.

Camp Etheridge, Tennessee, 22 June 1862

. . . Yesterday we had a great Union mass meeting here which the Colonel and I attended. The Honorable Marquis J. Parrott was the speaker and he was at his best. General Mitchell spoke also and said that it was his mission to restore order under the constitution and laws of the United States. He will compel the local inhabitants to rebuild the burned-out railroad bridges and hold them and their possessions responsible for all destruction of public property.

He will let those be hanged who violate their oath of allegiance to the United States. This is a comparatively loyal district, where out of 170 votes only 10 were cast for secession or withdrawal from the Union. There were many people present, a third of them women—the most prominent families in Tennessee. Many in tasteful and elegant costumes with beautiful figures and lovely faces.

Jennison's "Jayhawkers" are true to their old instincts and steal anything they can lay their hands on.[3] They make the secessionists scurry for their hideouts in a hurry. Yesterday they shot two young men who boasted of the fact that they hailed the Southern withdrawal from the Union. They say: "If you are a secessionist you do not deserve to live," and then shoot them down.

Camp near Humboldt, Tennessee, 26 June 1862

. . . After a march of eleven miles from Trenton yesterday we arrived here and pitched camp.

These Jayhawkers are in camp with us, while the rest of the troops are about a mile distant. There are, of course, no enemies in this part of Tennessee and what we are to do here, other than protect the secessionists, we are unable to understand. General Mitchell does everything he can for them, but he has a very undisciplined brigade. The Jayhawkers naturally do their best to circumvent his commands and lure Negroes away and confiscate rebel property for their own private profit—and "the 15th" does not seem to lag far behind. The 2nd Illinois Cavalry, the 7th and 8th Wisconsin Artillery, the 1st Kansas Artillery are all very expert jayhawkers, while the 22nd Missouri Regiment enjoys the reputation of being able to steal the eyes from the sockets of all of them.

We outdid even the Missourians yesterday. They came to the camp a couple of hours before us and stole every oat sheaf from the field. There were several beehives nearby where they posted a guard so they could steal them during the night—"three hours before daylight," as they said. Our boys were lurking about, and I told the sergeant who was watching the hives that he had better run and get some more guards, otherwise our boys would jayhawk the hives right under his nose. He did so; but before he returned, every hive had vanished. The Jayhawkers say they can steal honey at night; but to do this in broad daylight with the bees swarming around—that's beyond them.

General Mitchell, of course, wants to reimburse the owner no matter how great a traitor he may be. This makes us angry so we jayhawk anything within reach and lure away all the Negroes we can. I believe our government will discover some day—though it may take years—that the only way to crush the rebellion is to let those who started it and support it also smart for it.[4]

Slavery must be wiped out; it is of no use to speak of peace unless this happens, and the method employed by Jennison's men is undoubtedly the most effective to bring it about—and therefore also the best. The real war we are engaged in at present is between General Mitchell and the elements out of which his brigade is built. Colonel Heg is conservative and agrees with the general but Lieutenant Colonel [David] McKee—despite the fact that he is a former Democrat—is as radical as John Brown and does everything he can to hamper him. We will undoubtedly have some excitement. Colonel Anthony and a captain of the 7th Kansas Regiment were placed under arrest yesterday because of some Negro affair; and today some members of the General Staff tried to get a Negro out of their camp—an attempt that failed miserably. An order had been issued to send all Negroes, especially women, away from our premises.

Apparently we are not to go beyond the boundaries of this state, as [Gen. Henry W.] Halleck's plan is to lock the rebels up in the Gulf states and starve them into submission without pursuing them any farther. Undoubtedly they can be strangled in this way. Health conditions in the Regiment are excellent—not a man in the hospital!

Stevenson, Alabama, 24 August 1862

. . . Practically everyone in the area around Fort Scott and, in reality, more or less the whole population of Kansas are becoming rich because of this war. Wilson, Gordon, and Ray have a contract to supply the army with corn at $1.17 per bushel delivered at Fort Scott and Leavenworth. The newspapers of Aug. 12th list corn at 35 cents. When the new crop is ripe corn will be hardly be worth 20 cents in this state and much of it will be paid for in goods. That will net these speculators the enormous profit of about a dollar per bushel. There is a colossal fortune tied up in this one deal alone. The insane spirit of speculation and the shameless corruption that so long has reigned in Kansas will become a curse on the whole nation.

Buell has the best army that ever trod on Kentucky soil, and there was deep and noisy indignation yesterday when he let the enemy slip away.[5] I do not believe there will be any hasty moves if Buell retains the command. He is extremely unpopular with the army—from division generals to privates. Everyone thinks he is incompetent and many believe he is a traitor. Gossip has it that he commands two armies: his own and General Bragg's. That's the way it looks. When we caught up with Bragg at Green River a week ago his army could easily have been destroyed if an attack had been launched immediately. General Crittenden and General Thomas both offered to attack, solely with their own division. But Buell called a halt in front of Bragg's outposts, who were stationed ten miles away from the main army. He waited and fumbled away two days; and when finally on Sunday morning—he decided to attack, the enemy was gone. Our cavalry killed a few of their rear guards; and when Bragg changed direction by swinging toward the east, Buell continued on directly toward Louisville.

Our commanding general, Buell, is unpopular merely because he is slow and cautious—probably not such bad characteristics after all. He is an odd sort of general. He never appears before the troops and has no encouraging words for them. Nary a newspaper gets to the soldiers. But the opinion is spreading in the army that Buell manages the campaign well and that General Bragg's position is now becoming desperate.

NOTES

1. Stephen Oliver Himoe (Høimo) was born in Norway, March 10, 1832, and came to America at the age of thirteen with his father, who settled in Wisconsin. There the boy attended common school after which he graduated from Plattville Academy. Later he studied medicine at the St. Louis Medical College, and then moved to Kansas at a time when the struggle between pro- and anti-slavery forces was very intense. At the outbreak of war he was first placed with a cavalry regiment in Kansas, but when the Norwegian Regiment was formed he received a commission as army surgeon with that group. He was present at the battles of Perryville and Murfreesboro. During the battle of Chickamauga he was in charge of the field hospital at Crawfish Springs. He resigned in November, 1863, and was honored for his services by the Cumberland Army Headquarters. Thereupon he moved to Kansas City where he practiced medicine until his death on 19 April 1904. The letters were written to his wife. [Ager's note]

2. There was a fairly large Norwegian settlement in Texas from which many men entered the Confederate army. Many of them were captured early in the war and it is presumably to them that the doctor refers. [Ager's note] These prisoners were not exchanged and when the war ended the Confederate government had ceased to exist.

3. "Jayhawkers" was a term that originated during the "Free Soil" struggle in Kansas. They were members of guerilla bands that robbed and plundered settlers who wanted to make Kansas a slave state. [Ager's note]

4. At the outset of the war, property was protected, by both Grant in the West and [George B.] McClellan in the East, regardless of whether the owners were Unionists or Secessionists. After the battle of Shiloh Grant gave his troops greater freedom to plunder but individuals were protected. Even in areas where the armies needed the products, they were protected or paid for when seized. Where there was danger that the goods would benefit the Southern forces, they were destroyed. Sherman during his march to the sea and Sheridan in the Shenandoah Valley laid the land waste about them and brought the greatest suffering upon the inhabitants with the intention of bringing the rebellion to an earlier close. [Ager's note]

5. Dr. Himoe's characterization of General Buell of the Cumberland Army will be read with interest. [Ager's note]

From Morten J. Nordre's Diary[1]

Sunday, 29 May 1864. Thousands of wounded soldiers are arriving in Louisville on their way north. We left Louisville at 7 a.m., passed through Elizabethtown and came to Nashville, Tennessee.

Monday, 30 May. Left Nashville, passing through Murfreesboro and Tullahoma in Tennessee and Stevenson and Bridgeport in Alabama, arriving at Chattanooga, where we entered the Soldiers' Home and were treated to bread and coffee.

Wednesday, 1 June. The United States has performed a great work here by building a large bridge over the Tennessee River. Here we also met some of our comrades. We are staying at the Soldiers' Home, as the hotels charge $4.00 per day for board and room.

Thursday, 2 June. Arrived in Kingston at 9 o'clock last night. Theodore and I crept into a loft and slept there. Left Kingston at 2 p.m. and came to New Haven at 5 o'clock; found a loft where we spent the night.

Tuesday, 7 June. Joined our regiment at noon today. Can see the rebel camp from here.

Thursday, 9 June. Heard that Corporal Peter O. Harstad was wounded at the battle of Resaca on May 14th. He died on the 21st.

Friday, 10 June. In camp at Acworth, Georgia. It has rained hard all day.

Sunday, 12 June. Ate breakfast at 4 a.m. This is an ugly landscape, and we have not much to eat. We are again at the enemy's front line and battle for every inch of ground. We fight day and night and do not know at what hour we might fall.

Monday, 13 June. It has rained off and on for several days. When day dawns we are hungry, cold, and wet; and when night comes, it is the same. No chance to get into dry clothes. We have to lie under the open sky wet and in poor clothing. It is a hard life. Sometimes we go without food for a couple of days; and when we do get some, it is not enough to still the worst hunger.

Wednesday, 15 June. Today we fought a big battle. We took several prisoners, who told us that rebel General Polk has fallen.

Thursday, 16 June. Rested near Cedar Mountain. Advanced a mile, then we met a rebel force and drew up in battle order, awaiting an attack. When this did not happen, we had to charge them behind their barricades. The rebels tried to break through our lines but did not succeed.

Friday, 17 June. Today has been wet and cold. We were ordered out into an open field where we began at once to build breastworks. Soon we were ordered to conduct a raid. We had to wade across a stream. There we found a dead man—he looked horrible. A rebel bomb burst near us without doing much damage. But when the rebels sent a heavy shower of bullets against us we were forced to crawl into a ditch where we lay in water and mud—and called ourselves lucky for being able to lie there with a bit of protection against the rebel bullets that rained around us. He who has not experienced life in battle has no idea how hard it can be. It is so hard that money can in no way compensate for it.

Sunday, 19 June. The enemy has retreated. We have taken their breastworks and some prisoners.

Monday, 20 June. Today we were out skirmishing but were driven back over an open field.

Tuesday, 21 June. Today we were engaged in a hard battle. Corporal Nils P. Lund, Nils Starkson, and John Wasrud were wounded. We have now been in battle off and on for four days and parts of four nights without rest or sleep. We are in desperate need of rest and food.

Thursday, 23 June. Today we were under heavy fire from both artillery and rifles, so we were forced to stay close to our breastworks. Bomb fragments flew in all directions and some of our comrades were wounded. Now we have been stationed at a new position.

Friday, 24 June. Daniel Pederson was killed last night when a felled tree struck him.

Saturday, 25 June. Today the rebel general [Joseph E.] Johnston sent us a peace proposal requesting a two-day truce, but it was declined. All day we have bombarded the hill on which the rebels have taken a position and blown up some of their powder.

Sunday, 26 June. Today we had an intense fight with the rebels. Ivar Olson had both legs pierced by a rifle bullet.

Monday, 27 June. Have been in battle order all day at Loose Mountain awaiting a rally by the rebels. But those fellows knew better than to attack our barricades. Had they risked it, they would have got a pretty warm reception.

Tuesday, 28 June. It is terribly hot today. We are staying in some holes we have dug in the ground to shield ourselves from the rebel sharpshooters. But it is so hot in these holes that it makes life unbearable.

Wednesday, 29 June. Today we were sent out on a raid. Captain "Buckskinbreeches" opened fire on the enemy's breastworks, which was answered with a mighty thunder from their cannon. One man was killed.

Thursday, 30 June. This morning we were relieved by the 49th of our brigade. The rebels asked us not to shoot at them, and in return they would not fire at us. We agreed to this. We approached each other, talked a little, and exchanged newspapers even though our general has forbidden such actions.

Friday, 1 July. Although we have entered a new month, this war business of ours remains the same as before.

Monday, 4 July. This is a great day in all of the United States. But we had to get up at 4 o'clock and eat breakfast and prepare ourselves for an attack on the rebels. They retreated and destroyed the railroad and everything else that lay in their way. There is a distance of 128 miles from Chattanooga to Atlanta. The terrain between these two cities is uneven and hilly, and the soil is not as good as at home. Although the rebels have torn up the railway the whole distance between Kennesaw Mountain and Atlanta, the trains can run to the Chattahoochee River, and from there provisions for our army are transported in wagons.

Tuesday, 5 July. Today we were on the go at 3 a.m., drove the army over the Chattahoochee River, and took 95 prisoners.

Wednesday, 6 July. I was on a hilltop near the railway station today. There they had hanged a man—not with a rope but with a strip of bark. From this hill I got my first view of the city of Atlanta and at the same time saw the rebels attack our right wing. One of our men went to the river to bathe and was shot.

Friday, 8 July. We are now stationed near the Chattahoochee River on the south side of a large hill at the foot of which we found an excellent spring of water. From the hill we have a good view over the ranks of the rebels.

Saturday, 9 July. Last evening we launched the bloodiest and most murderous onslaught I have heard of in this war. We opened such fierce fire against the rebels that bullets by the thousands whirred over their barricades. No doubt it became too hot for them.

Sunday, 10 July. We were sent out in skirmish formations to the Chattahoochee River, where we relieved the 32nd Indiana Regiment. The rebels opened a frightful rifle fire at us; but as we did not reply, they soon ceased firing at us. Then one of the rebels stepped forth and said that if we would not shoot at them, they would not shoot at us. We immediately agreed to this. Then several of them came down to the river with some papers in their hands and asked if we would like to exchange newspapers. We were also willing to do this, but as the river lay between us it was not so easily accomplished. One of them then proposed that a man from each force should swim and meet in the middle of the river; but none of us had any desire for such a swim. Thereupon he read something from his paper, and when he had finished he said that he and many with him were tired of the war. It was not the common people, he said, but the ones in high authority who started this war and kept it going.

Thursday, 14 July. We had a rainstorm today, the likes of which I have never seen.

Sunday, 17 July. Received orders to proceed to the Chattahoochee River and drive the rebels away, thus giving General Hooker a chance to cross the stream. A messenger from General Hooker came and said the general was on the march. We took him for a rebel spy and brought him to headquarters. But he was a messenger, all right.

Wednesday, 20 July. Yesterday we marched to a creek four miles from Atlanta. Met a rebel force and several of our men were wounded. Marched to the same creek today. The other regiments have breastworks, but our poor 15th Wisconsin has to hold out on open ground. We threw up a barricade hurriedly. The rebels launched an attack and a slaughter ensued. A rebel general fell.

Friday, 22 July. The war trumpet awakened us at 3 a.m. The rebels have again left their entrenchments 2 miles from Atlanta. General McPherson attacked their right wing and was killed.

Saturday, 23 July. Camp Spring. The 25th Illinois Regiment and our regiment have built breastworks. The enemy kept up a fire against us all day and killed several of our men.

Sunday, 24 July. We heard today that the rebels have lost 15,000 men and we 8,000.

Monday, 25 July. Colonel Ole C. Johnson, who escaped from Dixie, came here today. We have strengthened our breastworks with sharp palings. Have drawn rations for three days.

Wednesday, 4 August. During the past few days we have fought battles off and on. Advanced toward Atlanta yesterday but had to pull back with a loss of 18 men. Every day some of our men get killed or wounded.

Saturday, 6 Aug. Brisk firing kept up without serious losses on either side.

Wednesday, 10 Aug. Even though it has rained all day, both sides have continued to shoot at each other.

Friday, 12 Aug. I must admit that the Southern ladies are brave and gallant women. Whole groups of them go among the rebel soldiers even during the heaviest gunfire, where every minute they stand the risk of losing their lives.

Saturday, 13 Aug. In the morning we can see gunsmoke rising like a fog from both camps. Because the woods have been cleared away, a stretch as open and clear as a city street lies between the two armies. There are heights here that resemble the mountains of old Norway. At 3 a.m. today we sent the rebels a rousing "good morning" as we showered hundreds of bombs over the city and their entrenchments. There was a thunder of cannons so terrible that you might think the city sank into the earth.

Wednesday, 17 Aug. Rebel General Wheeler broke through our "crackerline" and took 4,000 head of cattle that had been sent for the sustenance of our army. A member of the commissariat, Ola Olson, was presumably taken prisoner.

NOTES

1. Morten Nordre, who was also known as Lille-Morten, was a son of Jehans Mortensen Nyflødt from Ringebu, who settled in St. Lawrence, Wisconsin. Sergeant Nordre was mustered out with his company and died a score of years ago as a businessman in Alexandria, Minnesota. [Ager's note]

Letters from Colonel Heg and Others

Letter from Sergeant Ole Back[1]

Bird's Point, 13 March 1862

Dear Brother,

. . . As I have the time I will, for the sake of our mother, give you a brief account of our journey from Madison to the place where we now are stationed. On the 1st of March, at nine o'clock in the morning, we left Camp Randall by rail, bound for St. Louis. We traveled all day and all night and finally, at half-past ten Monday evening, we reached the Mississippi River, thirty miles above St. Louis, at a little town called Alton. We marched directly from the railway and boarded a steamer, preparatory to going down the river early the next morning. At twelve o'clock on March 4th we arrived at St. Louis. There we left our steamer and boarded another one which was lying directly by ours.

At the same time we arrived, another boat came up from the south carrying Union soldiers and 2,000 captive rebels who were to be sent to Chicago. Now, believe me, our boys had lots of fun buying oranges, apples, candy, etc. and throwing it over to the miserable and starved Confederate prisoners. They were so happy to get hold of an apple that we could hardly have been more pleased even if we had conquered the whole South. It was a real pleasure to see those fellows, crowded together on the desk, receive with outstretched arms the gifts our soldiers threw over to them. They were well satisfied with their captivity, it seemed.

I made use of the opportunity to look about in St. Louis and found it to be the most beautiful and well constructed city I have seen in America. It is located on a broad plain on the right shore of the Mississippi and has wide streets and unusually large buildings. I saw no house with fewer than three stories and they were constructed exclusively out of stone. The next morning, at five o'clock, we continued our journey, and at six o'clock a.m. on March 6 we were put ashore at a place in Missouri called Bird's Point. It is located directly across from Cairo, Illinois, where the Ohio empties into the Mississippi. During the winter 5,000 men were stationed here; but when we arrived, only one regiment remained, and it left today; so at present we are the only ones here, and we expect any day to receive orders to proceed farther south.

Before it was occupied by our soldiers, this camp site was a large farm of 20,000 acres worked by 30 slaves. The owner had a railroad station, a store, and many other things on the estate. During the siege his property was greatly damaged by trenches, fortifications, and barracks for the soldiers. They burned his granaries, destroyed houses, and took all the food supplies on the place. Because of this he naturally became angry and was seized by a desire for revenge. He declared that he was—and to all outward appearances seemed to be—a Union man. Because of this they allowed, him, for the time being, to retain his slaves. But at heart he was, and is unto this day, a confirmed rebel. During the whole winter he and his two sons sneaked about and murdered soldiers on outpost duty—a horrible deed; and the worst part of it is that he had driven his poor Negroes to do the same thing and—on pain of death—had forced them to keep quiet about it. The soldiers realized that there was an enemy in their midst when this happened time after time. They tried in all ways possible to find the culprit—but to no avail.

An old proverb says that "the apple falls when it is ripe," and so it went with this man. They finally decided to send out secret patrols, and one of them caught him red-handed shooting a man down with a revolver. At last they had the scoundrel, after many human lives had been lost. The man and his sons are now under lock and key in the camp and his slaves have been liberated. These poor people are very happy to be free, but they are like wild sheep, not knowing where to go. They are still in the camp and earn a living by washing clothes for the soldiers.

What do you think of it, brother? Now I am again a soldier, and this time in a land where war is raging. It really pains me to write this; but as an obedient son and brother, I hold it to be my duty. Now at least you know what became of me in case I should be unfortunate enough to fall in battle . . .

NOTES

1. Ole Back had been a soldier in Norway and served as an orderly under Colonel Heg, who offered to appoint him a corporal if he enlisted. He fell as a sergeant in the battle of Murfreesboro, 31 December 1862.

Letter from Colonel Heg[1]

Near Murfreesboro, Tenn., Feb. 15, 1863

Dear Mr. Adland!

The many valuable donations that have been received by the sick and wounded of my Regiment, from the Soldiers' Aid Society of Norway and Raymond through the efforts of your and other friends there, ought to have been acknowledged by me long ago. That I have neglected it is no reason why I should continue to do so.

The box I received from your brother, I succeeded in getting through myself, and it was immediately turned over to the hospital. It was nearly all on hand and used for the wounded after the battle. What there has been forwarded to us since has mostly gone directly to the hospital at Nashville, where a large number of our wounded and sick are at present.

Not to say anything of the comforts and blessings your liberal donations have bestowed upon the sick and suffering soldiers who so bravely have fought for a cause common to us, but, aside from all that, your kindness speaks to the heart of every soldier in the Army. What are men exposing their lives and health for in this great struggle, but a cause in which we are all interested?

What encouragements for men to undergo what they are daily called on to do here, but that they know their efforts are appreciated by friends at home? And what better evidence can be furnished that your hearts are with them than the valuable tokens of your kindness and generosity in caring for the sick and wounded? Our army is bound to crush this terrible rebellion, if the people of the North will only stand by the army, and by all their power encourage the soldiers.

And here let me add that I know from experience there is nothing equal to encouragement from home. You can do a great deal of good, not only by the efforts in which you have been so liberal, but I would ask you to encourage our soldiers by your kind letters. If a mother has a son, or a wife a husband in the army, her encouragement to him to do his duty is worth more than anything else; her continual complaints, and whinings, asking him to "come home," etc., has more to do with creating discouragement and finally sickness and disease than the hardships he has to endure.

I can see no daylight in any other direction than a suppression of the rebels by us. It is nothing else than simply this. Death and destruction to us, and our government, or their subjugation. The latter must be accomplished, no matter what the sacrifice may be—life, property, or anything else.

Hoping that the members of your society will continue to labor in the good cause they are engaged in, and that you will on behalf of the Fifteenth Wisconsin tender our friends our sincere thanks for your kind remembrances and favors, and trusting hereafter to be able to prove ourselves worthy of them I remain,

Very truly yours,
Hans C. Heg,
Col. Fifteenth Wis. Vols.

NOTES

1. This is not a translation, but a copy of Col. Heg's actual letter. Colonel Heg wrote the letter in English. [Catuna's note]

Letter from Captain Hans Hanson

Murfreesboro, 28 Feb. 1863.

Dear Friend,

I see by your letter that you are very anxious to hear about the results of the last terrible battle at Murfreesboro and especially to learn about the losses in Company C. It is now so long ago that I am certain you know all about it. Nevertheless I will give you the losses in my company. I went into the battle with four sergeants, five corporals, and twenty-one privates. Both my lieutenants were absent. I lost two sergeants, one corporal, and eighteen privates. Gunder E. Hansen, Knud Finkelsen, and Mathias Mathisen were killed immediately, while Berendt C. Osmundsen died a few days later from his wounds. The wounded were Corporal Samuel Johnson and the privates Knud Hansen, Jacob Jordahl, Lorentz Allen, Peter Jørgensen, Torbjørn Hansen, and A. Bergersen. Sergeant Hans Jacobsen was wounded in the head and shoulder and taken captive. Sergeant C. Heyer and four privates are missing and are thought to have been wounded and fallen into the hands of the enemy. This must be considered a great loss in view of the small size of the company. However, when I think of it, it seems a wonder to me that any of us escaped. As I know that through the papers you are aware of the conduct of our regiment during the battle, I will not say any more about it; but this I will mention, that when we finally were forced back, the enemy were not more than ten steps away from us. The rebels were then advancing in four close columns, firing salvo after salvo into our ranks.

I have no news to relate that will strike you as significant, except that Harvey Britton has been promoted to the rank of first sergeant in Company B, which he well deserved; and his relatives and friends will appreciate hearing that he has proved himself a brave and good soldier. The wounded boys are recuperating well, as far as I can gather. Concerning the prospects for an early end to the war—I can only say that they are gloomy and depressing. As regards me personally, I am sick of the whole affair and look with longing eyes toward the day when peace shall be declared—not the kind of peace the so-called "Peace-Democrats" desire, but a peace won by our armies, which, I believe, will be the only lasting peace. I would so gladly return to my home; but I am determined to play my part until the whole thing is settled, provided life and health be granted me.

I have nothing further to relate this time. I will close with a sincere greeting to all my friends and relatives.

Yours,
H. Hanson

Andersonville and Other Southern Prisons

Speech delivered by Ole Steensland
at a reunion of the 15th Wisconsin Regiment
at Chicago, 29 August 1900

Dear Comrades of the 15th Wisconsin: Is this not one of the most pleasant moments of your lives? To be able to come together like this and greet one another, when you recall the frightful days you went through from 1861 to 1865.

You will remember that when we passed through Chicago on the 2nd of March 1862 on our way to the front we were met by our countrymen, the Norwegians, who presented us with a beautiful flag. Why do they greet us with such a hearty welcome today? I believe it is because we defended that flag in more than one hard battle and took care that it never fell into enemy hands.

I will attempt to give a detailed account of what we did during our service in the army. You will remember how we were put ashore in the swamps above Island No. 10, how we surprised and captured the rebel camp at Union City, the time we took Island No. 10 and Madrid Bend. You remember, also, how eight companies of us set out on the long and arduous march that killed so many of our boys. We passed through parts of Mississippi, Alabama, Tennessee, and Kentucky—always in sweltering summer heat. You remember the sweat and the dust and the terrible thirst for water; and at times the rations were poor pickings.

You remember the charge at Perryville when we rushed over all those rail fences. You remember also how infested we were with lice; and how at Crab Orchard, when we had a bit of a rest, we boiled our shirts in the coffee kettles. You have not forgotten how on the way back to Nashville we attacked the rebel battery at Knob Gap, how we fought several days in succession at Stone's River, how we crossed the Tennessee River on that pontoon bridge under fire from the enemy and how we drove them back, how we dragged our battery and wagons up Lookout Mountain.

And never will you forget when we joined battle at Chickamauga on September 19, 1863, where our Chief of Brigade, Hans C. Heg, fell and so many of our officers and other brave men were killed, wounded, or taken prisoner. You remember the ominous morning of the 20th when the few of us who remained formed a battle line; how the enemy, four columns strong, attacked us, how they slaughtered us—killed and captured so many of us. There are some here today who were there, but they are few. I will never forget that day nor—I am certain—will any of the rest of you. Ole Milesten on my right was killed and Chris Thompson on my left was also killed. I had a bullet hole shot through my hat, which caused no pain; but then I was taken prisoner—and that was something that did pain me.

Sometimes when I was a prisoner of war I wished that I had been killed that day so I could have escaped suffering and rotting to death in the southern prisons. I had always followed my company and been ready for service, so I believe all of you will agree that I went through as many hardships as anyone. But what was that compared with the terrible suffering I had to endure during the next 19 months and 8 days in Confederate captivity. It was more than I can describe. I will say that those who did not see the horrors of that hell, Andersonville, cannot imagine the terrible sights and all the suffering found there. Neither could anyone who had been there longer than I come out of it alive and be with you here today. There are very few. I know a man who was in prison one day longer than I who is still alive (1900). He is Osmund Johnson of Company K, 15th Wisconsin Regiment.[1]

After we were captured we were taken to the Confederate rear guard. When we came to Chickamauga creek we found a camp of their wounded men. This made us feel a little better, as we realized that we too had done something for our country. The first night was spent at Tunnel Hill near Ringgold. From there we were sent off, packed into freight cars like those they ship cattle in nowadays. When we came to Atlanta we were sent to the "Bull Pen." That's what they called it, and the name was well chosen. Here they took our knapsacks, our canteens, and everything except our money. I will tell you about the money later.

The next day most of the prisoners were sent off in the same fashion to Richmond, Virginia, but some of us were sent to Belle Isle, an island in the St. James River. There they kept the prisoners from Gettysburg and they had managed to make them look pretty miserable already. We were shocked to see them; but worse sights were in store for us at Andersonville.

A few days later they took us to Libby Prison. It was full of officers just then, so they packed us into a tobacco warehouse nearby. Major Turner came in with some clerks, books, and tables and said to us: "Now, you Yankee prisoners, I know that some of you have money, and this is no safe place to keep money. You may lose it, or it may be stolen. We will take care of your money for you, and when you are exchanged, you will get back every cent. Go over to the clerks and they will enter it in their books. Give your name, regiment, and company. Those who will not hand over their money voluntarily will be searched and their money confiscated." Thus that scoundrel got hold of our money. I saw one man hand him $1,100. Naturally, not a one of us got a penny back.

The next development was that I and several others caught smallpox and were sent to the pesthouse, where most of them died. I was there about a month and was sent back to Pemberton Prison. There was not a soul there whom I knew and the place was so overcrowded that I could not even find a spot on the floor to lie down. When finally I tried to lie down I was told in no uncertain terms to get out of the way. I protested that the floor belonged to all of us; but before I knew what was happening I was knocked down and got the blackest eye I have ever had. You can imagine how I felt in such company.

The next morning I found out that there were some boys from my regiment in the adjoining section. There had been a door between the two rooms but the opening had been nailed shut with boards. We could, however, see each other and talk through the cracks. Then we knocked some boards loose and three men from our partition crawled into the other room and three from there came into ours. We figured this to be a fair exchange, and the boards were replaced. But someone must have tattled and we were discovered. There was an undersized New York rebel named Ross who was in charge of the roll call. He made a fuss over it, and then we were to be punished. First they decided to put us into a dark cell at Libby, but the final outcome was that we should be sent to Belle Isle. There they left us, in the midst of winter, without shelter of any kind. We had to tramp around all night to keep alive and sleep a bit during the day when the sun shone. They told us that before our arrival some men had lain down to sleep one night in what we call "spoon fash ion," and all of them were found frozen to death the next morning.

After a while we were sent back to Pemberton Prison. We were there when [General Hugh] Kilpatrick made his raid and nearly took Richmond. The rebels had been properly scared. There was no one to guard us except old men and young boys, and if any of us dared go near a window he risked being shot.

At times we got hold of some of the city newspapers, which carried tall tales that we did not believe. But when it was reported that all the Yankee prisoners would be sent to the swamps of Georgia where they would die little by little, then they told the truth for once.

On 8 March 1864 we were sent to Andersonville. They packed us into freight cars where we were so crowded together that we could neither sit nor lie down. How we cursed those rebels! Many also damned our government for not being willing to exchange prisoners. Our government presumably thought that it was best for the Union not to exchange prisoners as more men are always needed for attack than for defense.[2]

Our leaders had figured that thousands would have to die before the rebellion could be crushed, and they did not care particularly how the soldiers died. I think the rebels also realized that it was to the advantage of the North not to exchange prisoners; and I believe they treated us as badly as they could in order to arouse our people's sympathy and thus bring about an exchange. It is a fact, of course, that those who conduct a war can not permit themselves to waver because of sympathy for anyone.

No—our government was not very eager to get us prisoners exchanged, and it showed this by its actions. As "Commissioner of Exchange" it appointed a man whom the Southerners hated more than any other Northerner, a man whom they never called anything but "the Beast" [Benjamin F.] Butler—and you know that he was perhaps the best qualified wrangler for arguing with people that our government could find.

I will mention one incident that happened on the way to Andersonville. Two of the boys tried to escape at Raleigh, North Carolina; one of them was wounded during the attempt and gave himself up to the guard. When he was brought back, the captain shot him on the spot, exclaiming, "I will teach you how to escape, you damned Yankee scoundrel." The other fellow managed to get away but was caught later on.

Finally we arrived at Andersonville and were put into the stockade without shelter of any kind, and here the slogan was: "Root, hog, or die."

The stockade was built of large rectangular pine timbers set five feet into the ground and rising about twenty feet in height. The guards were posted at intervals along the top of the stockade; and there was a demarcation line about 16 feet from the walls which was called the death line. If anyone crossed it, he would be shot. About 16 acres were enclosed in this fashion. A stream flowed through the enclosure, and bordering it were about three or four acres of marshy ground. The first prisoners to arrive had been there some three weeks when we came, making a total number of about 2,000. There was enough firewood when the first prisoners arrived. It consisted of pitchpine, and those who lodged around those campfires were as black as Negroes. It was quite a sight to behold them as they sat there on the hillsides hunting for "grey-beasts" [lice].

Our rations consisted of cornmeal of the coarsest kind and a bit of meat and syrup. We were supposed to cook these things, but they never gave us anything to boil or bake them in. Those of us who were fortunate enough to get hold of half a canteen used it as kitchen utensil. The others ate their rations raw. If you had something to cook in, then the next problem was to secure firewood. The way in which we solved it was to seize every opportunity to help carry out the dead.

The Southerners used to gather up the corpses and place them in rows between the stockade and the death line. From there to the burial ground was a distance of 80 rods. There they dug a trench six feet wide so the dead could be placed side by side. We would stand by the corpses and watched the opportunity to carry one of them out and exchange it for firewood. It was a horrible sight to see those dead bodies—most of them naked—and the "grey-beasts" crawling over those skeletons.

Eventually so many prisoners died that the rebels did not bother the guards about removing them, and then we lost the chance of obtaining wood. They hauled the dead bodies to the burial grounds by the wagonload, exactly as we farmers haul fence posts.

As our armies advanced through the summer, our number also increased despite the appalling death rate, and robbery and disorder also grew worse. When new prisoners came in whom the rebels had not plundered then some of our own men would proceed to rob them. Consequently we could hear screams of murder and robbery every night. The most complete anarchy reigned. At last the better element organized and called themselves "Regulators." The rebels gave us permission to punish the robbers found within the enclosure. The Regulators arrested about a hundred culprits and the rebels told us we could deal with them as we saw fit.

The Regulators formed their own court, appointed a jury, and conducted trials. Six of the prisoners were found guilty of murder and robbery and were condemned to be hanged on July 11, 1864. The rebels had them under guard outside the stockade and on the appointed date they were handed over to our police. The first thing to happen was that one of the convicts tried to escape, but he was found in a marsh and brought back. Finally they were brought up on the scaffold and plunged into eternity— all except one, a hefty Irishman whose rope broke and he landed safely. You may believe me, that he pleaded for mercy; but there was no mercy for him. A man dubbed "Limber Jim" stepped forth and said: "You robbed me of $80 when I came here; and now, by God, you shall hang!" And hanged he was. We called these fellows "Raiders"; most of them were the dregs of New York City and they were generally dubbed "New Yorkers." There must have been about 30,000 prisoners within the stockade at the time, and everyone able to crawl out of his hole and stand on his legs wanted to see the hanging. It was a tremendous crowd, I can tell you. The hangings bore fruit. There were no more robberies; but, of course, petty thievery went on all the time.

If you good people could have seen where we got our drinking water you would have concluded that it was pretty messy stuff. There was enough of it, however. A stream ran through a marsh within the stockade, and this marsh served as a substitute for public rooms "Reserved for Gentlemen." It was a sight that I can not describe here.

We got better water after a while. Probably some of you have heard of "Providence Spring" in Andersonville. You may well call it that; it was a Godsend for us, but like every thing else it had a natural cause. We had such a terrible rain that it even washed away part of the stockade near the stream and the hill close by; and then the spring gushed forth near the stockade. It was a blessed rain because it also washed away a great amount of pollution from the marsh.

I cannot report in detail what happened later on. In September they moved us from Andersonville, as they feared that Sherman would pass through this region. Then we were to be exchanged—so they said. This they told us whenever we were moved from one prison to another. First they sent us to Savannah and thence to a stockade called Millen Prison. It was a stockade like Andersonville, without shelter of any kind. We were there during the election and the rebels wished to find out how the prisoners felt about it. So they wanted us to vote; and an election campaign was carried on in great fashion, exactly as if it were of real importance.

The New Yorkers went about with ballots shouting: "Vote for little Mac(Clellan) and let us secure peace so we can get out of here and not lie here and rot for Lincoln and the Negroes." We said: "Vote for Lincoln—a man who is true to the Union and will not give up until he has turned the Confederacy upside down."

We finished digging a tunnel but were discovered just as the first prisoners got through. I cannot tell you everything. General Sherman came our way and consequently we were sent back to Savannah and thence down to Blackshear, where we were kept in the woods, guarded by rebels and bloodhounds. Some prisoners were taken to Charleston or Florence and the rest of us went back to Andersonville.

Never will I be able to forget that night—near Christmas time—when for the second time I was sent to Andersonville. We had to march barefoot over the frozen ground and lie down on a plowed field, while the rest of my comrades were sent to Florence. I wept that night and was near giving up all hope. But the next day I met some old comrades; then I clenched my teeth and said to myself that the rebels would not take my life if I could do anything about it.

We had a hard winter. Some of the boys dug themselves into the ground like moles to protect themselves. At this time the rebels came and wanted us to enlist in their forces. I, for my part, said I would rather die where I was as an honorable man than sell myself to the devil. They did not get many takers. Those whom they got were New Yorkers, I believe.

Toward the end of April, 1865, we were released on our word of honor and sent to Jacksonville, Florida. We arrived at our destination on April 28—a miserable lot to behold. The only clothes I had were part of a shirt, a pair of pants, and a hat.

I had old clothes on when I was captured, and I had been barefoot almost eleven months. People talk mostly about our hunger, but that was less than half of our sufferings. Of course, we were practically always hungry. There was never any talk of sharing our rations—we devoured everything immediately. But bear in mind, we had to lie and wallow in filth all the time without shelter of any kind, nor did we have anything in which to cook our food—which they gave us raw. We did not receive any clothes even if we were naked. And, on top of it all there was the filth and the vermin that gnawed at us constantly—that drove men insane and foolish so they would eat all sorts of vile stuff.

Scurvy and diarrhea took the lives of most of the boys. I had a bad attack of scurvy and nearly gave up the ghost. My teeth were loose and my gums sore; I could see blood on the hard bread at every bite I took. My feet were so swollen that I could barely walk. Had I given up and merely lain down like so many others, then I would have died too, as they did. But I hobbled around and vowed that the rebels should not get my life if I could possibly prevent it.

Only one man was hanged for having treated us as they did, and that was Captain Henry Wirz. He was a devil. But the old saying is true that people hang the small thieves and let the great ones go. The high authorities knew that he was the worst man they could find, and therefore they kept him on the job. I cannot describe the horrors that took place. I saw men shot in broad daylight merely for crossing the death line to get cleaner water.[3]

How we were chased by bloodhounds! Frequently prisoners tried to dig their way out through tunnels, and you might believe that it would have been possible for someone to get away. But as far as I know not a single one got out of the stockade and escaped with his life. There was a man with bloodhounds whose sole duty it was to track down fleeing prisoners. The hounds were taken around the stockade every morning and they always picked up a scent. Then you should have heard the howls! There can be little doubt that Andersonville was the worst hell ever found on earth.

Forty-three members of our regiment died at Andersonville and fourteen in all the other prisons. Most of those who died at Andersonville were not confined there more than four or five months. Not one out of four came out alive even though nearly fifty percent of them had not been prisoners half as long as I.[4]

As for the old "Fifteenth," I can say that we always did our duty. I do not know of one prisoner from our regiment who was captured except after a hard fight.

And what do you think lay closest to our hearts? What, in the midst of our misery, engaged most of our conversation? We did not talk about the money we should make once we were free. Oh no! We talked about our mothers, wives, sisters—and sometimes about how well we should eat when we returned home. It seems that everyone of us had a good mother. We used to say that if our mothers or sisters could see us in our wretched condition it would break their hearts.

Thus far I have told you how the rebels treated us. Now I will say a little about the treatment I received from our own government. I enlisted for three years in October 1861; the pay was to be thirteen dollars per month and a bounty of $100. I served seven months beyond my period of enlistment—in Andersonville. Was our government willing to provide for my exchange? No! Did they give me a bounty as they did those who re-enlisted? No! If they had provided for my release at the time when my period of service expired, I could have got up to $1,000 for hiring out as a military substitute. Some men in our town received that much for re-enlisting after completing their service. As you know, you would have the right to sue a firm or a corporation that deprived you of such an opportunity.

Well, I had not tried very hard to get a pension until last year. I brought testimonies from a fellow prisoner, two lieutenants, and several neighbors, but the pension bureau treated all of us like a bunch of liars and the application was rejected. I must admit that it hurt me. The people in my town and county have looked upon me as an honest man and have elected me to various positions of honor and trust. They all feel that there must be something wrong with this pension business. I have never been able to stand very long or move about much on my feet since I got out of Andersonville. I feel certain that most of those who receive pensions are more able-bodied than I am. I have resolved, however, that I shall manage without a pension in the future, as I have in the past. I have the satisfaction of feeling that I served my country because of the principles involved and not for the money.

Well, boys! You must not believe that I am a "kicker." I have always stood up for my country, and today I am here with a big Hurrah for our soldier–president and comrade, William McKinley, as I was for Lincoln in 1860 and 1864.

NOTES

1. Osmund Johnson of Company K, 15th Wisconsin Regiment, whom Steensland mentions as having stayed longer in Andersonville than he did himself was from the Stavanger area in Norway. When the war broke out he was a married man and a farmer in Freeborn county, Minnesota. He enlisted with Captain Grinager in St. Paul. A younger brother of his was the well-known temperance speaker Knut Johnson, who served as an artilleryman during the war in a Minnesota battalion composed almost exclusively of Norwegians.

Osmund was taken prisoner at Chickamauga. The regiment came under a cross-fire when an advancing Union division—ignorant of the fact that the 15th was still holding its ground so far forward—opened fire on them, taking them for an enemy force. Then the regiment scattered, and in the confusion Osmund ran in the wrong direction until he came to a breastwork that he could not scale. He followed it some distance but when he saw rebel troops coming he threw himself to the ground, pretending to be dead. He even managed to smear some blood on his face. They understood, however, that he was merely feigning death and took him prisoner.

He had a lot to relate regarding his stay in Andersonville. At first he stirred his cornmeal and water in his cap; but when it developed a leak, he used one of his shoes in which he could stir a little at a time as his appetite demanded.

Among other incidents, he told about a German who lay near death. Osmund sat down beside him waiting for this to happen so he could inherit a blanket that the German happened to have. As Osmund sat there watching the dying man he began to feel sorry for him and chided him for giving up like this, he who had a wife and children. He even dug up the old story that they would soon be exchanged. Osmund's lecture had the effect on the German that he actually pulled himself together and recovered so well that he was on hand when the prisoners got out of Andersonville.

Old Osmund attended the next to last reunion of the regiment. His brother Knut met him on the steps of the Capitol in St. Paul and greeted him. The old fellow did not acknowledge the greeting but scowled at him and said: "You were never with the 15th Wisconsin." "No," Knut replied, "but you see, I am your brother." When the oldster had pondered this a while he came to the conclusion that a blood-brother might have as great a claim on him as a member of the regiment, and so they struck up a companionship. One peculiarity clung to old Osmund his whole life through after his experiences in Andersonville: he could not tolerate hearing anyone complain about food or talk about appetizing or unappetizing food. He died in the firm conviction that all food was edible. [Ager's note]

2. These prisoners were not exchanged and when the war ended the Confederate government had ceased to exist. [Ager's note]

3. It may be in order to mention here that General Grant's refusal to exchange prisoners placed the Southern states in a terrible dilemma: how were they to feed their thousands of prisoners? After the blockading of the Mississippi River few or no supplies arrived from the well-provisioned southwestern states, and at the time referred to by Steensland General Robert E. Lee's army at Petersburg lived on half rations similar to those received by the prisoners in Andersonville. Matters were made still more difficult because of the awkward transportation system and the poorly functioning commissariat. After a lapse of fifty years, history also deals more leniently with the memory of Captain Henry Wirtz. Under extremely difficult circumstances he tried to fulfill the obligations placed upon him, but with entirely insufficient means.

On July 25, 1864, the commandant, General Widener, telegraphed Adjutant General Cooper, saying that he had 29,400 prisoners and not a day's rations. He had to have on hand rations for at least ten days, he stated. In reply he was told that General Lee's army did not have more than a day's rations and it would be indefensible to demand ten days' rations for the prisoners.

Captain Wirtz must also have been better than his reputation. It has been revealed that he sent one complaint after the other because the rations were insufficient and the quality poor, and because the prisoners did not have any lunch pails in which to receive the food.

Originally Andersonville was thought of as a temporary establishment and was not designed for a vast number of prisoners. When General Grant refused to exchange prisoners, the numbers piled up—and there was such a shortage of provisions in the South that the Confederate soldiers did not get enough food to still their own hunger. Under these circumstances we can well imagine how the prisoners would fare.

The Confederacy did not attempt to conceal the extremely high mortality rate; and they sought time after time to exchange prisoners—man for man. But Grant refused. President Lincoln did not give his approval. This matter was under Grant's jurisdiction, however, and Lincoln did not want to interfere.

The death rate among southern soldiers in northern prisons was almost as appalling as that of northern soldiers in southern prisons. According to a report by Secretary of War Stanton to the House of Representatives, 25,436 Confederate soldiers died in northern prisons and 22,576 Union soldiers in southern prisons. But as there were more prisoners in the North than in the South it is difficult to give exact comparisons. The conservative northern historian J. F. Rhodes estimates the death ratio in northern prisons at a little above 12 percent and in southern prisons at 15.5 percent. As medicine was declared contraband of war, there was a great lack of the most essential drugs in the South, and this undoubtedly had its effect. [Ager's note]

4. Bjørn Aslakson from Willmar, Minnesota, who spent a long time in Andersonville and wrote an account of his experiences, gives the following information about fellow-sufferers from the 15th Wisconsin Regiment:

"The Norwegians I learned to know were members of the 15th or the so-called Norwegian Wisconsin Regiment. There was one man named Simon Pederson who, I believe, was from Ringebø, in Gudbrandsdalen. He suffered from a horrible attack of scurvy, the most common and the most debilitating of the diseased in the prison. Not only had his teeth fallen out but his limbs were so swollen and distorted that he had become absolutely deformed. When he tried to move, he was forced to crawl in the most miserable fashion on hands and feet that were so misshapen he had to place the backs of his hands on the ground. Besides, both hands and feet were blotched with large growths or boils, and gangrene had affected so many parts of his body that he looked like one living mass of sores. His sufferings were so indescribably that the most welcome guest was the miserable death which put an end to his torment." [Ager's note]

Battle of Murfreesboro or Stone's River

by Waldemar Ager

Hardly at any time during the whole history of the Civil War did it look darker for the North than during the last half of the month of December 1862. In Virginia there had been defeat after defeat. Even the Battle of Antietam, which in a way could be called a victory, was, when you think of the enormous losses the Northern states had suffered, hardly qualified to reassure the people. And now on 13 December, General Burnside, in whom the people had great confidence, had suffered a crushing defeat at Fredricksburg. In the West, however, they had been luckier. Fort Henry, Fort Donelson, Island No. 10, and New Orleans were shining examples. But now General Braxton Bragg had pushed into Tennessee and from there, if he was lucky, the way lay open into Kentucky and one could expect a hostile invasion. The Southern army under Bragg and the North under General Buell had played hide-and-seek nearly the whole summer. A single engagement like Perryville had taken place, which to those skilled in the arts of war was masterfully executed, but to the common soldier meant long, boring, and tiring marches back and forth through dust and mud. These marches thinned the ranks of the North more than battles did. Everywhere they went they left full hospitals and fresh graves. Army-cholera, typhoid, pneumonia, and other diseases raged and soldiers succumbed by the thousands.

Finally in October Buell was relieved by General W. S. Rosecrans, who was regarded as more capable. The army lay at Nashville and the Confederates had gone into winter quarters at Murfreesboro, 30 miles to the southeast. After the defeat at Fredricksburg, a certain element in the North who wanted the war to end and the South to be recognized as an independent federation were encouraged, and a victory somewhere was highly craved, if for nothing else than to strengthen the government. Here too, relations with Europe were involved. There was always the well-founded fear that England and France would recognize the South as an independent nation.

After some pressure from Washington, Rosecrans left Nashville on 26 December and marched toward Murfreesboro to take on the Confederates. They took a position a couple of miles from Murfreesboro after some small skirmishes.

The two armies were about equal in strength—between 40,000 and 45,000 men. The Northern troops comprised three corps: Crittenden's, Thomas' and McCook's. In the last corps, Davis' division and Carlin's brigade, stood the 15th Wis. Regiment. . . .

When Bragg discovered that Rosecrans had received reinforcements, he pulled back from Murfreesboro the next day, taking his prisoners and his spoils with him. The battle was a defeat for the North but, because of the fact that the last attack was driven back, it was deemed a victory and contributed to restoring the Northern states' sinking spirits.

As it turned out, it did in fact become a victory, as Bragg with his much battered army found it advisable to give up his invasion plans and get out of Tennessee.

The South's losses amounted to about 10,000 men, of whom 9,000 were killed or wounded. The North lost 13,000, of whom 3,000 were taken prisoner.

The 15th Wisconsin Regiment took a glorious part in this battle. The regiment here, in spite of two absent companies, was quite strong and counted about 500 men, a total they were never again to reach. They were in Carlin's brigade, Davis' division, McCook's Army Corps. This corps was the first to meet the enemy after the departure from Nashville. Ten miles from this city, near Nolansville, they met a force of Hardee's corps. These pulled back to Knob Gap where they set up a battery of 8 cannon. Colonel Carlin got orders to take this battery and attacked with the whole brigade, with the Norwegian regiment in the right wing. Here the regiment took the first cannon. It was so late in the evening that the enemy could not be pursued. In the morning, on 30 Dec., the battle line was formed and already that evening the brigade had an encounter with the enemy as they were ordered to take a hostile battery at their front.

Colonel Heg did all he could to encourage his men; he rode in the front where the hostile battery held sway over the terrain. Lt. Col. McKee called to him to be careful, but Heg pretended not to hear. His horse was then shot through the chest by a cannonball and the horse and rider fell to the ground in a heap, but the colonel was unharmed. Lt. Col. McKee, on the other hand, fell in this battle.

When the brigade took its position in the battle line, Company E of the 15th Wisconsin was sent forward to reconnoitre. Thus the battery at the brigade's front was discovered and Company E opened fire. It was, it seems, the first clash with the enemy, so it can be said that they opened the battle. At 2 o'clock in the afternoon the whole regiment was ordered forward with the skirmishers of Company E. It was in this battle that Captain Ingemundsen was killed. He commanded the skirmishers. The regiment stormed the battery under a terrific rain of bullets. Here they were attacked in the flank by a force on the right wing, while another hostile battery assailed the left. They fell back slowly, fighting steadily, about 300 yards and took a position behind a fence until darkness fell. Six were killed and 35 wounded in the first attack, before the real battle had begun.

Early the next morning the regiment stood in battle line again, after they had rested on their guns all night. When the South's violent attack took place in the morning and threw back Johnson's three brigades on the far wing, the regiment held the same position they had taken that night. When the battery on the brigade's right wing withdrew 300 feet, the regiment was ordered to support it. Therefore the regiment was separated from the brigade, as the battery withdrew farther back so that it would not fall into enemy hands. Colonel Heg then pushed the regiment back to the brigade and took a position behind the 28th Illinois Regiment, who were in battle with the enemy, and gave them support. When the regiment was pushed back, the 15th continued to fight the enemy, who were hardly 600 feet away and advancing in a column. Heg held his position until he saw himself flanked at the right. He had no choice but to pull back or be taken prisoner. The withdrawal took place over an open field and here many fell when followed by the enemy, who maintained a steady fire. Here he came upon the rest of Carlin's brigade, who had gathered near a house that was used as a hospital, a mile northeast of the place the brigade had stood that morning. From here the brigade retreated to Nashville-Chauseen, where they took up a position a few hundred feet from the pike, behind a fence where they opened fire on the enemy following them. Again they had to yield to a superior force; they took a position near a railroad line on the other side of the highway, where they awaited the enemy in a location well placed for defense. Here they remained over the 1st and 2nd of January until the evening, when they pushed over Stone's River out to the left wing under gradually lessening fire.

During the battle the weather remained extremely awful. It rained or snowed nearly the whole time and for five days the regiment had been under open skies, in slush and mud and without heat and on short rations. No one complained and the regiment had no shirkers. They had kept together and there was no panic when they retreated.

Besides Lieutenant Colonel McKee and Captain Ingemundsen, who were killed, captains George Wilson and Mons Grinager and Gustafson were wounded, also Lt. Simonsen. Many of the less seriously wounded did not go to the hospitals, and among many of the others who were declared missing there were quite a few who had fallen within the enemy lines and were buried in unknown graves.

Lieutenant Colonel McKee was a Scot and the only one within the regiment who was not a Scandinavian. It was said that J. A. Johnson (Ole C. Johnson's well-known brother) was to be elected to this post; but Johnson thought it was enough that two brothers (Ole and Hans) should go off to war, so he changed his mind. An American named K. Jones was then made Lieutenant Colonel. His wife was Norwegian and he considered himself Norwegian, as many of the others did. But Jones did not make out well with the rest of them so he withdrew. McKee then filled the post. He had taken part in the Mexican War and was a brave and popular officer who was respected and admired by all, both officers and privates in the 15th Wis. Regiment. It was a great sorrow to the regiment, when it became known that he had been killed.

The reports of losses were as follows: The North: Killed—1,730. Wounded—7,802. Missing—3,717. Total—13,249. The South: Killed—1,294. Wounded—7,945. Missing—1,027. Total—10,266. The North's force: 56,649. South's force: 47,978.

The latter had the advantage of having a self-appointed position and was able to attack before the Northern troops had reached the battlefield.

Ole K. Hanson of Company A was wounded five times but could not be induced to retreat. He pushed so far to the front that he was taken prisoner. After that no one heard from him. Evidently he died of his wounds. He was made an honorary captain for his gallantry.

An interesting appendix to the account of the Battle of Murfreesboro is a letter from Lieutenant P. W. Chantland written to his friend L. H.

Skavlem. The letter is written in good Norwegian. Mr. Chantland took part in the battle as sergeant and commanded Company E after its officers had fallen or were wounded.

Letter from Lt. P. W. Chantland

Camp near Murfreesboro, 11 Jan. 1863

Dear Friend!

. . . We left our camp near Nashville on the morning of 20 Dec. and marched ten miles in terrible rain and waded in mud up to our knees. When we had gone that far, we were ordered to fall into battle lines and our regiment was commanded to take a battery the enemy had put in a narrow gorge called Knob Gap. We stormed this battery and took a cannon and caisson and four horses and three prisoners. When this was done, we lay down right there where we were standing. It rained the whole night so it was impossible to sleep. The following day we had to pursue the enemy again, only about five miles, when they settled in at Murfreesboro and we had to wait for our train of provisions. We bivouacked in a small town called Nolensville, which the previous battle was named after.

On Sunday the 28th we got provisions, and on the morning of the 29th we were off to Murfreesboro, which was 16 miles away. We stopped within 3 1/2 miles of the town. On that day our cavalry had a clash with the enemy, and we pulled closer in on them. We were not allowed to build fires and it rained the whole night and we lay with our guns in our arms. On the morning of the 30th, we got orders to move forward and formed battle lines with two companies, the 21st Ill. Reg. and our company E, which advanced before the brigade. We went slowly forward and to the right, with stops now and then, until 3 o'clock in the afternoon, when we were ordered forward. Our troops were then in a strong line over three miles long. Here our brigade was ordered forward, and we went ahead as skirmishers and pushed the enemy's cordons back about 80 rods, until they found cover behind a stone wall and could not be driven off. We had to take our position in an open field, so they had a good view of us and it was not long before our captain got a bullet in the abdomen. He died within 15 minutes. Three others of our company were badly wounded. We then got orders to pull back and when we returned to our regiment we and the 21st Ill. pushed ahead with the other two regiments in the brigade that were held in reserve. We attacked a battery. The 21st Ill. began to weaken and fall back, as the fire from the enemy was unendurable; but I can tell you, in praise of our regiment, that none of them gave up until it was absolutely necessary. We now had no support; it was impossible to go on, as we were the only targets and the fire was horrible; but we were quite lucky even so, as not many were killed though many were wounded. When darkness came, the shooting held off until daylight. Then it started again and the enemy troops attacked our right wing commanded by General Johnson and drove them back. Our division made a defense as long as possible; but then they flanked us and got us under heavy fire and the whole wing was forced back. We pushed at their left wing. I must say that day was a great loss for us, when the enemy held the battlefield and our wounded had to lie out there two days before we could retrieve them. On New Year's Day it was quieter and we worked on barricades on both sides that day.

I must say that the 31st was a bad day. The enemy cavalry took our provision train too that day; but then our cavalry took it back. On the 2nd of Jan., in the afternoon, thunder began again on our left wing when General Rosseau attacked the enemy with two of his regiments to drive them from their barricades. On that day, we really let them have it. Three brigades of Rebel troops were knocked down, one after the other as fast as they came. This battle took place in about one hour and we drove them back more than two miles. Our brigade was so far to the right that we escaped this, but later we were ordered by Gen. Rosecrans to support those who pursued the enemy and later we got orders to take a position on the left wing. We did not arrive until after dark and had to set up barricades for the night. So here we lay, and kept up a scattered fire going with the enemy the whole day and the following night until the next morning, when we were sent to the right wing; by then the enemy had pulled back from Murfreesboro and left a few sentries to make us think they were still there.

I can tell you our brigade suffered much. We went in with 2,000 men and our loss was 821 wounded, killed, and missing. Our regiment lost 116, of whom two were officers. We had no officers left in our company and I am now alone to keep its records in order.

I for my part will say that this war is a terrible thing, and I would like to see an end to it now. It takes men of good constitution to stand these hard and inhuman marches, when one has to carry all one's clothes and three days rations at a time and lie outdoors in winter, in rain, and without fire for weeks at a time . . . .

The Second Day at Chickamauga
From a letter by Lieutenant Colonel Johnson

Lieutenant Colonel Ole C. Johnson commanded the 15th Wis. Reg. at the Battle of Chickamauga. As information regarding the Regiment's part on the second day of the battle (20 Sept.) has been insufficiently reported, we herewith print a letter that the lieutenant colonel wrote to his brother the Hon. John A. Johnson from Libby Prison in Richmond. The letter was dated 3 November 1863.

. . . . After dark, I walked to the hospital three miles away to see how things were going with our wounded. I was happy to see that so many of them were already getting nursing care. Those who had been able to walk had been released. I discovered that Col. Heg's wounds were mortal, and that he was not expected to live. He was very weak, and I talked to him for only a moment. He was prepared and calm about his approaching death. Between 10 and 11 o'clock I returned to my regiment with a heavy heart. I thought of the great loss we had suffered. Col. Heg, with his great goodness and gallant behavior, was always present where there was danger. He was something like an idol among us and his memory will always be held in high esteem by every man in the regiment. About 12 o'clock, I returned to the regiment and lay down for a few hours rest. On Sunday, at 3 a.m., we were again on our feet and marched west to the Chattanooga Pike, where we took a position on a hill. Here we made coffee and had breakfast. We were now in reserve and indulged in the hope that perhaps we would not be under fire that day; but no sooner had the combat begun at our front than we were ordered forward. When we neared the front, we had a slight pause; but, while the men ahead of us were sent off to other positions on the battlefield, we were moved forward and took a position at the front line, at 12 o'clock, behind a hastily erected breastwork. We had been there only a short time when the enemy attacked and tried to take this position. We had a good view of them as the field was open and we pushed them back with terrible losses. They assembled again and attacked once more but were again driven back. After the second time, I looked to the side and noticed that the regiment on our left wing (the 8th Kansas) already had fallen back and the enemy were crossing the breastwork. I was both surprised and frightened to see that the Rebels were not met with the slightest opposition there under the second attack; but then I knew there were lines behind us and I hoped that the Rebels would be stopped by them. On the other side, I found that the regiment that formed our other ring was also thrown back and we were almost encircled. Now, some of our men also began to retreat and in the next instant I was without much ceremony commanded to follow the Rebels to their rear. Another officer (Capt. Gustafson) and I with twenty-five men were captured together. The rest managed to escape.

That this battle was a big defeat is clear to everyone; but to point out on whom the blame lies is not so simple. On Saturday, our brigade was thrown into the battle completely without support on either wing and the result was that, after a terrible battle, we were thrown back. Another brigade was sent into combat at the same time with the same results, so we were thrown back one at a time. Anyone who is familiar with military affairs knows that that sort of tactics ends only in defeat and destruction. On Sunday, there was a space of about 600 yards between our divisions on the right and the next division. The fact is that the regiment on our right wing did not know that there were troops farther to the right. On our left it was exactly the same situation. The 8th Kan. Regiment formed the left wing of our division and that left was wholly unprotected. So, the enemy met hardly any opposition from these two regiments. If our lines had stuck together, we would never have allowed the enemy to drive us from this position.

The Battle of New Hope Church or Pickett's Mill

Those who know something of the Norwegian regiment's history know that the regiment lost over half of its men at New Hope Church in an attack on a fortified position, but how it really happened is almost impossible to ascertain. From veterans' accounts we know that after a long and exhausting march by the army's extreme left wing, they were ordered to storm a hill and they were met with terrific fire, that they advanced clear up to the enemy's barricades, that they almost lost their regimental banner, that they got no orders to retreat or they saw that this was more dangerous than to keep the battle going and that they took a position not far from the enemy front and held this position several hours until a counterattack threw them back.

P. G. Dietrichson tells in his book that the 4th Army Corps crossed Pumpkin Vine Creek near Dallas and entrenched themselves 250 yards from the enemy's fortifications, while skirmishers sought to drive the enemy out of its position. On the 27th [May] the division (Wood's) was sent four miles to the left to spy on the enemy's position and about 4 o'clock that afternoon Hanson's (Hazen's) brigade attacked but was driven back. The first rank of Willich's brigade (where the 15th Wisconsin stood) was sent ahead with the second line at its heels. The regiment crossed over a ravine that was raked by enemy artillery. Storming with "a shout" over the 2nd brigade (Hazen's) the regiment came so close to the enemy's barricade that several fell within ten feet of it. But it was impossible to rout the enemy, so the regiment crouched down 15 yards from the barriers and kept up a steady gunfire until 9 o'clock at night, when they got orders to pull back. When they attempted to take their wounded with them they were set upon by the enemy, who took a considerable number of prisoners, most of whom were wounded. The regiment then encamped on a hill 300 yards to the right and held on, after entrenching themselves, until the night of 5 June when the enemy retreated.

Editor Enander tells in his account of the Battle of New Hope Church that Sherman's right wing was attacked by the Rebels on 27 May and that he sent his left wing, which included Wood's division, to which the 15th belonged, and Hazen's brigade against the enemy's left wing (should be right wing—W.A.) to drive them from their position. So he records that Hazen's brigade was driven back and that Willich's fresh attack drew up to the enemy's fortifications—as in Dietrichson's account.

Buslett tells that Gen. Hooker began the battle in the passes in the Allatoona mountains after crossing the Etowah River with the enemy's advance guard. Gen. Schofield was to attack the front (center), while Sherman with the rest of the army went southwest (toward Dallas). So he describes the attack on Sherman's right wing and how Sherman sent his left wing against the enemy's right. Hazen's brigade fell back with great losses and Willich's brigade was ordered forward and reached the enemy's breastworks. Buslett calls it "the most desperate storm in the campaign" and records that many of the 15th were killed at the enemy's barricades and that they took a position 45 feet from the hostile breastworks and held this position under destructive gunfire, etc.

Lt. Col. Ole C. Johnson's official report deals with this information again, with how individual retreats took place. He relates that the regiment left Cassville on the 23rd to flank the enemy's left wing at the Allatoona Pass. On 25 May, at 4 o'clock in the afternoon, they heard strong gunfire at the front; the enemy had left its position in the Allatoona mountains and assaulted Hooker's (the 20th Army Corps). Johnson also reports that the brigade was ordered to form two lines behind [W. B.] Hazen's brigade on 27 May with the 15th Wis. in the center of the front line, along with the 89th Ill. and 32nd Ind; that they then marched 3 miles to the left and passed behind the 23rd army corps; also, that at 4 p.m. Hazen's brigade attacked and was driven back; that "the 15th" advanced across a valley and stormed forward over the 2nd brigade (Hazen's) and came so close to the barricades that several men were killed ten feet from them. Companies A and F had to form a front with a battery to the left. The rest coincides with the previous accounts.

With these conflicting reports, it is quite difficult to form a correct picture of the battle.

According to Enander and Buslett, Sherman's right wing was set on by the Rebels on 27 May. Actually this did not take place until the 28th and resulted when McPherson, leading Sherman's right wing, began to send men northeastward. Colonel Johnson states that the regiment was sent out to flank the enemy's left wing at Allatoona Pass. It must have been the right wing he meant; but the right wing on the 23rd was already over the Etowah River and on the 24th encamped 4 miles from New Hope Church, near the Allatoona pike. That the enemy threw themselves at Hooker on May 25th cannot be right either. The enemy had withdrawn four miles farther back and taken a position which Hooker repeatedly stormed on the 25th. It was these attacks that were the Battle of New Hope Church.

Even the name is erroneous. The Norwegian regiment did not take part in this battle at New Hope Church, which took place on May 25th, but the battle at Pickett's Mill five miles northeast of New Hope Church on the 27th of May.

And it is strange how little can be found out about this battle, which bears witness to such glorious heroism that there was hardly a more brilliant exploit in the whole campaign.

The Federal Army's commanding general W. T. Sherman bypasses it entirely in his memoirs and in "The Grand Strategy of the Last Year of the War" he scarcely mentions the fact that he was forced to fight on the 25th and 28th of May. (The last date indicates a comparatively insignificant attack by Hardee on McPherson's position at Dallas.)

The chief of corps General Howard marks the Battle of Pickett's Mill only as "something of a skirmish" in his "The Struggle for Atlanta."

Also it is difficult to find out the losses. "Battles and Leaders" otherwise gives the losses per brigade, but not in this instance. The army's strength as well as its losses has never been clearly tabulated.

If an explanation can be made, Sherman was not only a capable general—by many valued as the Union's most capable—but he also had an eye to the political effect of the reports that were given to the general public. Facing the enemy he never forgot the great newspaper reading public behind him.

The Norwegian regiment was now in Willich's brigade, T. J. Wood's division, 4th army corps, under General O. O. Howard.

The 1st brigade (Willich's) comprised 9 regiments, among them the remainder of Colonel Heg's brigade—the 25th Ill. Regiment and the 8th Kansas, which was led by Colonel Martin, who later became governor of Kansas. These along with the German 32nd Ind. Reg. made up the brigade's nucleus. They had been steadily in the field for two years and fought in many battles. Gen. Augustus Willich was a German, a devoted and capable brigadier chief, greatly esteemed by his men, bold in case of danger, and often wounded. He had no "pull" with the higher-ups and he is not mentioned once by his superiors in their accounts, while the chief of the 2nd brigade, W. B. Hazen, is often named.

The division was composed of three brigades (1st) Willich's, (2nd) Hazen's, and (3rd) Samuel Beatty's. Buslett errs in stating that Hazen's brigade belonged to Newton's division.

The Norwegian regiment was until 1st of June commanded by Major Wilson, a brave and capable officer. Lieutenant Colonel Ole C. Johnson had not returned from prison.

The Confederate Army was the so-called Tennessee Army under General Joseph E. Johnston; Gen. Polk, Gen. Hood, and Gen. Hardee each led a corps. Then came some state troops from Georgia along with cavalry and artillery. The latter was quite deficient.

Johnston had left the Resaca position on 17 May and had marched southward followed by the northern troops. At Adairsville and Cassville there was resistance. The army crossed the Etowah River on the 21st and took up a position that Colonel Presstman of the engineer corps had prepared at New Hope Church.

Hardee bivouacked near Dallas farther south and backed his left flank up against the turnpike to Atlanta. Next came Polk's corps, which was in contact with Hood, who had his center at New Hope church, which formed the Southern army's right wing. The line was about ten miles long and began at Dallas in the northeast, extending in a line about seven miles eastward to Pickett's Mill, then three miles east. A strong battery along with a cavalry unit completed the line. The position was along a continuous upward rise overgrown with scrub woods on top, while the slopes were bare. At the foot of the treeless slopes ran a narrow valley. The plan was to hold the enemy here until the engineer corps could build a new and stronger barricade in the Kennesaw Mountains and over Lost Mountain. From that position the railroad to Atlanta could be covered and protected.

Afterward, as the Northern troops went toward Etowah they spread out fanwise in order to control the whole Confederate front and later the different sections were moved so that McPherson stood against Hardee, Howard against Polk, and Hooker against John B. Hood. The 23rd army corps under Schofield lay a couple of miles back as reserve.

Hooker was the first to collide with the enemy on 25 May in the afternoon, when a splinter of his column met with the Confederate brigade (Stewart's) of Hood's corps, which lay as outpost until the ridge in back of them was sufficiently fortified. Hooker drove the brigade back and stormed the hill but time after time was thrown back. It was a terrible onslaught and took place in a thunderstorm with heavy rain.

The bad weather continued the next day and only skirmishes and small encounters took place.

On the 27th plans were made for an attack on the South's right flank. It is possible that Howard hoped to prevent the same tactics that Lee and Stonewall Jackson in May the year before had used at Chancellorsville, when Jackson with part of his army had made a circling movement and fallen on the North's flank and torn Howard's troops to pieces. What Lee and Jackson had done with 43,000 men against 106,000, they might do with 68,000 against 100,000.

Wood's division was taken out of Howard's corps and sent to the left. The 23rd army corps had come up from Burnt Hickory near Pumpkin Vine Creek and the division passed behind this. Meanwhile R. W. Johnson's division was sent out and marched *on echelon* on Wood's left.

The division formed attack columns behind the 23rd army corps and a

feint was made at the front to the east and they found the hill fortified.
The march continued a mile and Hazen's brigade stormed the slope with
his front to the south, while Johnson's division with Scribner's brigade in
front set out on the storm column's left to Pickett's Mill, where they were
attacked by the cavalry, which fought on foot. Meanwhile an attack
took place on Hood's center by Newton's and Stanley's divisions to draw
the enemy's attention away from the flank. Now Sherman and Howard
counted on Hood's division to avoid the enemy's right flank, but
Johnston had taken a devious route the night before and sent Cleburne's
infantry farther to the right. When Hazen and later Willich attacked,
they struck the newly formed center, where Cleburne's 5,000 infantrymen lay behind strong barricades with a powerful battery at their flank
and considerable cavalry strength.

Like Jackson at Chancellorsville, Howard had ordered the attack in
storm columns by brigades or half-brigades, instead of the usual spread-
out formation. These storming columns formed a part of Cleburne's entrenched position, which was quite long, and from its flank gunfire
spilled obliquely towards the deep columns.

Hazen's brigade was soon broken up and through the opening burst
General Willich's brigade led by the Norwegian regiment. It was 5:30 in
the afternoon. The Norwegian regiment pushed clear up to the enemy's
barricades and several men fell scarcely ten feet from it.

While the Northern generals have refrained from mentioning this
butchery, there has followed some recognition; the Confederate com-
mander-in-chief Joseph E. Johnston has written about it in his account of
the campaign. In regard to the ferocity with which the battle was fought
at Pickett's Mill, he says that the leading regiment in the storm columns
came as close to the barricades as 20 feet, while the flagbearer broke
rank and planted the regiment's flag in the ground 10 feet from the entrenchment and was shot. First one man, then two more crept forward
to rescue the flag and were shot one after the other until the fourth man
succeeded in carrying it away.

There is hardly any doubt that he was speaking of the Norwegian regiment, as it came closest to the barricades and the man who rescued the
flag was Major Wilson, who lost some fingers on one hand, but brought
the flag back through the brushwood. That about a wounded hand is possibly erroneous.

There was also a Tord Foleson in the regiment who planted the flag in the ground after he was wounded and three men fell when they tried to rescue it.

The regiment was not able to drive the enemy from its position, but they dug in 45 feet from the barricade where the slope of the hill formed a sort of cover, and they kept the battle raging with gunfire until nine o'clock at night, when orders came to withdraw. When they sought to carry their wounded away, the enemy attacked and drove them back.

Here in a short time the regiment lost half of its men and among the survivors many were wounded. Few came out of this battle without a memento.

The commanding general has been reproached for not giving orders to retreat sooner. It is possible that the reserve division's (Johnson's) difficult position was the reason for that. It stood tightly packed in a narrow depression and was attacked fiercely at the front. It had to leave this trap very carefully.

It is regrettable that Sherman does not mention this battle and that Howard calls it only "something more than a skirmish." Big preparations were made and four divisions took part in this maneuver aimed at a decisive defeat for the Confederate army.

Sherman's orders on May 27th went out that all batteries belonging to the 20th, 23rd, and 4th army corps should start fire on the enemy early in the morning and continue until 9 o'clock. (Official Records). The cannonade that reached over more than two-thirds of the whole line was obviously intended to divert the enemy's attention from the threatening flank or to keep him in ignorance of where the attack would come. With all this artillery besides the four divisions in action, Howard could merely characterize it as something of a battle while Sherman in his memoirs reports on hundreds of more meaningless things.[1]

There is considerable disagreement in regard to the Norwegian regiment in the reports of the flag incident.

Otto Steen, who took part in the battle as sergeant and who is now a business man in Wahoo, Neb., wrote this to Mr. Albert E. Rice: "I want to tell you the facts of what occurred at Pickett's Mill on 27 May 1864. It is as alive in my memory as if it had happened yesterday. I remember how we advanced through the woods and had some difficulty in keeping the regiment in formation. So we crossed a deep ravine and as we worked our way up a steep incline the line kept falling apart and every man had to look out for himself. Corporal Gulbrand Løkke, and another man of

Co. E, with a new recruit named Jensen, and I lay down behind some bushes. We had not lain there a minute before Løkke and Jensen were killed and the third fellow had gotten a bullet in the hip and I was the only one untouched. I looked back and found I was a good distance ahead of the regiment, so I crawled back and found cover behind a log. We kept up fire until it was dark and then we took some of the wounded back to the ravine with us. I met Major Wilson and asked if we were to remain there all night. He answered, 'No, we are expecting to be relieved any minute.' (This was after the battle was over.)

"Lieutenant [Ellend] Erikson of Co. K, Lieutenant Simonsen and I sat down and discussed what had happened and who had been killed and wounded, when we heard a noise ahead of us. We knew that none of our men were there, and fired. Soon after, a man sprang into view. He wore our uniform, but he was a Rebel. He said, 'For God's sake, don't fire on them, you are shooting at your own men.' I had just loaded the gun and had my fingers in the box of percussion caps. I looked up and there was a Rebel regiment before us with bayonets pointed a couple of feet from our chests. We were forced to surrender and we did. I think about 20 of our regiment were taken prisoner. The rest, including Major Wilson, retreated and escaped capture.

"When I was taken away I was led through three tight lines of Rebel soldiers, but there were no breastworks. At Pickett's Mill there was no attack from either side. We just lay down on one spot and fired. The flag was never out of the bearer's hands."

The Hon. Albert E. Rice writes that that account coincides with his memory up to the time he was wounded.

Mr. B. Nelson, corporal, who also took part in the battle in Co. I writes: "The 15th was in the first line or arranged in two lines. We were numbered 1, 2, 3, 4,—1 ahead of 2, 3 ahead of 4, etc. We had no reserves. We came over a field with a small rise and could not see the enemy who lay in the woods and had barricades. These we could not see till a day later. As I recall, our brigade was on the right wing. When we reached the hill the enemy opened fire on us. From the sound of the gunshots it must have been a whole division. We also opened fire and lay down on the slope. Here the flag was set in the ground, while we lay there loading and shooting. To fall back was sure death. At dusk the Rebels came yelling and shouting and we had to retreat as fast as we could. Who it was that picked up the flag I don't remember. Hans

Hanson and I were about the last, the flag was ahead and six Rebels behind us. None of us had a chance to load our guns; we ran across the field and came to a small grove. Here were some of the men of our brigade, so we had help.

"As far as I recall, Wilson was wounded three times; in the leg, in his side, and on the hand, though they were not serious wounds. Who carried the flag I just cannot seem to remember. After Anders Urness who was wounded at Chickamauga, there was a man named Colbjørnsen who was flag bearer, later one from Co. I named Petter Long; but if he carried the battle flag here, I am not sure. He became ill and was sent home and did not return, but perhaps that was later."

This tallies with the verbal account Lieutenant Gilbert gives of that incident, where Gilbert states that repeated attempts were made to rescue the flag when it was left standing in the ground a distance from the place where the regiment had taken cover while they continued to fight.

The enemy from their entrenchments had the best opportunity to see what was going on at the front and it is hardly credible that they would report on heroic exploits in the opponents' ranks, had they not taken place.

W. B. Hazen, who led the first attack with his brigade, was quickly stopped and when Willich's brigade attacked it passed through Hazen's troops. General Hazen mentions the incident of the flag planted in the ground but makes no claim that it belonged to one of his regiments. Books that have since come out about the Norwegian regiment say that the regiment advanced so close to the enemy's entrenchments that several fell scarcely ten feet from them. There could not have been any other regiment ahead of the Norwegian. Orders were to attack in deep formation, but, under the gunfire of the Southern lines, which reached far out on both sides, the formation burst open so that the regiment spread out in longer lines. Under these circumstances it has been difficult for anyone to know what actually happened along the lines and especially when nearly every man had to drop flat on the ground and search for whatever cover the slope could give. Therefore it is possible that whatever happened to the flag could have taken place without anyone seeing it.

It is very peculiar that in the regiment there are few accounts of any individual heroism. One gets the impression from the letters that no one saw that any one stood out beyond any one else and what one did, the other fellow could have done also. There is a remarkable lack of emphasis on individual gallantry, except for officers like Heg and Wilson, whose honor also belonged to the whole regiment. A large number of the regiment are listed on the Roll of Honor for heroism and promoted to honorary captain, etc. which was earned instead of the European armies' medals and decorations.

Charles (Karelius) Olson (Co. K), who was severely wounded in the battle, writes: "I do not remember much except that our regiment was the spearhead in that battle. I was wounded about 6 o'clock in the afternoon and had to drop out of the ranks, but the others advanced and the battle went on. I do not recall any particular details about how the flag was planted in the ground. Our flagbearer was Anders Urness and perhaps it was he who stuck it in the ground, but I am not sure."

Erik Barsness was in the fight and was at one time the regiment's flagbearer. A teacher, Erik Dalager, visited him in March 1916 for information. He writes: "Barsness is very ill now and possibly will not live long. He complains about the pain from the bullet he carries for the Cause and his memory is poor. As far as he recalls, he says it was his friend Anders Urness and another boy who were flagbearers at New Hope Church. This boy, whose name he has forgotten, was killed and Anders came back with both flags. After that time Urness and Barsness each carried a flag."

Therefore, it seems of the highest certainty that Gen. Joseph E. Johnston's report of this heroic exploit did take place somewhere in the Norwegian regiment's front line under observation, so the enemy noticed it but only a few of the regiment itself.

The reason I have fixed myself so strongly on this track is that one has to go back a thousand years in Norway's history to find a similar evidence of wartime honor or gallantry such as this little episode that the Battle of Pickett's Mill witnessed.

W. A.

NOTES

1. Gen. W. B. Hazen, who led the 2nd Brigade, has also mentioned this. He says, among other things, "This battle seems scarcely worth the mention in the commanding Union General's reports, and Sherman omits it in his memoirs; but it was nevertheless the most terrible, bloodiest, untenable attack pressed upon our troops in the whole Atlanta Campaign, and the Confederates, who were the victors, have written about it in detail." (Narrative Mil. Service, p. 256)

Gen. Minty wrote 9 Oct. 1864 from the battlefield: "We are now bivouacked on the battlefield at Pickett's Mill. The battle took place on 27 May between some of Hooker's (Howard's) Corps and the enemy. Between the two lines the fire has been the strongest and the most destructive that I have ever seen, as nearly every other tree has been killed by bullets. In one tree I found 157 bullets, in another 133, and in a third, 101. In the first tree, 130 bullets were only 6 inches from the ground. Some of the smaller trees have branches so splintered that those that remain look like brooms." [Ager's note]

The Battle of Chattanooga

by Waldemar Ager

Vicksburg and Chattanooga were the two most important strategic points in the western war theatre. Gen. Grant took Vicksburg on 4 July 1863, but Rosecrans had a terrible defeat at Chickamauga Creek on the 19th and 20th of September. After the defeat he fell back to Chattanooga and was besieged there by the Southern army under General Braxton Bragg.

Chattanooga lent itself to being besieged. The city lay in a bend of the Tennessee River; toward the west lay the lofty Lookout Mountain, which jutted out like a steep and mighty fortress over the town. Toward the south was Missionary Ridge, another mighty mountain chain running parallel with Lookout Mountain but reaching four miles farther east so it formed a strong barrier to the south. Between the two mountain chains lay a plateau about four miles wide, split in the middle by the Chattanooga River, which ran down the valley and made a sharp bend to the north at the foot of Lookout Mountain. Both of these mountain chains and the plain between were beset by Southern troops and strongly fortified. The Tennessee River was to both the north and the south of the city and was controlled by Southern troops. The siege lasted two months, which time Rosecrans used to fortify the town with trenches and forts.

One mile north on Missionary Ridge lay the Southern troops' first trenches, not far from the Federals', and they were propped here by a height, Orchard Knob, which was in their possession and which must be taken first before Missionary Ridge could be stormed.

From a military standpoint the South's position here seemed almost invulnerable; but General Bragg made several mistakes of which the worst was that he sent his best corps of 20,000 men, under his most efficient general, James Longstreet, on a fruitless expedition north to Knoxville to besiege that city, held by the North under General Burnside. Bragg's men had been much diminished at the futile victory at Chickamauga and from the heights above the city one could see that the siege was not effective and that the North had got reinforcements, while they had sent their best general and best troops away. If Bragg had been waiting for Gen. Grant, who had now taken command, to weaken the Chattanooga army by sending reinforcements to Burnside, he made a mistake. But even with the force he had, he had grounds to believe that his position was invincible.

On 23 Nov., at noon, Gen. Grant stood with generals Thomas, Hooker, Granger, Howard, and other officers and Assistant Secretary of War C. A. Dana on a parapet at Fort Wood and saw Wood's division with the help of Sheridan storm Orchard Knob.

Orchard Knob was a steep and rugged hill overgrown with small trees and lay midway between the North's and South's barricaded lines. On the west side of the height was a quarter-mile belt of woods that stretched out from the foot of the mountain. In front of this was an open field, without the slightest cover, that the attacking troops had to cross.

From the North's side one could see Wood's division prepare to attack and it looked like a peaceful manoeuvre as they readied themselves for review and marched forward in the best order under full music and flying banners. It looked as if the enemy did not know the meaning of this. Wood went in with Willich's and Hazen's brigades in front and Beatty's in reserve. Willich, who had the Norwegian regiment in his brigade, went straight up the height, drove the enemy out of their trenches and pushed up the hill. Hazen met strong resistance on his side but the hill was taken. Gen. Wood now placed them in a defensive position for a possible counterattack and Hooker's corps marched forward up the hill on the left side.

The capture of the Knob was the first act of the Battle of Chattanooga.

The second came on the following day at 4 o'clock in the afternoon when Gen. Joe Hooker drove the enemy from Lookout Mountain.

But the worst remained and that was to drive the enemy from his strongly barricaded position on Missionary Ridge. That battle took place the day after the assault on Lookout Mountain, on 25 Nov.

Between Orchard Knob and Missionary Ridge was a valley partly overgrown with brush. At the foot of the hill were strong barricades, well fortified, which could easily be seen from Orchard Knob.

Over this valley stormed Thomas' corps of 20,000 men, among them the brigade that included the Norwegian regiment. General Grant had ordered that the trenches at the foot of the mountain be taken, while the mountain itself should be taken under the cover of Sherman's corps. This failed, as Sherman was detained, but by good fortune Thomas' corps, after taking the trenches, followed the enemy up the heights without command. "Who ordered them to storm the hill?" asked Gen. Grant angrily, as he stood and watched the battle with Gen. Thomas. "I don't know as I have given any such order," said Thomas. "Have they really done it?" He then asked Gen. Granger. "No," he answered, "but it looks as if those fellows started out at such a fast pace they could not stop."

The Confederate troops seemed gripped in utter panic and fled head over heels. Gen. Bragg said later that he could not explain that blot on his army's honor. The line at the top could have been held by a cordon chain, he said. When we recall that the Federal troops were physically exhausted when they neared the top it should have been an easy matter to have thrown them back.

General Bragg was relieved by Gen. Joe Johnston after a fairly orderly retreat was brought about.

The Norwegian regiment under these attacks was commanded by Captain John A. Gordon, as Major Wilson had not recovered from the wounds he received at Chickamauga and Lieutenant Colonel Ole C. Johnson was in prison.

The Norwegian regiment, along with other troops, was soon after the battle sent northward to assist Burnside at Knoxville, which was besieged by James Longstreet.

Losses in the Norwegian Regiment in the Civil War

by Waldemar Ager

When one speaks of the losses in the Civil War, one thinks first of the battlefields; but terrible as the losses were there, they hardly came to a fraction of the actual losses. Where bullets struck one, army cholera, pneumonia, typhoid, and other diseases took three or four.

Sanitary conditions must have been awful and wastefulness of human lives shocking. The United States was a young country and no one thought to economize, least of all with human lives, while ship after ship emptied its loads of immigrants on our wharves. When one soldier's usefulness was over, men did not make a fuss over it. It was easier to enlist a new man than to cure a sick one. However, something was done for the ill, more in the east than in the west. There were both hospitals and hospital ships; but service was poor and it seems the mortally ill soldiers had to subsist on the same fare as soldiers in the field. If they wanted a glass of milk, they had to pay for it out of their own pockets at exorbitant prices.

In any case the death rates were horrifying. As an example, the Norwegian Company H of the 27th Wisconsin Regiment mustered in with 80 men and 40 of these died of sickness and not on the battlefield. It was worse than even Andersonville, where every third or fourth man died of disease and where they would arrive weakened and often wounded after a battle. The 25th Wis. Reg. lost two men on the battlefield and 259 from disease. The 32nd Reg. lost 27 on the field and 243 from sickness. The 25th Regiment lost 376 men from sickness and the 27th 23 in battle and 222 from disease, or nearly ten times as many. Of total losses of nearly 10,000 from all the Wisconsin regiments, only 3,028 found death on a battlefield or from wounds.

The Norwegian regiment lost 82 men who were killed in battle or died of wounds soon after, but 217 were taken by disease. To these can be added those listed as "missing." Of these the largest number were prisoners and some deserters; but not a few fell on battlefields that came into the enemy's possession and were buried in nameless graves. Here we employ only the totals from official reports.

A great many of the soldiers of the 15th Wis. Reg. had poor knowledge of English and were frightened of hospitals and everything foreign to them. They felt most at ease among their own kind and were reluctant to be ill. As those on the battlefield frequently "stood" too long, so they also "went" sick too long. When it happened and they sought help, it was often too late.

Also, they were driven hard. Often after a long and fatiguing march, when the rest of the division or brigade got a well-earned rest, the Norwegian regiment was sent out on an expedition in the neighborhood to forage for food or on outpost duty.

In almost every battle they were placed where they got the first hard push. In the bloody battle at Murfreesboro, it was the 15th that got the order to face the first fire while two days before they had had instructions to storm the battery at Knob Gap. At Chickamauga they were under fire among the very first and at Orchard Knob they were in the front ranks. At Rocky Face they received orders to attack the apparently impregnable position at the top of a steep cliff. At Resaca and Pickett's Mill we again find them at the spearhead of an attacking column.

Losses can often be blamed on accidental occurrences; but it is interesting to note that the losses on the battlefield almost always were the greatest in that brigade where the Norwegian regiment happened to be. Where they were, there was much heat—that much we can learn from these figures.

The word went around regarding that regiment, that they always "stood" too long.

The Battle of Murfreesboro

			Killed	Wounded	Total
Davis' Division:	*Carlin's Brigade*		129	498	627
	Post's	"	25	144	169
	Woodruff's	"	32	179	211
Johnson's "	Willich's	"	90	373	463
	Dodge's	"	99	344	483
	Baldwin's	"	59	244	303
Sheridan's "	Sill's	"	104	365	469

		Killed	Wounded	Total
Schaefer's	"	71	281	352
Roberts'	"	62	343	405

(These nine brigades comprised the Federal Army's right wing, and Carlin's brigade, where the Norwegian regiment stood. Not only did they have the greatest losses here but they also had the greatest losses of any brigade in the whole army.) Sill's brigade, Sheridan's division, included the 36th Ill. Reg. with a nearly whole company of Norwegians, led by Porter C. Olson, who later fell at Franklin, Tenn. as a Brigadier General.

The Battle of Chickamauga

		Killed	Wounded	Total
Davis' Division:	*Heg's Brigade*	70	519	589
	Carlin's "	54	299	353
Johnson's "	Willich's "	63	355	418
	Dodge's "	27	200	227
	Baldwin's "	57	385	442
Sheridan's "	Lyttle's "	55	321	376
	Layboldt's "	38	243	281
	Bradley's "	58	374	432

Heg's brigade, in which the Norwegian regiment stood, had the heaviest loss of dead and wounded of any brigade in the 20th Army Corps and next to the greatest loss in all the brigades in the whole Federal Army. There were three brigades with a greater loss, but two of these—Croxton's of Negley's Division (14th Army Corps) and Steedman's of the Reserve Corps—had respectively five and six regiments to Heg's four. Ferd[inand] Van Derver's Brigade of the 3rd Division, 14th Army Corps, with four regiments had a loss of 738 dead and wounded—the greatest loss in the army.

The Battle of Chattanooga and Missionary Ridge

		Killed	Wounded	Total
Wood's Division:	*Willich's Brigade*	46	291	337
	Hazen's "	92	430	528
	Beatty's "	14	160	174
Cruft's "	Whittaker's "	17	63	80
	Grose's "	4	60	64
Sheridan's "	F. T. Sherman's "	30	268	298

	Killed	Wounded	Total
Wagner's "	70	660	730
Harker's "	28	269	297

There were two brigades in the Army Corps with greater losses than Willich's, where the Norwegian regiment now stood. (F. T. Sherman's brigade was previously led by Gen. Sill, who fell at Murfreesboro. In this battle the brigade was led by Porter C. Olson, who had been promoted to Lieutenant Colonel.)

Losses in the Atlanta Campaign have not been possible to ascertain through the sources available to me, but with the bloody battles at Resaca, New Hope Church, and Kennesaw Mountain in mind, there is no doubt that Willich's brigade had as great a loss, if not greater, as any brigade in the whole campaign. At the Battle of New Hope Church they lost at least a third of their men, and the Norwegian regiment 92 men in two hours.

The Largest Percentage-loss in Wisconsin

Out of 52 regiments mobilized in Wisconsin during the war, there were four that totaled more deaths that the 15th Wis. Reg. They were the 7th, 11th, 16th and 25th regiments. But all of these were much larger than the 15th, which was the smallest of all the regiments mustered in Wisconsin during the war. In terms of percentage, it reads thus:

	No. of men	Loss		Percent
15th Wis. Regiment	905	299	or	33.04
7th " "	1794	391	"	21.79
11th " "	1735	343	"	19.7
16th " "	2086	369	"	18.0
25th " "	1420	418	"	29.44

Among the Wisconsin regiments that took part in the Virginia campaigns there was a greater loss on the battlefields than that of the 15th Wisconsin Regiment but they did not have the large percentage of deaths from disease that the western war theatre had. They did not have the long, killing marches; and sustenance was much better because of the shorter communication lines. The above lists include those who wore themselves out on the long treks as well as those who fell on the battlefield. The losses do not include those "missing" or deserters.

The notice affixed to the Norwegian regiment's flags in the historical museum at Madison lists the following losses: Fallen or dead of wounds and sickness 331, by accident 14, total 345. That gives the Regiment a percentage of 38.1 or nearly double the average loss for all Wisconsin regiments, which was about 19 percent.

Incidental Observations

by Waldemar Ager

I have included these incidents as I believe they have some value in showing a fuller picture of the regiment. In regard to drinking, we find ourselves in a period when temperance work in the form we know now was unknown to the soldier, and drinking was common on the field when it was available. As to foraging by night, one must remember that the soldier found himself in enemy territory with poor provisions, which made him passionately desirous of a decent meal now and then. In the regiment's four-year service, there is evidence of only one example where a soldier stole anything when it wasn't intended to sate his hunger. He was severely punished. There is no incident of murder or rape committed by any of the Regiment.

Another thing to be taken into consideration is that when several hundred energetic young men under the somewhat excited state that prevails in wartime are placed in constrained idleness, it is evident they will be up to something, which in many cases shows considerable enterprise.

And that there were some wild characters among so many Norwegians and that their exploits are best remembered from camp life is natural.

Life at Camp Randall

It was at Camp Randall, Christmas 1861, that those who liked beer got the opportunity to purchase some for the holidays. On Christmas Eve, a whole wagonload of kegs stopped near our barracks. Casper Hansen of Co. I, whom we called Jolly Brother, took care that when the driver went in with the keg he took one off the wagon, placed it on his shoulder, brought it into our barracks, and hid it well under a bed until the driver had left the camp. Then the keg was brought out and we celebrated Christmas Eve. There were 20 men in each section, and we had some left over for the next day. After a while the beer took effect on some, so there was a brawl.

The other two regiments—the 16th and the 17th—were not a bit better off, especially the 17th, which was called the Irish Regiment. They were also unruly and a bit worse off than the 15th. The 16th was supposed to do police duty, but it came to nothing as they had not been given guns. The turmoil continued until the beer was gone, and the next day there were many sore noses and black eyes to be seen.

Camp Life on Island No. 10

A small steamer came with provisions and other things for Memphis. It stopped overnight here, so, naturally, we had to place guards to see that nothing was stolen. Now the receiver is no better than the thief. We got hold of a jug of very fine brandy, which probably was meant for the officers. We hid it in the woods, but that wasn't all. The boys heard that there was a half-cask of whiskey on the boat, so then one of the barrel-bands was removed and a hole bored and a pipe set into the hole so the whiskey ran nicely into canteens. When we were finished we plugged up the hole and put the band back in place. The next day many were drunk. Jolly Brother walked around smiling and very happy, as he always was when he had had something good to drink. That brandy was first class, he said. Gunder Hane was also in a good mood and the Totning imagined himself back home in Norway. It was not only these four, unfortunately, who were in a good mood. Co. A from Chicago included a good number of seamen and they were not backward when it came to drink. They were also as good as any to come up with chickens, fresh meat, and such things. The officers had some suspicion of where the whiskey came from, so there had to be an inquiry. Capt. [Andrew] Thorkildsen was installed as judge, as he had been a police officer in Chicago before the war, and, like King Saul, he was a head taller than the rest of the men. He had two other officers with him. We got wind of this and all who had whiskey in their canteens hurried and emptied them and filled them with water. Company A was the first to be questioned. The canteens were searched but nothing was found but water. Now they were asked where they got the whiskey, and they said it came from Cairo, and the other companies agreed.

A few days later the boat returned. As the captain had missed a jug of brandy which was on a requisition slip, it was then agreed that it must have been left in Cairo. Then the captain of the boat was asked if he had brought whiskey for the boys of the "Fifteenth." No, that he had not done. "Well then," said Thorkildsen, "the five gallon keg must be here." Then, the captains got orders to search every tent in their quarters and every place where a jug of brandy could be hidden, but it was not found. The jug lay a good half mile away.

The 17th of May, 1862

On the 17th of May we got some whiskey in the morning. It was about 3 drams for each of us. I was sick at that time because of the poor water. In my diary I had jotted down: "The Toten roars, the Hane [rooster] crows, Jolly thirsts, Brother coughs." There was a man from Toten named Christian Olson in Company B. We called him the Totning. He had such vocal power his voice could be heard over the whole camp. Then there was one whose name was Gunder Hane who used to crow like a rooster when he was drunk, and he was most likely drunk that day. So was Nils Hansen. He was called "Jolly" and was always thirsty, and then one fellow in Company I was called "Brother Jolly." His name was Casper Hansen. These two Hansens were not blood brothers but were old friends from Waupun. I sold my portion of whiskey to Casper for 25 cents. Others also sold theirs, as we newcomer boys did not like this raw fiery-tasting whiskey.

Later in the afternoon there was to be a parade; but there was no orderly arrangement because Company A from Chicago wanted to be first and foremost, and Company B wanted to be just as important, so it ended up in a fight. Then the other companies got involved too. Who won is hard to say, but those who were sober were ordered to take care of the drunks and the most disorderly were put in the guardhouse.

Foraging

We were getting poor food so we set out in an attempt to get fresh meat. We were 10 or 12 of us and we took off to go about 5 miles. As it was dark it was hard to tell how far we went. This time we took sacks with us as it was chickens we were after. We found a good-sized hen-house with many chickens. We placed guards at the door of the home and some men went into the coop to wring the necks of the chickens. The chickens set up a terrible squawk, and a woman opened the door where I stood guard. I immediately ordered her to go back and lock the door, which she did. We got 1 1/2 sacks-full. Then we went to another place and a third. In the morning we returned with six sacks of hens. That was not so much for 10 companies, but we had a good meal of delicious soup.

When the owners came to complain, we had to be very careful about the feathers and could not cook the chickens the first day. We blamed the soldiers who were in a garrison at New Madrid and they of course blamed us when they did the same thing. So that way, we always got out of it.

Lt. Nils J. Gilbert tells this: "I was a sergeant and had been on guard duty and while I was gone the boys of my platoon had found a beehive and set it inside a tent without my knowledge. The intention was to close all openings and smoke the bees out. I did not know this and was standing outside having some coffee. The boys had just made coffee and it tasted good after my watch. In the meantime the farmer who had lost his beehive came to the camp and before we knew it, Colonel Heg came striding forward on his long legs, followed by the farmer. He asked me about the beehive and I knew nothing. Of course the boys knew nothing either. Unfortunately, he went over to search the tent along with the farmer, and no sooner had they stuck their heads into the tent when both were attacked by furious bees. Heg was angry and I got a proper overhauling, though I was innocent. As none of the boys could explain how the bees got there, nothing more was done about it.

There was a farmer who lived a half mile from our camp who had a large flock of beautiful geese. Day after day the boys went over and drooled over these geese, but the farmer had a big, vicious dog who watched them well.

A council of war met and laid the following battle plan: some would go over and pet the dog and make friends with him. Another group would visit the farmer's apple orchard, and four men would sneak over to the goose house. The boys figured the farmer would be so busy saving his apples he would forget about the geese.

The geese were inside a strong log house with a large heavy door. Everything went well. The orchard was on the other side of the farm and the farmer was on guard. Unluckily, the geese set up a frightful squawk when they were disturbed and the farmer ran to their coop. When he made sure there was no one inside, he slammed the big oak door shut and propped it on the outside with a scythe that crossed over the whole door. Then he set out for camp to relate his story and to get someone to come with him and nab the four sinners in action. While he was away the boys found a crooked log in the rear wall. The space where it did not fit the other log was filled with dirt and such. Here they made a hole, and with a spike bent the log out and were able to crawl out. The geese were passed out through the opening. Then the log was put back in place again. When the farmer returned he got a reprimand for having lured a guard far out into the country for nothing.

This happened in southeastern Tennessee. We had driven the Rebels over to North Carolina and some of the boys had found a molasses mill about 1 1/2 miles from camp. Some of the 15th and the 32nd Indiana (the German regiment) took off to get a barrel of syrup, which they rolled the whole way back to camp. At one place, they had to build a bridge in order to get the barrel across a stream.

There was a big cheer when they arrived and a couple of hundred men swarmed around the barrel and smeared each other with syrup and had great fun.

Complaints came to Division General Wood and the blame was placed on Willich's Brigade. And here where every other man stood licking his lips, there was no use denying it.

General Willich was named inquisitor. When he found such a fuss was made over a barrel of syrup, he became very angry and with his poor command of English, he told them he thought it was paltry of the Army to deny him a barrel of syrup "to sweeten my Brigade with." The division general laughed and Willich left the battle a victor for his "sweet" Brigade.

Arne Ellebakken (Grøndahl) told a story about Nils Luraas. Once when they lay back of a barricade and were very hungry, a whole flock of sheep passed between their lines and the enemy's. "If you want one, I will get it," said Nils and therewith sprang into the flock, took a sheep and brought it back while bullets whizzed about his ears.

But the best of all was one named Funkelien. He stole a bottle of brandy out of the pocket of an officer of high rank while he was conferring with other officers of the regiment.

A Romance at Whiteside Station

Sergeant J. H. Johnson of Company G was our chaplain. He was so well known he was counted as one of us. But it so happened that he was a

Methodist and we were Lutherans, which formed a sort of rift between us and seemed to make us more indifferent to religion.

The last three months, when guarding the railroad bridge at Whiteside Station, I got better acquainted with him. On Sunday afternoons he went out into the country a few miles and preached to the people, as there were both Methodists and Baptists there. We went along too, to listen and look—perhaps mostly to look.

A widower of Company H was also a frequent attender. His name was Anfin. I do not remember his last name. It was not long before we discovered that there was something that lured Anfin out there on Sundays and weekdays.

It was an older girl he had fallen in love with; but it was too bad because Anfin could not speak English and could barely manage it at all, even though he had been in this country seven years. He had to get help to get his desires expressed to the girl and one person took the task of interpreter.

It went right smoothly. She agreed at once and they were engaged. Shortly after, they were married by Chaplain Johnson. Who was the victor in regard to language it is hard to say. She evidently had to learn Norwegian, as Anfin could not learn English.

Anfin and his wife came home with us and as far as I know they settled in Dane county. (B. Nelson)

Occupation of Island No. 10[1]

". . . We went down to Island No. 10 on April 6 (1862) quite early in the morning. We were not in the slightest danger and did not fire a single shot. I think it was the cavalry that went ashore first. But before that, naturally the gunboats had slipped down quietly during the night. The first had a large barge loaded with wet bales of hay on the sides. It worked out pretty well as there was rain and bad weather. It seems they did not see the first boat; but when the second passed by, then, believe me, it really started. As it was dark, with rain, thunder and lightning, it helped with the plan's success. They fired over 70 salvos from their big batteries on our gunboat and surely thought that they could sink it; but the gunboat put on steam and sped downstream. When they saw this, they must have thought it was the Devil himself that had come down there and they must have given up all hope of holding the island. They certainly seemed to believe that we were much stronger than we actually were, and also they were afraid that Gen. Pope would cut them off if he should retreat on the other side. There were a great many Rebels who tried to desert and many of them succeeded; yet even so, nearly 6,000 men were taken prisoner.

"You can be sure that the steamboats then came to life again. Left behind were all sorts of provisions, such as pork, beef, flour, rice, sugar, coffee—yes, in short, all kinds of foodstuffs. I remember they said at home that the Rebels would soon be starving, but as far as I can see, these soldiers had better fare than we have had. We have never had it so good since we entered the service as we have had it here, and we expect to live in style now, as long as these provisions last. Here are powder cellars full of ammunition worth several thousand dollars and horses, mules, wagons, and a lot of bedding and bed linens and wearing apparel of all sorts."

NOTES

1. From a letter by Johannes H. Stokke to his wife. J. H. Stokke belonged to Company E and had enlisted with Capt. Ingemundsen. He was wounded in one knee at Chickamauga, recovered, and was able to go through the whole war. He was 29 years old and married when he volunteered. He and his wife live in Chaseburg, Wisconsin. [Ager's note]

Additional Letters

Three miles north of Island No. 10[1]

7 April 1862

Dear father!

. . . . On Sunday 31 March, we got orders to go by steamboat to Hickman, which lies on the Kentucky side, and from there to march farther inland to Union City, where the Rebels presumably had a large camp. We were with the 42nd Ill. Regiment and some artillery and cavalry. We had not reached the town when we spied the Rebels' tents in the woods; their outposts fired at us a couple of times, then ran off; but at the same time our artillery opened fire, and soon the whole regiment was on its way, and we swung in good order into their camp, where we found a great many guns, swords, and other weapons, as well as flags and drums, etc.; also horses, wagons, and mules. They had run from it all. We were not allowed to leave the ranks, so we did not get more in exchange than what we could pick up at our feet. Then fire was set to the whole place and it burned with a bright flame. We hurried out of the camp quickly; inside the tents guns and bullets began to explode and fly into the air. As a large Rebel force lay in the vicinity, who would soon come upon us, we felt we were too few in number to withstand an attack. We boarded the steamship and returned here, proud of our victory, and hoped to soon repeat it.

We are so close to the island that when we are on outpost guard, the Rebel shells fly over our heads.

I am in good health and content, as this is a glorious life.

Your devoted son

Oscar

NOTES

1. A letter from Oscar Thompson to his father. Oscar Thompson, who was from Beloit, enlisted on Dec. 2, 1861. He was 18 years old. He fell at New Hope Church on May 27, 1864, shot through the head. [Ager's note]

Letter from Serg. Jørgen Jørgenson Sanda[1]

Chattanooga, 27 Nov. 1863

Dear mother!

After coming out of another big battle, I will write you a few lines. On the 23rd we were ordered out with two days rations and 100 rounds of ammunition. We marched out at one o'clock in the afternoon and drove the enemy's outposts and the front line two miles back. That night we erected some barricades and lay there and waited for the Rebels, who did not come. The next day our regiment was sent out as sentinels and it was all quiet on our side, but we could hear rifle fire and the roar of cannons the whole day. On the morning of the 25th our regiment was sent out to skirmish. We advanced about a half mile when the enemy opened fire. We drove them back and at 3 p.m. the whole line advanced and stormed Missionary Ridge, captured it, and a good many prisoners, and all their cannon – I think 64 all together. Our regiment did not lose any. How many dead or wounded there were in the Brigade, I don't know. Last night we returned to our old camp, as Bragg has turned his back on us, but now we have marching orders . . . .

Jørgen Jørgenson Sanda

NOTES

1. Sergeant Sanda or George Georgeson, as he was called in the roster, was from Boone county, Ill. and enlisted in Company A in October, 1861. He died in a hospital at Chattanooga on October 5, 1864. He is listed on the Roll of Honor for gallantry in action. [Ager's note]

Letters from Lt. Svend Samuelson[1]

Manitowoc co., Wis., 8 July 1861

Dear brother!

. . . . You most likely have seen in the newspapers that we here are headed for a very serious and uncompromising war, if the developing entanglement is not settled peacefully. The reason for this war I will try to describe for you briefly. As you know, we elect a president for the United

States every four years. Last fall an election took place for the next four years and it was a terrific campaign, one of which they have never seen the like in America before. There were four candidates, but the southern Slave States and the northern Free States were the leading parties. The southern states worked hard to get a man who was in favor of Negro slavery. We in the north worked hard to get a good president, who was against slavery spreading further than it now exists; we believe that no man's government has the right to go to Africa and steal Negroes and bring them to America to be sold or traded like goods or beasts of burden or worse. In short, the northern states won the victory and elected Abraham Lincoln president. Right away some of the southern states wanted to withdraw from the Union and elect their own president. That the North would not tolerate, so war was declared and both sides have armed themselves mightily, and some small military encounters have already taken place.

In regard to last year's harvest, it was remarkably good, but we needed it as it was very poor the year before. This year it looks good too.

Here there is, however, a great shortage of money. Prices on provisions are low now. Wheat flour is $4 a barrel (200 lbs.) Pork is 5 or 6 cents a pound, butter 6 cents, coffee 18 cents, sugar 10 cents, a milk cow $15 or $16, and a good young workhorse $60 to $80. Good clothes are expensive here. A good suit costs up to $16 and trousers $6 to $8, and other things in proportion. Wages are high. A good worker (on a farm) cannot be gotten under $15 a month and at harvest time I am sure he will get $2 a day with board.

. . . My chief employment since I came here has been farming, which has given me poor returns, except this past year; but I have earned a little by writing after I became familiar enough with the English language that I could speak and write it. As I stated before, the people here elect their public officials annually, and separately for each town. A town is about one Norwegian mile square (Old Norse mile). I was elected town clerk four years ago. In Norway that would be the same as *Sekretær*. My job is to register all transactions, also to record expenditures for the town with school and highway boards, officers' salaries, mortgage bonds, and so on. To be sure, I stand on a friendly foot with all the people in my district; I know that in the past three elections I got every vote from my countrymen, Germans, Irish, and Americans. I was also made Justice of the Peace, wherewith I had the right to judge in small affairs and perform marriages, etc. But this I got tired of and gave it up. I tied the knot in what I foresee as an untieable bond between an American of 60 years and a Norwegian girl of 20.

With a longing heart I hope I again shall see my beloved Fatherland, relatives and friends with whom I spent my childhood days. Here, to be sure, I have, as long as my health holds, a good position and a good future and can live well with food and drink and all the other necessary conveniences, which is called the Good Life; but there needs but something which nothing here can replace, namely all that childhood memories are indelibly affixed to . . . .

Your ever devoted Svend Samuelson

Eaton, Manitowoc co., 1 Jan. 1865

Dear brother-in-law and sister!

. . . As you probably know, I returned from the war a year ago. I had served over two years and in that time I was lucky, as I had taken part in many of the worst battles without being wounded, while many of my best friends and comrades fell by my side. I am now married to a daughter of Bore Christiansen of Borebakken near Christiania and was very fortunate in my choice, as you will see when you come here.

I wonder a great deal about what I see in the Norwegian newspaper reports by those who clearly support the South. One can hardly believe one's eyes that a people who speak of having the freest nation with a free constitution should take the side of the rebels and the most barbaric aristocrats and slave traders in the world.[2]

True, slavery was not the foremost reason for this war; but if slavery had not existed, I am sure this war would never have started.

Selling human beings and flogging these poor Negroes to death in order to get them to work beyond their strength showed that the landrich and the proud regarded all those who worked equal to Negro slaves; therefore they wanted to separate themselves from the United States and form their own slave republic; but they have no more right to do that than Norway has to separate itself from Sweden, as long as they keep their constitution inviolate.

The war is now, I think, soon over, as the Rebels can hardly hold out much longer; while we in the north could hold out ten more years without causing agriculture or commerce the slightest hardship.

. . . There are good opportunities for work now that will surely last because of the war. This winter a man can earn a dollar a day with board, but next summer it will probably be double that. Prices for commodities are as follows: wheat flour 4$^1/_2$ cents a pound, pork 12 cents, beef 4$^1/_2$ cents, butter 30 cents, coffee 50 cents, sugar 25 cents, and other things in proportion. Clothing material costs from $2 to $4.50 a yard and a pair of boots $5.50 to $9. Cotton cloth is 60 cents a yard. Brandy is very expensive. There is now a half-dollar tax on each bottle of brandy and a drink costs from 5 to 10 cents and a glass of beer is 5 cents. A good horse costs from $150 to $200 and a good milk cow $30. . . .

Always your devoted

S. Samuelson

NOTES

1. Second Lieutenant Samuelson from Eaton was mustered in at Madison on Jan. 14, 1862, 36 years old and unmarried. He left the service on Nov. 15, 1863, unfit for further duty because of illness. He was born on the farm Mitsum in Krogstad parish and came to America in 1854. These letters were used as they show an intelligent man's view of the war, as held at the beginning and toward the end. The letters were kindly lent to us by headmaster M. Andresen of Oslo, Norway. They were written to relatives in Norway. [Ager's note]

2. Most of the Norwegian newspapers during the Civil War took their war news from the Confederate-friendly English newspapers. The whole time, the South maintained that the reason for the war was that the rights that the U.S. Constitution warranted them had been violated and in this purely technical interpretation, they had some right. It was this view that was mostly publicized in the English newspapers, and from there spread to the Norwegian. But Lt. Samuelson is correct and historians confirm that the basic reason for the war was the slavery of Negroes, which later became an accepted interpretation. It was only a small fraction of the South that could afford to have slaves, and that they were so unanimous was due to the fact that they were deceived by their leaders in regard to the real cause of the war. [Ager's note]

Religious Provisions for the Regiment

In Buslett's book about the Regiment one finds a chapter written by Pastor C. L. Clausen, the Regiment's first chaplain. He readily admits that at first he believed it would be a very difficult task to accomplish anything among such a group of recruits, most of whom did not seem to take any interest in the Word of God. But he discovered that underneath the seeming indifference or even disdain flowed a strong current of religious sincerity. The letters from the soldiers give that impression, as the great majority of them express a religious spirit. It is quite certain that a large number of the men carried their hymnbooks and other religious books with them and used them diligently. And when they lay sick or wounded in the hospitals, then the hymnbooks came forth. The often quite raw camp life did not check this religious undercurrent. Beyond any doubt there were many sincere Christians in the regiment who openly professed their faith.

The regiment was especially fortunate in its chaplains. Both Pastor Clausen and Pastor Johnson were able and very gifted men who later occupied prominent positions in their respective denominations: The Norwegian Lutherans have few more highly honored pastors than C. L. Clausen and likewise the Norwegian Methodists have no one more highly respected or esteemed than J. H. Johnson.

Pastor C. L. Clausen was Danish by birth but he found his field of activity among the Norwegian pioneers. As a young man – after completing his education in Denmark – he went to Norway with the intention of becoming a schoolteacher. In Norway, however, he heard about the need for religious teachers among the Norwegian immigrants in America. Consequently he left in 1843 and came to the new settlement at Muskego, where the first Norwegian-Lutheran congregation in America was organized. Clausen became its pastor, and here began his work as one of the most persevering and devoted pioneer pastors. Like other early leaders such as H. A. Stub, [Nils O.] Brandt, [Laur.] Larsen, [U. V.] Koren, [H. A.] Preus, and [Elling] Eielsen he traveled widely and organized congregations in the new communities; yes, he even helped to found settlements. When the Norwegian-Danish Conference was formed, he became its first president.

His work as chaplain was brief, however. While the soldiers were at Camp Randall it was Pastor Preus who served them. Clausen resigned for health reasons in November 1862. A bomb that exploded near him caused a nervous disorder from which he never fully recovered. He was born in 1820 and died 20 February 1892.

Pastor Johan Henrik Johnson was born at Fjøsne farm in Ætnes parish in Bergen diocese 18 July 1837. His parents were Johan Vogt and Susanne Torbjørnsdatter. After working as a salesman in Norway he left for America in 1857 and settled in Perry, Wisconsin. He had received a good education in Norway and must have learned the English language quickly because only a year after his arrival we find him established as a schoolteacher. In 1859 he was converted to the Methodist faith and became a highly respected lay preacher. When the war broke out he enlisted and was commissioned a sergeant in Company G. As such he shared the soldiers' life and performed his military duties. When the Regiment was divided, with two companies remaining on Island No. 10, the chaplain accompanied the other eight. Johnson then assumed many pastoral duties on the island such as hospital visits and related services. When Clausen later returned, Johnson was recommended for chaplaincy by the regiment's officers and assumed that position. Not being ordained, Johnson retained his sergeant's rank and took part in the fighting like any other soldier.

As he was a Methodist while the Regiment consisted almost entirely of Lutherans, there was always something of a difference to overcome. His work was further hampered by the fact that no priestly dignity elevated him above the rest of the soldiers. To listen to a duly ordained Lutheran pastor was one thing—but to worry about things preached by Sergeant Johnson was something else again.

This young man, full of zeal for spreading the gospel, was never disheartened. Besides working within his own regiment, he went out into the countryside and preached the Word of God to the "enemies" and to the Negroes. It was probably these poor innocent, enslaved human beings who interested him the most. Among them he found no prejudice or veneration of priestly authority; and when, with his eloquence, he gripped them both body and soul so they laughed and cried and clapped their hands then he undoubtedly found inspiration also for his own sensitive soul.

Johnson stayed with the regiment until it was discharged – from the first to the last. He took part in several battles, but he was never wounded. The rumor was abroad that his Bible, which he carried in his breast pocket, had once saved his life by stopping a bullet. This he denied. The first part of the rumor was true—he always carried a Bible, but not for protection against some bullet. However, he might add with his characteristic friendly smile, it had protected him against much greater dangers than the rebel bullets.

Johnson entered the ministry and became known for his brilliant eloquence. After having served several congregations in this country he was sent to Norway where for eight years he functioned as presiding elder,

1880–1888. Upon his return to America he occupied a similar position in various districts. He passed away in October 1896 in Chicago, where he was pastor of the First Norwegian Methodist Evangelical Church. He was married soon after the war to Miss Anna Frydenlund, who died in 1915. They had five children who are still living [1916].

Colonel Hans C. Heg

by Waldemar Ager

Colonel Heg's father, Even Heg, came to America in 1840 and settled in the well-known Muskego settlement, where the first Norwegian-American church was built and the first Norwegian newspaper in this country *[Nordlyset]* was founded. Even Heg was one of the leading men in the community and to his home all newcomers found their way. Here [James D.] Reymert, [Frederick] Fleischer, [Knut] Langeland, and others were frequent visitors; here the first pastors were welcomed. Hans Christian Heg was eleven years of age when he arrived from Norway; and in his home, as in the settlement generally, Norwegian was spoken almost exclusively. Even Heg's well-known barn, where so many new arrivals found shelter, and Søren Bakke and [J.] Johannesen's store in the Indian mound could well be considered the Norwegian-American capital and cultural center during the 1840s. Here the intelligentsia gathered. That in such surroundings an alert boy like Hans Heg would develop into a typical "hyphenated American"—in the best sense of the word— goes without saying.

In 1849 he, together with another Norwegian, left for California to dig for gold and was thus a "forty-niner." During this trip he wrote letters to *Nordlyset*. He returned in 1851. Since his father was dead, he took over the management of the farm and married Gunhild Einung, a girl of the community. In 1859 he moved to Waterford and with two Americans founded a business that had very good prospects. In the fall of that year he was nominated for the position of prison supervisor, which at the time was an elective office, and won by a large majority.

He was the first Norwegian elected to a state office in this country. As prison supervisor he performed his duties well. Law and order were maintained, sanitary conditions improved, revenues increased, and expenses lessened. It aroused attention that his accounts were correct, and at the time of his death one of Milwaukee's leading citizens said to Knut

Langeland: "He is the only supervisor who has left an honest account at the state prison." He was renominated for the position with strong approval—and then came the war.

There was talk about organizing a Norwegian regiment and Heg made up his mind. He declined the nomination and took on the job of recruiting. A man with a good position and a family might have had many reasons for staying at home, but Heg did not hesitate to enter the service. He began recruiting among his own relatives, several of whom joined the colors.

There is not much a person can have recourse to when attempting to give a characterization of this man. There was nothing glamorous about him—he was above everything else a man with a strong sense of duty. Quiet and correct in all his behavior, he did not commit himself entirely to anyone and seems to have had no intimate friends. Apparently he placed the greatest demands upon himself.

There are moments, however, when we catch glimpses of a distinct personality. In battle he might be all fire and flame—something akin to the Viking's sheer joy in a good fight. At Knob Gap we notice his eagerness to have his regiment capture the first cannon. Another time we find him attacking and capturing two Confederate guards despite the fact that he was armed with only a sword and was accompanied by two unarmed men. Characteristic is the fact that he arranged to have his regiment be the first of the whole force to cross the Tennessee River on a pontoon bridge in the face of enemy fire. To take the lead in crossing a broad river on a narrow floating bridge with the enemy directly in front is surely nothing to wish for. But it seems as if Colonel Heg, unobtrusive as he was, in no way liked to see anyone but the enemy *ahead of him and his regiment.*

In a sense he was a dual personality—he gave an impression of calm confidence on the one hand and of rashness on the other.

One big question undoubtedly haunted Colonel Heg right up to the first battle: how will these Norwegian boys—many of them recent immigrants—and their untried officers behave under their first trial by fire. Time after time during the early period of the war panic seized the inexperienced recruits—panic and headlong flight. His boys had undoubtedly heard exaggerated tales about the brutality of the Confederate troops; the land and the language were, in a measure, strange to them. They would have had a feeling of uneasiness here even during times of peace.

What if they should desert? After all the talk about Nordic heroism and Viking blood and all that—what a blot it would leave on the honor of his countrymen, a blot difficult to erase.

This probably explains why during their first serious battle at Murfreesboro (Stone's River) he dashed into the line of fire ahead of his regiment while the bullets whizzed about him. He wanted to bolster their courage by showing them that matters were not as dangerous as they seemed. Certainly he was not inspired by bravado. Nothing was more foreign to this man than swagger and swashbuckling.

The famed Southern general "Stonewall" Jackson had done the same thing at Bull Run and thereby given his brigade the stability that caused General Lee to exclaim: "There stands Jackson like a stone wall!"—a term that has ever since been attached to Jackson's name.

As "Stonewall" Jackson transformed his wavering brigade into a 'stone wall' by riding slowly back and forth at the front line, so Heg also made a stone wall out of his regiment. He had a horse shot from under him, but what of it? If there is any assertion that expresses good Norwegian philosophy it is this one: "Whatever another Norwegian can do, I can do too."

Heg had the born commander's psychological ability to reassure his men.

At Chickamauga he showed the same qualities. He was not a general of the type for whom soldiers give their lives. He was one of those who die for their men.

In a letter from him printed earlier in this book we find another proof of the fact that he had a clear and correct understanding of the soldiers' psychology. He cautions mothers and wives back home against writing letters that arouse worry and homesickness among the men at the front. He goes so far as to claim that such complaints and laments in letters from home lessen the soldiers' power of resistance to disease and injure their health by undermining their morale. This sounds very modern. A few days before this was written—in the year 1916—an almost identical assertion was made by one of the World War's greatest commanders.

We have before us the picture of a tall, blond, calm, and reserved man who seems to be present everywhere, who sees everything but says little. He kept his distance from the privates and did not try to be their comrade. This aloofness was undoubtedly assumed out of consideration for discipline, because he was quite companionable outside the service. He knew his men.

During the battle of Viniard's Farm at Chickamauga he spent little time with his own regiment. He felt he could depend on it and wanted to be where he was most needed. But after he received a mortal wound, he still rode a quarter of a mile and placed himself at the head of his own regiment.

Colonel Heg—marked by death—with sword and reins in one hand and swinging his hat with the other, probably wanted to die leading his own regiment; and when exhausted through loss of blood he fell off his horse, it was Norwegian hands that caught him and carried him out of firing range.

He had done his duty here also and left behind him a squared account.

He was above everything else a man bound by a strict sense of duty and what in Norway is called *retlinjet* [integrity]. He forgot nothing and neglected nothing. He was a brave and intelligent officer. He did little to win the hearts of his soldiers, but they had *his* heart and he wanted to stay in the saddle until he was among them. When strength failed him, the final accounting with his own flesh and blood should come to an end in their presence. It is difficult to think of any other reason for his dangerous ride to the front of the Norwegian regiment after being struck by the fatal bullet.

On the place where Heg fell veterans have raised a monument in the form of a pyramid made of cannon balls. His body was taken to Wisconsin and buried in the family plot in Muskego.

Colonel Heg's widow is still alive when this is written and lives in Newark, New Jersey. One of his sons is practicing medicine on the West Coast.

The Norwegian Society in America has appointed a committee to erect a statue of Colonel Heg and the plan is to donate a cast of the statue to Drammen, Norway. Heg was born at Lier near Drammen.

After Colonel Heg's death the regiment continued to maintain its position as one of the best in the army. But anyone who has delved into its history will have noticed that with Heg's passing it seems as if the regiment was reduced to a simple war machine. The "Norwegian" element became less noticeable. The joy of combat had been replaced by a sense of duty. The regiment was not the same after Chickamauga as it was before that battle.

Opinion has been divided as to exactly where and when Colonel Heg was wounded. Editor [Johan A.] Enander says in his book that an eye-witness told him Heg was wounded in the evening after he had shown conspicuous heroism all afternoon and always been at the right spot at the right moment. Several times he steadied the yielding ranks of the brigade and personally led the attacks against the enemy, always escaping unharmed. According to this eyewitness Heg was wounded by a stray bullet after darkness had fallen. Heg fell from his horse but was soon up again, ran after the horse, caught it, sprang easily into the saddle but then fell forward over the horse's neck. This does not agree with other accounts. The brigade was spread out over a rather long line and Colonel Heg spent hardly any time with the Norwegian regiment but stayed with the other wing where he felt that his presence was more needed. All are in agreement, however, that he fell off his horse in front of the Norwegian regiment, and even the above-quoted "eyewitness" was an officer in the 15th.

In a letter sent to the Madison *State Journal* soon after the battle it is definitely stated, as proof of his endurance, that he rode a quarter of a mile after being wounded. It is certain that he personally led the 15th Wisconsin Regiment in a bayonet attack on the enemy position and that during this assault he fell from his horse.

There is every reason to believe that he first prepared one wing of his brigade for attack on the rebels and after being wounded rode to the other wing to see how matters stood there, and then used his last bit of strength to lead the attack.

This happened before the brigade dispersed and the 15th was caught in a crossfire. When they assembled after this catastrophe, it was Lieu-tenant Colonel Johnson who led them to a grove where the regiment sought cover and from which still another attack was launched and enemy cannons and a blockhouse were taken. Later the regiment supported most vigorously the last assault by the Union forces, which drove the Southern troops away from most of the ground they had won earlier in the afternoon.

According to this sequence of events Heg must have been shot at the time when the rebel general Fulton launched his terrific attack and was met by a counter charge. Heg was struck in the abdomen by a bullet that entered one side of his body and went out the other.

An officer who visited him together with Captain Grinager at the hospital relates: "Colonel Heg was fully conscious and in good spirits but his deathly pale face and the deep furrows over his eyebrows told of the terrible pain he was suffering. He spoke of the brave boys in the Fifteenth—and brave they were, even if I say so myself with much pride. I told him that I had heard about him that afternoon and his gallantry in action, and added that it would have cheered the boys in his own regiment if they could have caught a glimpse of him. 'Tell my boys in the Fifteenth,' he said, 'that I stayed where I was needed, and I knew they did not need me!' The only thing that made it hard for him to die, he said, was that he had to leave his family. He lived through that night and died the next day at 10 o'clock."

In a Madison daily a man who was present at his deathbed gave the following gracious characterization of Colonel Heg: "From his earliest childhood a bright disposition and patience were his most marked characteristics. A person could not associate with him without becoming aware of the magic power he had of dispelling despondence and sadness. This quality did not leave him even in his last moments. The same considerate friendliness which had surrounded him during his life also cast a glow over him in death."

Colonel Ole C. Johnson

by *Waldemar Ager*

Colonel Johnson was born at Skipsnes near Lake Nordsjø in Holden [now Holla] parish, Upper Telemark in the year 1838. In 1844 the family emigrated to America. There were nine children, the oldest only 12 years of age. They came to Milwaukee and left there for Walworth county, where they obtained land. The children learned to read at home and also received instruction in a Norwegian ambulatory school. In 1852 the family moved to a place near Stoughton, Dane county. Ole's elder brother was the later well-known businessman and politician, J. A. Johnson. He taught common school and also gave instruction to his brother, who later attended Albion College. When the war broke out, one of the brothers enlisted in a Minnesota regiment and died of disease during the war. As J. A. Johnson was one of those who most earnestly had worked for the establishment of a Norwegian regiment, it was self-evident that Ole would join that group. He enlisted as a private but the governor appointed him a recruiting officer, and when he had assembled Company B he became its captain. Thereafter promotions followed quickly. Major Riis retired and Johnson became a major. When Lieutenant Colonel McKee fell at Murfreesboro, Johnson took his place and when Colonel Heg was made brigadier general, Johnson assumed command of the regiment.

Johnson was an able officer. At Chickamauga he was taken prisoner on the second day of battle. The account of his stay in Libby prison at Richmond and the subsequent adventurous flight when four officers cut their way through the floor of a railroad car and let the train pass over them reads almost like fiction.

Johnson did not return to the regiment until almost a year after his capture. Subsequent to his discharge from the 15th he attempted to recruit a new regiment and was appointed colonel of the 53rd Wisconsin. It never saw action, however, as the war ended before its organization was completed.

Johnson had strong Norwegian interests and was an intelligent, brave, and capable officer. He was conscientious and fearless, but was reputed to be stern and proud. Like Heg he demanded order and discipline. Officers with these characteristics are easily misunderstood.

For further information about Colonel Johnson we can refer to a book his brother J. A. Johnson wrote about the Regiment and likewise to Buslett's volume about the Fifteenth Wisconsin. He died in 1886, having never recovered completely from his stay in the Southern prisons. He was survived by his wife and one son. During his later years he adopted the name Skipsnes.

The Last Reunion

At the big 17th of May festival in 1914 on the fairgrounds between St. Paul and Minneapolis the 15th Wisconsin Regiment held perhaps the last reunion of its organization.

The veterans met at the so-called Log Cabin on the fairgrounds on Saturday May 16th in the afternoon:

E. Rice Co. K Willmar, Minn.

O. P. Olson Co. B New Richland, Minn.

August Møller Co. E New Richland

N. J. Gilbert Co. A Eleva, Wis.

Elias Thompson Co. C Brookings, S. D.

Michael Thompson St. Ansgar, Iowa

J. Burkee Evansville, Minn.

John Johnson Co. D Hennings, Minn.

Halvor Larson Co. H Elkader, Iowa

Henry Knudson Heron Lake, Minn.

Johs. H. Stokke Chaseburg, Wis.

Daniel Anderson Co. D New Rome, Wis.

Halvor O. Halvorson Co. D Stevens Point, Wis.

O. P. Anderson, Granite Falls, Minn.

A. Tofte Grasston, Minn.

Lewis Swenson, Montevideo, Minn.

T. Rossing Co. E. Decorah, Iowa

Gulbrand A. Dahl Co. E. Minneapolis

Martin Jørgenson Co. A Willmar

Tollef Anderson Co. K. Glenville, Minn.

Geo. Goodridge Co. E Lake Park, Iowa

James Julson Vandrie, S. D.

Andrew Johnson Co. A Cambridge, Neb.

August Anderson

Nils Anderson
Th. Thompson
Halvor Lee Co. D Minneapolis
Herman Anderson Co. I Muscoda, Wis.
Ex-Governor Rice was reelected President; First and Second Vice-
    Presidents: T. A. Rossing and Lewis Swenson; Secretary: N. J.
    Gilbert.

Editor W. Ager brought to the exhibition the whole collection of photo-
graphs, arms, maps, flags, and other things that were to be taken to the
Jubilee exhibition in Norway. Most of the veterans took advantage of
the opportunity to visit this exhibit and refresh their memories.

On Sunday the 17th of May there was a big program at the Hippodrome and those veterans who remained were invited to attend. A
Norwegian newspaper reported that about 60,000 people were assembled on the festival grounds on Sunday. The attendance exceeded by far
'the big days' at the State Fair. Every place was filled.

The folk festival at the Hippodrome also gathered a full house and although the building holds 12,000 it was packed to the utmost and thousands who could not get in remained outside.

The Rev. H. K. Madson gave the main address and his mighty resonant
voice was almost the only voice that could be heard over the whole area.

A terrific storm of applause rose through the hall when some old veterans of the Norwegian 15th Wis. Regiment were brought up on the platform and former Lt.–Gov. A. E. Rice unfurled their old regimental flag.
Cheers and applause sounded like a hurricane over the gathering and the
old warriors seemed very much moved by the ovation, which they had
well earned. Twenty-two of them had met the day before; but now many
had left for home. Here it must be mentioned that the regiment's
Norwegian flag, which is owned by the Lodge Nora in Chicago, also arrived, but it was not exhibited until Monday when most of the old veterans had gone home except for a couple who lived nearby. The rest did
not see the old Norwegian flag, as it was called.

There were also about 50 other Civil War veterans at the festival. On
Monday they organized the Scandinavian Civil War Veterans Associa-
tion with Mr. Oley Nelson of Slater, Iowa, as chairman, Captain Geo.
Jackson of Chicago as Vice-Chairman, and Lt. N. J. Gilbert of Eleva,
Wis. as Secretary.

The 15th Wis. and the other Civil War veterans held a joint meeting on Monday and passed the following resolution, which *Reform*'s editor W. Ager was requested to take along to Norway:

"We Norwegian-born veterans of the American Civil War, gathered at a general reunion during the Centennial 17th of May celebration May 1914 at the Minnesota State Fairgrounds, wish to send our heartfelt and respectful greetings to the Norwegian people, with wishes that God will protect old Norway, its King, Parliament, and people, that they will retain a fortunate, free, and esteemed land, whose sons and daughters in the future, as in the past, may go forward with straight backs and lofty brows, both at home and abroad, in war and in peace. God bless old Norway, our fathers' fair land."

This resolution was printed in Norwegian newspapers in Oslo and publicly announced at a large gathering in church on the Fairgrounds.

Of the regiment's officers we know that the following are alive in
    1916:
Captain Torkild Rossing, Decorah
Lt. Ivar A. Brandt, Decorah
Lt. Nils J. Gilbert, Eleva
Lt. Ole P. Olson, New Richland, Minn.
Lt. Ellend Erikson, Albert Lea, Minn.
Adj. [Otto A.] Risum, Los Angeles
There are perhaps 30 Privates left. Several live on the Pacific Coast.

Hospital Memories

by "a Veteran"

I believe that this is the place to tell about a touching incident that occurred in the hospital. Everyone in the regiment knew the Urness brothers. There were three of them. Anders Urness was the flag carrier or "Color Bearer." He was also mature in his attitude. One could not find a more gallant soldier in the regiment that he. Likewise, his brother Ole, who after the war came to Douglas county and was the sheriff for many years. But their youngest brother, a little young boy, his name [Peter] I don't remember, was one of my best friends, especially in the hospital, where there were many from our regiment. But this little Urness fellow was always regarded by all of us as a kind of pet. His winning nature made him beloved by all. He had the habit of washing his feet every day. One day, when he sat by the fire washing, he said to me that he did not have long to live. I laughed at him and said that was only his imagination, which I believed. But I had to help him to bed, which we never had to do before, and at his request I removed from under his pillow a portfolio with some letters and a photograph of his sister. These objects I promised to give to his brother Anders, which I also did later, along with his brotherly greetings. He called the nurse and asked her to call all the Norwegians to his bedside, which was also done. When they came he could no longer see; but he called us by name and asked us to come closer. Then he took us each by the hand and thanked us for the love we had shown him. When he had said goodbye to all, he folded his hands on his chest and recited the Lord's Prayer clearly for us all. We stood around his bed and thought he must have tired himself, that he had fallen asleep. But to our great astonishment, he was dead. I have seen many die and dying; but never had I seen anyone die so peacefully and it seemed as painlessly as he.

(Peter Urness volunteered for service on Jan. 28th, 1862, when he was 18 years old. He died in a Nashville hospital on October 19th, the same year.) W. A.

210

Crossing the Tennessee River

by Waldemar Ager

On the 24th of June [1863] began the campaign towards Chattanooga in which Rosecrans "with a masterly strategic manoeuver" forced Bragg to leave central Tennessee and pull back over the Cumberland Mountains to Chattanooga. On the 3rd, McCook's Division, to which the 15th belonged, made camp near Winchester, where the regiment bivouacked in a beautiful grove. On the 17th the army broke up and went over the Cumberland Mountains to Stevenson, Alabama, where they arrived on the 20th and lay over till the 28th. Heg's Brigade was ordered to lay a pontoon bridge and to be the first to cross the Tennessee River on the 27th, and this was carried into effect. The 15th Wisconsin was the first regiment to step on the Southern shore.

The regiment's then chief, Colonel O. C. Johnson, told of that crossing in his "Memories of the War" which he presented to the Veterans Club in Beloit in 1880.

"The main force of the Cumberland Army stood, in the beginning of 1863, at Stevenson, Alabama, and Rebel General Bragg with his main force was at Chattanooga. In the afternoon we received orders to stand ready to march at three o'clock the next morning, and at the appointed time we were in marching order. Colonel Hans Heg, of the 15th Wisconsin, functioned at that time as Brigade Commander, and to him was delegated the glorious task of being the first to cross the Tennessee River, which ran barely 3 miles from Stevenson. In one sense we naturally felt honored to be selected for this dangerous task, but many surely thought, too, that this honor could be dearly bought, if we found the opposite shore of the river tightly beset with Rebels; these fellows had the habit of shooting and we had learned to have proper respect for them on such occasions. The pontoon Army Service was also on hand and as soon as it was light enough to see, we started to put the boats in the water and shortly after sunrise the command was given and all the boats moved in battle formation over the river.

"The Tennessee River's water was quiet and still and glistened in the morning sunlight and, despite the moment's seriousness, I could not fail to wonder at the beautiful scene, as the boats glided lightly over the water.

"Later, as we neared the other shore and no sign of the enemy could be seen, we started little by little to feel a competitive urge to see which boat could be first to reach the opposite shore, and it was with a feeling of great satisfaction that I helped members of my own regiment to be the first to set foot on land. We had not dared to hope that the enemy would let us land without a struggle, and we were therefore agreeably surprised to find the only sign of them was a half burned-out watch fire where there evidently had been two or three cavalry sentinels, who took to their heels when we started our crossing. They had left in such haste they had forgotten to take along some particularly good fried fish, which some of our boys got hold of and declared quite remarkable."

A Poem About The "Fifteenth"

(Mr. Bersven Nelson jotted down the following poem from memory. It is not a masterpiece; but he says there were several who worked on it and maybe that was what was wrong. I have placed it here, because Heg's Boys liked it. It has been sung by campfires and more than one of the boys perhaps shortened the long hours on guard duty by humming it. —W.A.)

A poem I'll compose now to Heroes of the North,
Free-willing in their fosterland they eagerly set forth
Their courage to deliver and exploits to display;
We'll really show those fellers, that I'm glad to say.

I'm but a lowly Private in this fine regiment.
We use the rifle boldly, ourselves to represent.
Among the other Nations, we'll surely gain a name
We'll never make excuses, but storm ahead to fame.

A regiment so pleasant and Norsemen are we all
The name, Fifteenth Wisconsin, we proudly do recall
It was on March the second, to war we marched away
In eighteen-hundred sixty-two, that's the year they say.

That's when we left our campground, the name was Camp Randall
Yes, many Norsemen parted then from friends and pals, as well
As parents and his sisters and brothers dear they left
Their sweethearts too, forever, alone and sad bereft.

The parting was so heavy with relatives around
When off we trudged ahead, down to the station ground,
And straight into the railroad cars, to places us assigned,
While snow and storm and wintry cold, around us blindly whined.

The train away it chugged, but soon it lost its speed;
The snow's great masses made it stick very fast indeed.
Another horse came to its aid, a large and stronger beast
That pulled us out, that was for sure, to the city in the East.

Chicago was its name; through evening there we stayed
While through the streets so smartly, we marched in big parade.
So many Norsemen's daughters came out for us to view
While in the middle of the town a halt was called there too.

And on the city's avenues, great honor came with fuss.
The Norsemen of Chicago a flag presented us.
Yes, large and handsome, so it was, a lion on it stood.
We thanked them all so nicely, the love they showed was good.

Two flags from State Wisconsin, us also given were
One with stars along and stripes so red and clear,
As clean as Heavens' arches shine, white and gleaming are,–
The other was a blue one, and that we also bear.

Beneath that flag above us, we Norse our duty'll do
Among the other nations, and win our victory too.
We'll not retreat in battle, nor fire's hottest fight
But stride ahead as Heroes and win our cause for Right.

List of Officers and Men in the 15TH Wisconsin Volunteer Regiment

Prepared by A.L. Lien

Colonel Hans C. Heg, Waterford, enlisted 30 Sept. 1861, wounded at Chickamauga, 19 Sept. 1863, died the day after.

Lieutenant Colonel Ole C. Johnson (Skipness), Stoughton, Captain, Co. B, 12 Nov. 1862, Lieutenant Colonel, 26 Feb. 1863. Taken prisoner at Chickamauga, 19 Sept. 1863. Colonel, 21 Feb. 1865, discharged 10 Feb. 1865.

Major Charles M. Reese, Danish, Madison, enlisted 1 Dec. 1861, discharged 8 June 1862.

Major George Wilson, Madison, enlisted 12 Nov. 1861. Second Lieutenant, Co. B, promoted Captain, Co. H, 14 May 1862, wounded, promoted Major 11 March 1863, wounded at Chickamauga. Discharged 6 Jan. 1865. Commissioned Lieutenant Colonel 25 Feb. 1867 from 21 Feb. 1865.

Adjutant Hans Borchsenius, Danish, Baldwin, enlisted 7 Dec. 1861, discharged 28 Sept. 1862.

Henry Hauff, Stoughton, First Lieutenant, Co. I, 14 Dec. 1861, promoted Adjutant 1 Oct. 1861, Captain, Co. E, 8 May 1863, fell at Chickamauga 19 Sept. 1863.

Lewis G. Nelson, Oconomowoc, enlisted 30 Oct. 1861, First Lieutenant, Co., D, promoted Adjutant 27 May 1863 and Captain, Co. D, 31 Aug. 1864, discharged 13 Feb. 1865.

Otto A. Risum, Spring Valley, enlisted 16 Oct. 1861, veterinarian, Sergeant, promoted Sergeant Major 1 Jan. 1864 and Adjutant 24 Sept. 1864. Discharged 10 Feb. 1865.

Quartermaster Ole Heg, Waterford, enlisted 28 Oct. 1861, discharged 6 June 1862.

Physician Stephen O. Himoe, Lawrence, Kans., 11 Nov. 1861, discharged 13 Nov. 1863.

A.F.S. Lindsfeldt (Swedish, wife Norwegian), Sheboygan, 27 Nov. 1863, discharged 2 Feb. 1864.

First Assistant Physician Søren J. Hanson, Utica, 11 Nov. 1861, discharged 20 Oct. 1862.

Co. A:

Captain Henry Siegel, Chicago, 27 Sept. 1861, First Sergeant, promoted First Lieutenant 16 Dec. 1862, dated from 8 Jan. 1862 on detached Service at General Davis headquarters as Provost Marshal, Captain 1 Sept. 1862, without review, discharged with Co. A, 12 Dec. 1864.[1]

First Lieutenant N.I. Gilbert, promoted First Lieutenant 1 Sept. 1864, dated 22 July 1864, without review, discharged 20 Dec. 1864.

Captain Andrew Torkilsen, Chicago, 11 Nov. 1861, accepted discharge 19 Oct. 1862.

Captain John M. Johnson, Madison, 9 Dec. 1861, from Second Lieutenant, Co. E, Captain 20 Oct. 1862, fell at Chickamauga 18 Sept. 1863.

First Lieutenant Emanuel Engelstad, Chicago, 15 Nov. 1861, discharged 19 Oct. 1862.

Second Lieutenant Oliver Thompson, Chicago, 15 Nov. 1861, fell at Chickamauga 20 Sept. 1863.

Gahr Amundson, Madison, 29 Oct. 1861, moved to Veterans Reserve Corps 1 Sept. 1863.

Fredrick Aargaard, Chicago, 9 Oct. 1861, Corporal, Sergeant. Second Lieutenant from 20 Sept. 1863.

Field pastor Claus L. Clausen, St. Ansgar, Iowa, 11 Dec. 1861, discharged 26 Nov. 1862.

Field pastor John H. Johnson, Primrose, 19 Oct. 1864.

Sergeant Major Torkild A. Rossing, 11 Dec. 1861, Sergeant Major 1 July 1862, First Lieutenant 3 Sept. 1862, Captain Co. E, 7 April 1864, discharged 20 Dec. 1864.

Martin A. Erickson, Sparta, 22 Oct. 1861, First Sergeant Major 1 Jan. 1863, promoted to Second Lieutenant, Co. H, 27 May 1863, taken prisoner at Chickamauga, discharged 20 April 1865.

Nils Johnson, Oconomowoc, 25 Oct. 1861, Corporal, Sergeant, promoted Sergeant Major 15 Oct. 1864.

Quartermaster Sergeant Ole R. Dahl, Blooming Prairie, 29 Oct. 1861. Quartermaster Sergeant from Co. H, 1 July 1862, promoted to First Lieutenant, Co. B, 30 Jan. 1863, taken prisoner 1 March 1864, discharged 12 March 1865.

Com. Sergeant James Larson, Perry, 25 Jan. 1862, promoted to Second Lieutenant, Co. C, 9 July 1862, First Lieutenant 19 Oct. 1864, without review, discharged 13 Dec. 1864.

John Gysler, Chicago, 25 Oct. 1861, from Co. A, Sergeant, promoted, 1 Sept. 1862, discharged 20 Dec. 1864.

Hospital Steward Anthon O. Oyen, Chicago, 8 Oct. 1861, Hospital Steward 18 Nov. 1861, taken prisoner at Chickamauga, discharged 25 May 1865.

Ole P. Olson, Coon Prairie, 23 Sept. 1861, Sergeant, First Sergeant, Second Lieutenant 1 Nov. 1862, discharged 22 June 1863.

Principal musician, Jørgen Isaacson, Mt. Morris, 1 May 1862, transferred from Co. A to B, 1 Aug. 1862. Died as a prisoner of war in Richmond 1 Jan. 1864.

Carl C. Evenson, Madison, 1 Dec. 1862, from Co. B to H, 1 Dec. 1864.

Jacob Abrahamson, Chicago, 20 Feb. 1862, to Co. H, 20 Dec. 1864 to Co. I, 13th Infantry, discharged.

John T. Anderson, Boone Co., Ill., 17 Oct. 1861, Corporal, discharged 20 Dec. 1864.

Lars B. Anderson, Chicago, 9 Dec. 1861, discharged 20 Dec. 1864.

Ole Anderson, Boone Co., Ill., 3 Jan. 1862, taken prisoner at Stone River, moved to Veterans Reserve Corps 1 Aug. 1863. Discharged 16 Sept. 1863.

Nels Arneson, Chicago, 31 Oct. 1861, discharged 20 Dec. 1864.

Ole Back, Chicago, 11 Oct. 1861, Corporal Sergeant, died 16 Jan. 1863. Wounded.

George A. Boge, Chicago, 25 Nov. 1861, musician, discharged 20 Dec. 1864.

Ole C. Branstad, (?), 20 Aug. 1862, taken prisoner at Chickamauga, discharged 26 Jan. 1865.

George O. Branstad, Chicago, 26 Oct. 1861, Sergeant, wounded and captured at Chickamauga, died in Andersonville Prison 6 Aug. 1864.

Peter Brekkan, Chicago, 8 Oct. 1861, discharged 20 Dec. 1864.

Fredrick Brown, Chicago, 9 Oct. 1861, discharged 23 June 1862, sick.

Lars P. Christenson, Chicago, 11 Oct. 1861, discharged 20 Dec. 1864.

Tobias Christenson, La Crosse, 16 Feb. 1862, taken prisoner at Chickamauga, died in Andersonville of sickness 18 Oct. 1864.

Charles A. Dahl, Chicago, 18 Oct. 1861, discharged 20 Dec. 1864.

Edward Edson, Boone, Ill., 16 Oct. 1861, died at Chattanooga, Tenn., 4 Feb. 1864.

Henry Ellingson, Boone, Ill., 16 Oct. 1861, died at Nashville 21 Feb. 1863.

Andrew Ellingson, Madison, 27 Oct. 1861, discharged 20 Dec. 1864.

Fredrick Fleischer, Chicago, 26 Oct. 1861, Corporal, discharged sick 20 Aug. 1863.

Peter H. Funkly, Jefferson, 7 Nov. 1861, discharged sick 30 June 1863.

George Georgeson, Boone, Ill., 16 Oct. 1861, Corporal, Sergeant, died at Chattanooga 5 Oct. 1862.

John Gysler, Chicago, see Commissary Sergeant, discharged with Co. A, 20 Oct. 1864.

John Haldorson, Chicago, 16 Oct. 1861, discharged sick 20 Dec. 1862.

Martin Halvorson, Chicago, 16 Oct. 1861, discharged 20 June 1863, sick.

Oliver Halvorson, Madison, 30 Oct. 1861, died at Corinth, Miss., 16 Sept. 1862.

Ole K. Hanson, Boone, 15 Oct. 1861, Sergeant, discharged 27 May 1864.

Hans C. Hanson, La Crosse, 16 Oct. 1861, veterinarian, moved to I, 13th Infantry, discharged 3 July 1865.

Peter Hanson — 16 Dec. 1861, discharged 20 Dec. 1864.

Hans J. Henderson, Houston, Minn., 9 Jan. 1862, discharged 20 Dec. 1864.

Edward Holberg, Chicago, 18 Oct. 1861, discharged 20 Dec. 1864.

Edward Howland, Chicago, 11 Nov. 1861, discharged 20 Dec. 1864.

Hans Ingebritson, Chicago, 11 Oct. 1861, Corporal, moved to Veterans Reserve Corps, discharged 1 Sept. 1863.

Tobias Ingebretson, Bad Ax, 3 Jan. 1862, discharged sick in Oct. 1862.

Andrew O. Jenson, Chicago, 25 Oct. 1861, moved to U.S. Navy 5 May 1864.

Andrew Johnson, Boone, 10 Oct. 1861, Sergeant, discharged 20 Dec. 1864.

Christian Johnson, Chicago, 24 Oct. 1862, taken prisoner 21 Sept. 1863 at Chickamauga, discharged 20 Dec. 1864. Died at Dwight, ND, 1911. Farmer and merchant.

John Johnson, Boone, 22 Oct. 1861, died at Chattanooga 17 Dec. 1863.

Austin Johnson, La Crosse, 16 Dec. 1861, died at Iuka, Miss., 25 Aug. 1862.

Edward Johnson, Boone, 3 Jan. 1862, died at Nashville, Tenn., 2 Dec. 1862.

Christian Johnson, Winneshiek Co., Iowa, 8 Jan. 1862, died at Nashville, Tenn., 2 Feb. 1862.

Ole Johnson, Winneshiek Co., Iowa, 8 Jan. 1862, died at Nashville, Tenn., 13 Nov. 1862.

Knut Johnson, Winneshiek Co., Iowa, 8 Jan. 1861, Corporal, died at Louisville, Ky., 9 Nov. 1862.

Lars Johanneson, Chicago, 30 Sept. 1861, Corporal. Discharged 20 Dec. 1864.

Christian Johanneson, Houston, Minn., 16 Feb. 1862, moved to H, 20 Dec. 1864. Discharged 13 March 1865.

Halvor Jørgenson, Chicago, 26 Oct. 1861, discharged 7 April 1863, wounded.

Martin Jørgenson, Chicago, 28 Oct. 1861, moved to Veterans Reserve Corps 15 Feb. 1864. Discharged 20 Dec. 1864.

Ole Knudson, Winneshiek Co., Iowa, 8 Jan. 1862, discharged sick 17 Nov. 1863.

Lars Kydland, Chicago, 28 Oct. 1861. Discharged sick 27 June 1863.

Andrew Larson, Chicago, 30 Sept. 1861, moved to U.S. Navy 5 May 1864.

Ole Larson, Winneshiek Co., Iowa, 8 Jan. 1862, died at Nashville 26 March 1863.

Elias Lodgaard, Chicago, 9 Dec. 1861, died in Andersonvile Prison.

Ole J. Lorentzen, Chicago, 9 Dec. 1861. Discharged sick 15 Dec. 1862.

Herman Lundgreen, Winneshiek Co., Iowa, 30 Sept. 1861 from D. Discharged 30 June 1864.

John M. Lindgren, Chicago, 25 Nov. 1861, wounded at New Hope Church 27 May 1864. Last report lay sick with wounds.

Andrew Luraas, Chicago, 17 Oct. 1861. Died at Mound City, Ill., 10 April 1862.

Anton Monson, Chicago, 25 Nov. 1861, moved to Veterans Reserve Corps 6 Oct. 1864.

Jonas Norem, Chicago, 9 Oct. 1861, taken prisoner 24 Dec. 1862. Discharged 20 Dec. 1864.

Peter Norman, Chicago, 8 Oct. 1861. Died at Bowling Green 22 Nov. 1862.

Olaf Olson, Chicago, 8 Oct. 1861, moved to U.S. Navy 5 May 1864.

Amund Olson, Bad Ax, 14 Nov. 1861, discharged 20 Dec. 1864.

Nels P. Olson, Bad Ax, 16 Nov. 1861, discharged 20 Dec. 1864.

Michael Olson, Bad Ax, 16 Dec. 1861, died at Chicago, Ill., 28 July 1862.

Amund Olson, Jefferson, 28 Jan. 1862, died at Nashville 27 July 1863.

Knut Olson, Pleasant Spring, 16 Jan. 1864, moved to Co. I, 13th Infantry. Sick, absent at discharge.

Ellef Pederson, Chicago, 11 Oct. 1861. Discharged sick 28 July 1863.

Knud Pederson, Chicago, 9 Oct. 1861. Died of wounds 13 April 1863, Nashville.

Osmund Peterson, Chicago, 26 Oct. 1861, Corporal, Sergeant. Discharged wounded 28 July 1864.

Thomas Sampson, Boone, Ill., 16 Oct. 1861, died at Island No. 10, 23 May 1862.

Samuel Sampson, Boone, Ill., 16 Oct. 1861, died at Island No. 10, 30 May 1862.

Gabriel J. Somme, Chicago, 5 Oct. 1861, Corporal, discharged 6 Dec. 1864.

Arnoldus Schlambush, Chicago, Sergeant, taken prisoner at Stone River, transferred to Flaaden in May 1864, died in Sheridan, Ill., 1906.

Gabriel E. Somme, Chicago, 24 Dec. 1861, prisoner at New Hope Church, in captivity at discharge 20 Dec. 1864.

Henry Sporland, Chicago, 11 Oct. 1861, moved to Veterans Reserve Corps 15 Aug. 1864.

Oliver Stahl, Boone, Ill., 17 Oct. 1861, discharged 20 Dec. 1864.

Andreas Swenson, Chicago, 27 Sept. 1861, wounded, discharged sick 10 Feb. 1863.

Jacob Syverson, Madison, 26 Dec. 1861, fell at New Hope Church 27 May 1864.

Isaac Syvertson, La Crosse, 3 Jan. 1862, discharged 20 Dec. 1864.

Ole Syvertson, La Crosse, 10 Jan. 1862, discharged sick 5 May 1863.

Henry Syvertson, Chicago, 20 Feb. 1862, Sergeant, moved to Veterans Reserve Corps 27 Aug. 1863. Discharged 28 Feb. 1865.

Ditlef Tharaldson, Janesville, 30 Dec. 1863, moved to I, 13th Infantry, discharged 30 June 1865.

Lewis Thompson, Boone, Ill., 16 Oct. 1861, died at Island No. 10, 7 May 1862.

Jonas Thompson, Chicago, 11 Nov. 1861. Discharged 19 Feb. 1864.

Ole G. Thompson, Chicago, 28 Dec. 1861, First Sergeant, Second Lieutenant, Co. B, 14 May 1862. First Lieutenant 1 Nov. 1862, discharged 30 Jan. 1863.

Thomas Thompson, Chicago, 28 Dec. 1861, Corporal, Sergeant, moved to U.S. Navy 5 May 1864.

Co. B:

Joseph Mathisen (Danish), Madison, 12 Nov. 1861, First Lieutenant, promoted Captain in Nov. 1862. Discharged 1 Dec. 1864.

Ole G. Thompson, Chicago, from Co. A, promoted 1 Nov. 1862 First Lieutenant. Discharged 30 Jan. 1863.

Ole R. Dahl, Blooming Prairie, First Lieutenant 26 Jan. 1863, taken prisoner 1 March 1864, discharged 12 March 1865.

Halvor Anderson, Cambridge, 10 Oct. 1861. Died at Island No. 10, Tenn., 25 May 1862.

Syvert A. Anderson, Madison, 22 Oct. 1861. Discharged 16 Sept. 1863.

Ole Anderson, Sr., Stoughton, 22 Oct. 1861. Discharged 16 Dec. 1862.

Ole Anderson, Jr., Door Creek, 11 Dec. 1861, prisoner in Chickamauga 25 April 1864, prisoner in Danville, Va.

Andrew C. Anderson, Madison, 5 March 1862. Discharged 18 Aug. 1864.

Nils Anderson, Berlin, 8 Nov., moved to 8th Battalion Light Artillery 29 July 1863. Absent at discharge.

Andrew E. Anderson, Deerfield, 15 March 1864, moved to K, 13th Infantry. Discharged 2 Nov. 1865.

Kittel Amundson, Winchester, 28 Oct. 1861. Discharged sick 6 Oct. 1862.

Erick Asbjørnson, La Crosse, 23 Dec. 1863, moved to I, 13th Infantry, discharged 14 Nov. 1865.

Andrew Asperheim, Windsor, 22 Dec. 1861, fell 14 May 1864.

Erick M. Basness, Koshkonong, 3 Dec. 1861, Corporal, discharged 2 Dec. 1864.

Knut Bragen, Vermont, 21 Oct. 1861, from Co. C. Discharged 1 April 1862.

Ole O. Burke, La Crosse, 23 Sept. 1861, died in Andersonville Prison 11 June 1865.

Anders J. Burke, Koshkonong, 8 Feb. 1862, to Veterans Reserve Corps 4 Oct. 1863. Discharged 8 Feb. 1865.

Carl L. Colbjornson, Madison, 14 Sept. 1861, Sergeant. Discharged 23 March 1863.

Anders Christopherson, La Crosse, 26 Aug. 1862, to 24th Wisconsin 13 Feb. 1865.

Christian O. Dahl, McFarland, 4 Dec. 1861, died 2 Aug. 1863.

Anders Ellefson, Mt. Morris, 25 Nov. 1861, died in Andersonville Prison 26 April 1863.

Anders Erickson, Door Creek, 11 Dec. 1861, discharged 2 Dec. 1864.

Knut Erickson, Neshonoc, 5 Jan. 1864, moved to Co. I, 13th Infantry. Discharged 24 Nov. 1865.

Lars Erickson, Buffalo City, 17 Feb. 1864, to Co. K, 13th Infantry, discharged 24 Nov. 1865.

Christopher Erickson, Black Earth, 30 Oct. 1861, died in Andersonville Prison 19 Aug. 1864.

Hans Fostad, Stoughton, 26 Oct. 1861, discharged 13 Feb. 1865.

John H. Fostad, Stoughton, 26 Oct. 1861, died at Nashville 22 Nov. 1862.

Peter Frogness, Pleasant Springs, 5 Nov. 1861. Discharged sick 19 Dec. 1862.

John Gilbertson, Gale, 21 Jan. 1864, moved to Co. I, 13th Infantry. Sick at discharge.

Lars Halvorson, Stoughton, 23 Sept. 1861, died at Island No. 10, 25 May 1862.

Halvor Halvorson, Winchester, 6 Jan. 1862, died at Cincinnati 1 July 1862.

Lars Hambal, Merton, 28 Sept. 1861, Sergeant. Discharged sick 21 Dec. 1862.

Lars Hanson, Stoughton, 15 Nov. 1861, died in Andersonville 3 Sept. 1864.

Christian Hanson, Stoughton, 25 Nov. 1861, Corporal. Discharged 2 Dec. 1864.

Christian Hanson, Manitowoc, 25 Nov. 1861. Discharged sick 11 Oct. 1862.

Soren L. H. Hauge, Sterling, 14 Dec. 1861. Wagoner, discharged 2 Dec. 1864.

Ludwig L.H. Hauge, Sterling, 25 Jan. 1862, discharged 2 Dec. 1864.

Hans Hendrickson, Madison, 8 Nov. 1861. Discharged 2 Dec. 1864.

Christopher Hoff, Christiana, 10 Nov. 1861, discharged 2 Dec. 1864.

Jørgen Isaacson, Mt. Morris, 25 Nov. 1861, musician, taken prisoner Jan. 1864, died at Richmond, Va., 20 March 1864.

Jacob Jacobson, Milwaukee, 20 Aug. 1862, moved to Co. H, 1 Dec. 1864.

Engel Johnson, Leeds, 24 Sept. 1861, moved to H, 1 Dec. 1864. Discharged 2 Dec. 1864.

John H. Johnson, Cambridge, 7 Nov. 1861, died at Island No. 10, 3 July 1862.

John Johnson, Door Creek, 11 Dec. 1861, died of wounds 19 Sept. 1863.

Osten Knutson, Winchester, 19 Nov. 1861, fell at New Hope Church 27 May 1864.

Ole Knutson, La Crosse, 5 Jan. 1864, fell at New Hope Church 27 May 1864.

Hans Lageson, Alamakee Co., Iowa, 18 Jan. 1862, discharged 2 Dec. 1864.

John Larkee, Neenah, 21 Oct. 1861, First Sergeant. Discharged sick 14 Nov. 1862.

Edwin Larson, Madison, 8 Sept. 1861, discharged sick, 8 April 1863.

Peter O. Larson, Coon Prairie, 23 Sept. 1861, Corporal. Sergeant, discharged, wounded 4 April 1863.

Jens C. Larson, Columbus, 10 Oct. 1861, Corporal. Died in Nashville 22 Nov. 1862.

Erick Larson, Deerfield, 22 Oct. 1861, died of wounds 22 June 1864.

Stark Larson, Pleasant Springs, 26 Oct. 1861, discharged sick 11 May 1863.

Mads Larson, Stoughton, 13 Nov. 1861, died in Andersonville Prison 1 Sept. 1864.

Ragnald Lasseson, Christiana, 22 Oct. 1861, died in Murfreesboro, Tenn., 6 April 1863.

Sophus Listo, Madison, 1 Sept. 1862, discharged sick 23 Feb. 1863.

Bernt Madson, Cambridge, 1 Oct. 1861, Sergeant. Discharged 27 Jan. 1865.

Torgrim Mikkelson, Vermont, 17 Oct. 1861, Corporal. Fell at Stone River 3 Dec. 1862.

Ole Mikkelson, Vermont, 8 Nov. 1861, died in Miss., 10 Aug. 1862.

Andrew Milson, Vermont, 17 Oct. 1861, died at Winchester 4 Aug. 1863.

Knut J. Mjelde, Madison, 7 Sept. 1861, Corporal. Discharged sick 3 Nov. 1862.

Jens O. Moe, Columbus, 19 Feb. 1862, died at Island No. 10, 19 May 1862.

Iver Monson, Christiana, 11 Jan. 1862. Discharged 2 Dec. 1864.

Torger Monson, La Crosse, 25 Feb. 1864, moved to Co. I, 13th Infantry, 24 Nov. 1865.

Ole Nelson, Koshkonong, 8 Oct. 1861, discharged sick 27 July 1863.

Lewis Nelson, Cambridge, 28 Oct. 1861, fell at Bald Knob, Ga., 28 July 1864.

Albert Nelson, Pleasant Springs, 12 Oct. 1861, Sergeant. Discharged 2 Dec. 1864.

Andrew Nelson, Stoughton, 17 Oct. 1861, died at Winchester 4 Aug. 1863.

Rasmus Nelson, Holland, 28 Oct. 1861, to Veterans Reserve Corps 9 April 1864.

Christian Nelson, Holland, 28 Sept. 1861, discharged sick 22 Oct. 1862.

Ole A. Norby, Cambridge, 10 Oct. 1861, Sergeant. Discharged sick 29 Oct. 1862.

Nils Olaus, Winchester, 6 Jan. 1862, discharged 18 June 1865.

Gunder Olson, Stoughton, 20 Sept. 1861. Fell at Chickamauga 19 Sept. 1863.

Tideman Olson, Vermont, 15 Oct. 1861, discharged 7 Aug. 1862. Wounded by accident, Birds Pt., Mo.

Peter Olson, Christiana, 10 Oct. 1861, discharged 25 Sept. 1863.

Ole M. Olson, Vermont, 15 Oct. 1861, died in Andersonville Prison 11 July 1864.

Ellend Olson, Brager, 17 Oct. 1861, discharged 2 Dec. 1864.

Michael Olson, Stoughton, 22 Oct. 1861, died in Andersonville Prison 9 Nov. 1864.

Thomas Olson, Stoughton, 18 Oct. 1861, discharged 2 Dec. 1864, died 1901.

Lars Olson, Stoughton, 18 Oct. 1861, died in Murfreesboro 16 Jan. 1863.

Soren Olson, Wellers Creek, 12 Dec. 1861, to Veterans Reserve Corps 11 Sept. 1863.

Christian Olson, Winchester, 2 June 1862, moved to H, discharged 8 Feb. 1865.

John S. Opdahl, Leeds, 14 Sept. 1861, died in Andersonville Prison 22 June 1864.

Peter Peterson, Primrose, 16 Oct. 1861, discharged 2 Dec. 1864.

Herman Peterson, Spring Prairie, 31 Oct. 1861, died in Chattanooga 13 June 1864.

Harder Rossing, Christiana, 13 Nov. 1861, to Veterans Reserve Corps 11 Sept. 1863.

Ole N. Skjelde, Cambridge, 24 Oct. 1861, died at Island No. 10, 14 May 1862.

John S. Skjeldstad, Perry, 3 Oct. 1861, discharged 2 Dec. 1863.

Brown Syvertson, Deerfield, 22 Oct. 1861, Corporal, died of wounds in Chattanooga 6 July, 1864.

Anfin Syvertson, Windsor, 11 Nov. 1861, discharged 2 Dec. 1864.

Carl Syvertson, Cambridge, 2 Nov. 1861, to Veterans Reserve Corps 6 Oct. 1863.

Syvert Syvertson, La Crosse, 5 Jan. 1864, moved to Co. I, 13th Infantry. Discharged 24 Nov. 1865.

Herman Thoreson, Pleasant Springs, 28 Oct. 1861, discharged 2 Dec. 1864.

Anders J. Urness, Vermont, 28 Oct. 1861, Corporal. Sergeant, discharged 2 Dec. 1864, died 1905.

Peter Urness, Vermont, 21 Jan. 1862, died at Bowling Green, Ky., 19 Oct. 1862.

Ole J. Urness, Vermont, 5 Jan. 1864, Corporal, moved to Co. I, 13th Infantry. Discharged 30 June 1865, died 1902.

Jørgen C. Velle, Milwaukee, 30 Dec. 1861, transferred to 8th Wisconsin Battalion 29 July 1863.

Peter Walin, Fox Lake (Swedish), 15 Nov. 1861, Corporal, to Veterans Reserve Corps in Nov. 1863, discharged 22 Nov. 1864.

Syvert Wilkinson, Buffalo City, 17 Feb. 1864, moved to I, 13th Infantry, 1 Dec. 1864, discharged 24 Nov. 1864.

Company C:

Fredrick R. Berg, Milwaukee, 19 Nov. 1861, Captain. Discharged 12 June 1862.

Hans Hanson, Norway, 19 Nov. 1861, First Lieutenant. Died in prison in Atlanta, GA, 13 Oct. 1863.

James Larson, Perry, promoted from Com. Sergeant, Second Lieutenant, First Lieutenant, 19 Oct. 1864, discharged 3 Dec. 1864.

Peter Anderson, Sr., Raymond, 20 Oct. 1861, discharged 31 Dec. 1864.

Peter Anderson, Jr., Norway, 5 Nov. 1861, discharged 31 Dec. 1864.

Martin Anderson, Norway, 5 Nov. 1861, Corporal, to Veterans Reserve Corps 31 Dec. 1863. Discharged 31 Dec. 1864.

Arne Arneson, Milwaukee, 19 Oct. 1861, died at Madison, Wis., 10 Feb. 1862.

Ole Bergeson, Norway, 18 Nov. 1861, discharged sick 13 Jan. 1864.

Knut Brownson, Norway, 25 Feb. 1862, discharged 21 Dec. 1864.

Edward Burke, Sr., Waterford, 1 Nov. 1861, discharged sick 21 May 1862.

Edward Burke, Jr., Waterford, 20 Aug. 1862, discharged 19 Dec. 1862.

Enock Christopherson, 18 Oct. 1861, discharged 31 Dec. 1864.

Daniel Danielson, Muskego, 10 Dec. 1861, died at Racine, Wis., 15 Oct. 1863.

Andrew Ellickson, Pleasant Springs, 14 March 1862, moved to Co. I, 13th Infantry, discharged 21 March 1865.

Albert Emerson, Norway, 11 Oct. 1861, Corporal, Sergeant, discharged 1 Jan. 1865.

Thomas Emerson, Norway, 31 Oct. 1861, died in Stevenson, Ala., 20 Oct. 1863.

Erick Erickson, Norway, 31 Oct. 1861, discharged sick 7 Feb. 1863.

Joseph Fjeld, Norway, 5 Nov. 1861, Sergeant, discharged sick 25 Aug. 1863.

Gustav A. Fjeld, Norway, 4 Dec. 1863, moved to H, 1 Jan. 1865, to K, 13th Infantry, 10 June 1865.

Knut Finkelson, Norway, 11 Nov. 1861, fell at Stone River 31 Dec. 1862.

Peter George, Racine, 21 Oct. 1861, Sergeant, discharged sick 5 July 1862.

Oscar Gibson, Waterford, 9 Nov. 1861, Corporal, died at Richmond 2 Feb. 1864.

August Goodale, Vernon, 1 Jan. 1862, discharged 31 Dec. 1864.

Elias Halvorson, Norway, 11 Nov. 1861, discharged 31 Dec. 1864.

Christopher Hanson, Waterford, 14 Oct. 1861, discharged 31 Dec. 1864.

Andrew Hanson, Raymond, 5 Nov. 1861, discharged 31 Dec. 1864.

Gunder E. Hanson, Norway, 5 Nov. 1861, fell at Stone River 30 Dec. 1862.

Knud Hanson, Norway, 2 Nov. 1861, discharged sick 5 Aug. 1863.

Jacob B. Holm, Raymond, 15 Oct. 1861, died at Murme Brigade, Ariz.

Torbjørn Hanson, Madison, 25 Feb. 1862, died at Richmond, Va., 27 Jan. 1864.

Ole Hanson, Racine, 29 Nov. 1862, moved to K, 13th Infantry, discharged 24 Nov. 1865.

Tosten Hendrickson, Norway, 10 Dec. 1861, discharged 9 Nov. 1865.

Christian Heyer, East Randolph, 9 Nov. 1861, Sergeant, First Sergeant, Second Lieutenant, 3 July 1863, discharged 31 Dec. 1864.

Elling Iverson, Norway, 10 Dec. 1861, died at Bowling Green 19 Dec. 1862.

Hans Jacobson, Norway, 11 Nov. 1861, Sergeant, discharged 31 Dec. 1864.

Salomon Jacobson, Norway, 22 Dec. 1861, discharged 30 Jan. 1865.

Rasmus Jenson, Racine, 22 Nov. 1862, died of wounds in Atlanta 2 Feb. 1864.

John Johnson, Norway, 15 Oct. 1861, died in Andersonville Prison.

Peter Johnson, Rochester, 15 Oct. 1861, discharged 10 June 1865.

Hendrick Johnson, Norway, 31 Oct. 1861, died at Bowling Green 25 Feb. 1863.

Carl J. Johnson, Norway, 5 Nov. 1861, discharged sick 19 Aug. 1862.

Rasmus Johnson, Norway 5 Nov. 1861, Corporal, discharged sick 15 April 1864.

Niels Johnson, Norway, 12 Nov. 1861, Corporal. Sergeant, discharged 31 Dec. 1864. Commissioned Second Lieutenant 25 Feb. 1867, time of service counted from 19 Oct. 1864.

Jacob Jordahl, Norway, 10 Dec. 1861, discharged 31 Dec. 1864.

Martin Johnson, Waterford, 29 Feb. 1864, moved to I, 13th Infantry, discharged 20 Nov. 1865.

Peter Jørgenson, East Randahl, 2 Dec. 1861, to Veterans Reserve Corps 1 Dec. 1863, discharged 31 Dec. 1864.

Knud Knudson, Norway, 11 Oct. 1861, missing at time of discharge.

Ole Larson, Oakland, 21 Oct. 1861, died at Nashville 15 Dec. 1862.

Lorens C. Larson, Norway, 12 Dec. 1863, moved to Co. I, 13th Infantry, discharged 24 Nov. 1865.

Mathias Mathiason, Norway, 11 Oct. 1861, fell at Stone River 31 Dec. 1862.

Paul Mathiason, Norway, 4 Nov. 1861, discharged 31 Dec. 1864.

Andrew O. Moe, Madison, 21 Oct. 1861, moved to Co. E, discharged 10 May 1863.

Jacob Nelson, Norway, 5 May 1861, died at Island No. 10, 28 June 1862.

Nels Nelson, Raymond, 9 Nov. 1861, discharged sick 22 Aug. 1862.

Lars Nelson, 15 Nov. 1861, died in Chattanooga 3 Dec. 1863.

Hans Nelson, Raymond, 21 Nov. 1861, died at Iuka, Miss., 5 Sept. 1862.

Ole Olson, Sr., Norway, 9 Oct. 1861, Sergeant, discharged sick 14 Nov. 1862.

Ole Olson, Jr., Norway, 5 Nov. 1861, discharged 31 Dec. 1864.

Thore Olson, Milwaukee, 8 Nov. 1861, discharged 31 Dec. 1864.

Lorents Olson, Milwaukee, 12 Nov. 1861, discharged 13 May 1863.

Erles J. Osmundson, Norway, 28 Nov. 1861, discharged 23 June 1862.

Bernt C. Osmundson, Norway, 30 Aug. 1862, died of wounds at Murfreesboro 9 Aug. 1863.

Jens Overson, Norway, 14 Oct. 1861, Corporal. Discharged 9 Aug. 1864.

Ole Peterson, Sr., Norway, 14 Oct. 1861, discharged 31 Dec. 1864.

Ole Peterson, Jr., Racine, 14 Oct. 1861, died at Murfreesboro 19 April 1863.

Christian Peterson, Raymond, 4 Nov. 1861, discharged 11 Oct. 1863.

Lewis Rolfson, Norway, 14 Dec. 1861, discharged 31 Dec. 1864.

John Simonson, Norway, 10 Nov. 1861, died 30 Sept. 1863.

Peter Soderberg, Waterford, 31 Dec. 1863, moved to Veterans Reserve Corps 22 Nov. 1864, discharged 26 Aug. 1865.

Hans Sorenson, Whitewater, 25 Oct. 1861, discharged 31 Dec. 1864.

Peter Sorenson, Racine, 29 Nov. 1862, died at Nashville, Tenn., 11 Nov. 1863.

Peter E. Stangeland, Norway, 4 Nov. 1861, discharged 31 Dec. 1864.

Erick O. Stensby, Norway, 31 Nov. 1861, discharged 31 Dec. 1864.

Lars Stinson, Milwaukee, 9 Oct. 1861, died at Louisville, Ky., 4 Nov. 1862.

Ole Storland, Madison, 29 Dec. 1861, moved to E in May 1863, discharged 20 Dec. 1864.

Ole Svendson, Norway, 6 Nov. 1861, discharged 31 Dec. 1864.

Samuel Svendson, Norway, 7 Nov. 1861, died at Chattanooga 28 Nov. 1863.

Herman Berg, 2 Dec. 1861, taken prisoner at Bardstown, Ky., transferred to Veterans Reserve Corps April 1863, discharged.

Martin Amundson, 6 Nov. 1861, Corporal, to Veterans Reserve Corps, sick, discharged 1 Dec. 1863.

Co. D:

Albert Skofstad, Waterford, 14 Jan. 1861, First Lieutenant, Captain, 20 April 1862, discharged 2 March 1864.

Lewis G. Nelson, Oconomowoc, 10 Dec. 1861, First Sergeant, First Lieutenant, 20 April 1862, Adjutant 27 May 1863, Captain 1 Aug. 1864, discharged 13 Feb. 1865.

Nels G. Tufte, Pine Lake, 10 Dec. 1861, Corporal, Sergeant, Second Lieutenant. 27 May 1863, First Lieutenant. 25 Aug. 1864, discharged 13 Feb. 1865.

Christian E. Tanberg, Oconomowoc, 14 Jan. 1862, First Lieutenant, 27 May 1863, discharged 31 Oct. 1863.

Rollef Amundson, Pine Lake, 31 Oct. 1861, discharged 13 Feb. 1865.

Anders Amundson Bolstad, Springdale, 22 Jan. 1862, moved to Veterans Reserve Corps 10 July 1864, discharged 25 Jan. 1865.

Martin Anderson, Butte Des Moete, 25 Nov. 1861, Corporal. Died at Bowling Green 4 Dec. 1862.

Daniel Anderson, Strong Prairie, 27 Dec. 1861, discharged 15 Feb. 1865.

Arne Arneson Eldebakken, Springdale, 15 Nov. 1861, discharged 15 Feb. 1865.

Ole M. Bendikson, Columbus, 27 Nov. 1861, Corporal. Sergeant, discharged 13 Feb. 1865.

John Bever, New Lisbon, 28 Oct. 1861, discharged sick 10 April 1863.

Christian Bjorneby, Strong Prairie, 28 Nov. 1861, died at Madison 17 Feb. 1862.

Knut Bjorgulfson, Oconomowoc, 17 Jan. 1862, discharged sick 18 Dec. 1862.

Iver A. Brandt, Oconomowoc, Corporal, Sergeant, First Sergeant, Second Lieutenant 31 Aug. 1864. Discharged 13 Feb. 1865.

Andrew Clement, Waupun, 5 Oct. 1861, Sergeant, First Lieutenant, Co. K, 10 Oct. 1862.

Andrew A. Dahl, Lewiston, 2 Dec. 1861, Corporal, Sergeant, discharged 13 Feb. 1865.

Andrew J. Dutton, Waupun, 14 Nov. 1861, died at Nashville, TN, 19 April 1864.

Martin Fjeldstad, Waupun, 23 Oct. 1861, Sergeant. Died at Bowling Green, Ky., 18 Nov. 1862.

Ole Fredrickson, Stoughton, 15 Dec. 1861, moved to H, 13 Feb. 1865, veterinarian, to K, 24th Infantry, discharged 24 Nov. 1865.

John Gulbrandson, New Lisbon, 28 Oct. 1861, discharged 13 Feb. 1865.

John Haldorson, Chicago, see Co. A.

Martin Halvorson, New Lisbon, 21 Oct. 1861, veterinarian, moved to H, 24th Infantry, 9 March 1865, discharged 1 May 1865.

Halvor Halvorson, New Lisbon, 28 Oct. 1861, fell at Chickamauga 19 Sept. 1863.

John Halvorson, Oconomowoc, 30 Oct. 1861, discharged sick 22 Oct. 1862.

Halvor J. Halvorson, Oconomowoc, 30 Oct. 1861, musician, discharged 1 Feb. 1863.

Christian Halvorson, New Lisbon, 4 Nov. 1861, Corporal, discharged 2 Nov. 1864.

Hans Halvorson, Neenah, 5 Nov. 1861, discharged 25 March 1865.

Halvor O. Halvorson, Kilbourn City, 30 Oct. 1861, Corporal, discharged 4 March 1863.

Gutorm Halvorson, Moscow, 30 Oct. 1861, discharged sick 10 May 1862.

John B. Hoveland, Oconomowoc, 11 Nov. 1861, Corporal. Died at St. Louis 17 March 1862.

John Hoyer, Strong Prairie, 28 Oct. 1861, Corporal, discharged 13 Feb. 1865.

Christian Ingebretson, New Lisbon, 2 Nov. 1861, died at Madison 18 Feb. 1862.

Isaac Isaacson, Pine Lake, 9 Dec. 1861, moved to Veterans Reserve Corps 15 Feb. 1864.

Hans L. Jacobson, Pine Lake, 30 Oct. 1861, died at Pine Lake, Wis., 3 Feb. 1862.

Jacob L. Jacobson, Oconomowoc, 25 Nov. 1861, discharged 13 Feb. 1865.

Andrew L. Jacobson, Oconomowoc, 25 Nov. 1861, died at Chattanooga, 5 Nov. 1863.

Ole Jacobson, New Lisbon, 23 Dec. 1861, Corporal, died in Andersonville Prison 15 June 1864.

Lars Jenson, Oconomowoc, 30 Oct. 1861, discharged 13 Feb. 1865.

Iver Joanson, Oconomowoc, 30 Oct. 1861, died at Jackson, Tenn., 4 Oct. 1862.

Engebret Johnson, Oconomowoc, 25 Oct. 1861, died at Nashville 2 Dec. 1862.

Nels Johnson, Oconomowoc, 25 Oct. 1861, Corporal, Sergeant, promoted Sergeant Major 15 Oct. 1864, transferred to the staff, 20 Nov. 1864.

Peder Johnson, Oconomowoc, 5 Feb. 1864, discharged 25 May 1865.

Andrew M. Johnson, Chicago, 27 Dec. 1861, discharged sick 14 Feb. 1862.

Svend Johnson, Chicago, 25 Oct. 1861, discharged 15 July 1862.

Hans Kammen, Springdale, 9 Jan. 1862, discharged 8 July 1862, sick.

Frederick Kammen, Springdale, 9 Jan. 1862, discharged sick 15 July 1862.

Ole Kittelson, Chicago, 12 Feb. 1862, discharged 13 Feb. 1865.

Knut Kittelson, Leland, 25 Feb. 1862, moved to Veterans Reserve Corps 14 Oct. 1862.

Syvert Larson, Neenah, 5 Nov. 1861, discharged 13 Feb. 1865.

Halvor A. Lee, Springdale, 14 Jan. 1862, Corporal, discharged sick 1 March 1863.

Ole A. Lee, Springdale, 10 Feb. 1862, fell at Stone River 31 Dec. 1862.

Herman Lundgreen, Winneshiek Co., Iowa, 30 Sept. 1861, see Co. A.

Andrew Mikkelson, Lewiston, 25 Nov. 1861, wagoner, discharged 13 Feb. 1865.

Julius Monson, Oconomowoc, 25 Nov. 1861, Sergeant, discharged 29 Oct. 1862.

Anton Monson, Oconomowoc, 4 Dec. 1863, moved from D to I, 13th Infantry, sick at discharge.

Halvor Museus, Oconomowoc, 8 Jan. 1862, discharged 13 Feb. 1865.

Hans Museus, Oconomowoc, 8 Jan. 1862, discharged 7 Aug. 1862.

Jacob Nelson, Bad Ax, 16 Oct. 1861, discharged 14 Feb. 1863.

Nels Nelson, Spring Prairie, 23 Nov. 1861, fell at Stone River, Tenn., 31 Dec. 1862.

Knut Olson, Chicago, 1 Oct. 1861, died at Chattanooga 1 Feb. 1864.

Nels Olson, Oconomowoc, 25 Oct. 1861, died at Jackson, Miss., 22 Sept. 1862.

Nils S. Olson, Pine Lake, 8 Dec. 1861, discharged 15 July 1862.

Ole Olson Hoiseth, Springdale, 15 Dec. 1861, died at Jackson, Miss., 28 Sept. 1862.

Halvor Olson, Springdale, 14 Jan. 1862, discharged 14 Oct. 1864.

Thomas Olson, Moscow, 11 Feb. 1862, discharged 13 Feb. 1865.

Hans Pederson, New Lisbon, 28 Oct. 1861, died at Columbus 23 Sept. 1862.

Peder Pederson, Oconomowoc, 30 Oct. 1861, died at Nashville, Tenn., 8 Dec. 1862.

Elias Peterson, Portage City, 27 Nov. 1861, died at Portage, Wis., 10 June 1862.

Torger Peterson, Scandinavia, 30 Oct. 1861, from Co. I, discharged 13 Feb. 1865.

Simon Peterson, ?, 28 Dec. 1861, discharged 13 Feb. 1865.

Erick Reierson, Chicago, 3 Dec. 1861, discharged 14 Feb. 1862.

Edwin C. Shaw, Waupun, 8 Nov. 1861, Sergeant, First Sergeant, discharged 6 Oct. 1862.

Lewis Solberg, Chicago, 30 Sept. 1861, moved to Veterans Reserve Corps, 1 Sept. 1863.

Ole Sorenson, Waupun, 23 Oct. 1861, died at Danville, Ky., 6 Oct. 1862.

Jens Strom, Oconomowoc, 8 Jan. 1862, discharged sick 23 Oct. 1862.

Thomas Thompson, Spring Prairie, 11 Nov. 1861, discharged 13 Feb. 1865.

Nils M. Tobiason, Oconomowoc, 11 Nov. 1861, Corporal. Died in prison in Richmond, Va., 2 Feb. 1864.

Lars Tallakson, Portage, 28 Nov. 1861, died at Chattanooga 4 Dec. 1864.

Sven Torgerson, Oconomowoc, 11 Nov. 1861, discharged 13 Feb. 1865.

John Warp, New Lisbon, 28 Oct. 1861, discharged 13 Feb. 1865.

Thomas Hollan, reported deserted.

Christian Schow, deserted.

Co. E:

John Ingemundsen, Neshonoc, 29 Dec. 1861, Captain, fell at Stone River 30 Dec. 1862.

Henry Hauff, Stoughton, 14 Dec. 1861, First Lieutenant, Co. G, Adjutant Captain, 8 May 1863, fell at Chickamauga 19 Sept. 1863.

Torkel A. Rossing, Wiota, 11 Dec. 1861, Sergeant Major, 1 July 1862, First Lieutenant 3 Sept. 1862, Captain 7 April 1864, discharged 20 Dec. 1864. Lives in Bode, Iowa.

Iver William Tjentland, Moscow, 9 Dec. 1861, First Lieutenant, discharged 8 Sept. 1862.

John N. Brown, Christiana, 17 April 1861, Co. K, 3rd Wisconsin Infantry, Second Lieutenant 10 Dec. 1862, discharged 9 April 1863.

Peter W. Chantland, Primrose, 8 Dec. 1861, First Sergeant, Second Lieutenant, 9 April 1863. Discharged 13 Nov. 1863, died in Fort Dodge, Iowa, in 1905.

Simon Amundson, Coon Prairie, 23 Nov. 1861, Corporal, died a prisoner in Richmond.

Iver Anderson, Preston, 7 Nov. 1861, fell at New Hope Church 27 May 1864.

Peter Anderson, Preston, 7 Nov. 1861, died at Washington, D.C. 11 Sept. 1864.

Andrew Anderson, Neshowoc, 5 Jan. 1864, to Co. I, 13th Infantry, ill at discharge.

Lawrence Arneson, Hamberg, 13 Jan. 1861, died of wounds at Atlanta, Ga., 22 June 1864.

William Bergerson, York, 2 Nov. 1861, died at Nashville, Tenn., 9 Nov. 1863.

Nicolai Bestrup, La Crosse, 8 Dec. 1861, Corporal, to Veterans Reserve Corps, 1 Sept. 1863.

Halvor O. Brenden, York, 17 Dec. 1861, discharged 20 Dec. 1864.

Andrew S. Bronken, La Crosse, 24 Feb. 1864, moved to H, 20 Dec. 1864.

Ole Christopherson, Berry, 8 Dec. 1861, died at Cincinnati, Ohio, 6 Sept. 1862.

Even Christopherson, Ettrick, 10 Feb. 1864, Sergeant, moved to I, 13th Infantry, died at San Antonio, Tex., 15 Oct. 1865.

Gudbrand Dahl, Moscow, 31 Dec. 1861, discharged 20 Dec. 1864.

Ole E. Dahl, Springdale, 4 Jan. 1862, died at Island No. 10, 30 April 1862.

Torger Erickson, Coon, 25 Oct. 1861, discharged 20 Dec. 1864.

Lewis Erickson, Portland, 12 Nov. 1861, discharged 9 June 1862.

Torbjørn Erickson, Moscow, 28 Nov. 1861, died at Edgefield Jct., Tenn., 15 Nov. 1862.

Peter Erickson, Viroqua, 16 Dec. 1861, musician. Died at Richmond 1 Dec. 1863.

Ole Erickson, Arendahl, Minn., 18 Dec. 1861, died at Nashville, Tenn., 14 Feb. 1864.

Ole Erickson, Sr., La Crosse, 26 Feb. 1864, fell at New Hope Church 27 May 1864.

Ole Erickson, Jr., Onalaska, 26 Feb. 1864, fell at New Hope Church 27 May 1864.

Helge Espelie, York, 25 Nov. 1861, discharged sick 6 Aug. 1862.

Syver K. Foss, St. Peter, Minn., 5 Oct. 1861, discharged sick 15 July 1863.

Gunder Gunderson, Primrose, 12 Nov. 1861, Sergeant. Discharged 20 Dec. 1864.

Christian Gunhus, Primrose, 13 Dec. 1861, died at Green Co., Wis., 4 Aug. 1862.

Edvin Hadley, Perry, 10 Oct. 1861, Corporal. Fell at New Hope Church 27 May 1864.

Lars T. Halling, Spring Valley, 12 Nov. 1861, discharged 23 June 1863.

Ole Halvorson, La Crosse, 11 Dec. 1861, died at Bowling Green, Ky., 24 Sept. 1862.

Jens Hanson, Onalaska, 23 Oct. 1861, discharged sick 6 Aug. 1862.

Neri Hanson, York, 18 Oct. 1861, discharged 20 Dec. 1864.

Nils Hanson, Neshonoc, 14 Nov. 1861, discharged 30 April 1864.

Hans Hanson, Moscow, 25 Nov. 1861, died at Chattanooga, Tenn., 12 Dec. 1863.

Anders Hanson, Freeborn Co., Minn., 27 Nov. 1861, Corporal, discharged sick 9 March 1863.

Anstein Hanson, Neshonoc, 29 Feb. 1864, moved to I, 13th Infantry, discharged 24 Nov. 1865.

John Hutland, Freeman, 4 Nov. 1861, sick, discharged in St. Louis.

John Hoff, Hamburg, 26 Nov. 1861, moved to Veterans Reserve Corps 1 Sept. 1864.

Peter Homlebek, Primrose, 14 Dec. 1861, died at Bowling Green, Ky., 12 Oct. 1862.

John N. Hovrud, Perry, 23 Nov. 1861, discharged 20 Dec. 1864.

Ole K. Hovrud, Perry, 24 Dec. 1861, discharged sick 16 Oct. 1862.

Lars Ingebretson, Hamburg, 1 Dec. 1861, died at Chickamauga 21 Dec. 1863.

Halvor Jenson, York, 1 Oct. 1861, discharged sick at Nashville, Tenn., 12 Jan. 1863.

John Johnson, Onalaska, 23 Oct. 1861, died at New Albany, Ind., 14 July 1861.

Guldbrand Johnson, York, 27 Oct. 1861, died at Cairo, Ill., 3 Oct. 1862.

John M. Johnson, Primrose, 1 Nov. 1861, discharged 20 Dec. 1864.

Andrew Johnson, Primrose, 6 Nov. 1861, Corporal. Died at Albany, Ind., 18 March 1863.

Peter Johnson, Sr., Primrose, 20 Dec. 1861, discharged 20 Dec. 1864.

Peter Johnson, Jr., Coon, 5 Dec. 1861, died at Bowling Green 11 Jan. 1863.

Knut Johnson, Viroqua, 16 Dec. 1861, discharged 20 Dec. 1864.

Lewis C. Johnson, Buffalo City, 22 Feb. 1864, moved to I, 13th Infantry. Discharged 24 Nov. 1865.

John Jørgenson, Perry, 18 Jan. 1862, discharged 20 Dec. 1864.

Simon Jørgenson, Ettrick, 10 Feb. 1864, moved to I, 13th Infantry, sick at discharge.

Edwin Julson, Perry, 8 Nov. 1861, Corporal. Died at Chattanooga, Tenn., 2 Jan. 1864.

James Julson, Perry, 8 Nov. 1861, discharged 20 Dec. 1864.

Amund Kelsevig, York, 29 Nov. 1861, discharged 20 Dec. 1864.

Ole Kjostenson, Coon, 22 Nov. 1861, sent to 8th Battery Light Artillery, 29 July 1863, absent at discharge.

Henry Knudson, Moscow, 2 Dec. 1861, moved to 4th U.S. Cavalry 24 Nov. 1862.

Thore Knudson, Perry, 7 Dec. 1861, musician, discharged 20 Dec. 1864.

Ole Larson, Neshonoc, 26 Feb. 1864, died at Nashville 10 Dec. 1864.

Jacob J. Lee, Perry, 20 Nov. 1861, moved to Veterans Reserve Corps 28 April 1864.

Christopher H. Lee, York, 5 Dec. 1861, died at Murfreesboro, 17 Jan. 1863.

Ole Lenvig, Rushford, Minn., 18 Dec. 1861, Corporal, Sergeant, fell at New Hope Church 27 May 1864.

Hans Lenvig, Rushford, 18 Dec. 1861, fell at Rocky Face Ridge, Ga., 1 May 1864.

Henry Lewis, Perry, 28 Oct. 1861, Corporal, discharged sick 9 April 1863.

Ole Lindbo, York, 24 Oct. 1861, died at Nashville 27 Aug. 1863.

Tobias Logan, Moscow, 28 Oct. 1861, discharged sick 6 Aug. 1862.

Guldbrand Lokke, York, 10 Nov. 1861, fell at New Hope Church 27 May 1864.

Ole H. Milestun, Perry, 23 Dec. 1861, fell at Chickamauga 20 Sept. 1863.

Anders O. Moe, Madison, 23 Oct. 1861, from Co. C, discharged sick 19 May 1863.

August Moller, Rushford, 12 Nov. 1861, discharged 20 Dec. 1864.

Nels Nelson, La Crosse, 25 Aug. 1862, moved to 24th WI, discharged ?

John Nelson, Primrose, 1 Nov. 1861, died at Iuka, Miss., sick 31 Aug. 1862.

Osmund Olson, York, 23 Oct. 1861, moved to Veterans Reserve Corps, 26 Sept. 1863.

Lars Olson, Neshowoc, 11 Nov. 1861, discharged sick 10 Oct. 1862.

Charles Olson, Buchanan, 14 Nov. 1861, died at Nashville 14 Jan. 1863.

Rolin Olson, Argyle, 8 Dec. 1861, Sergeant, 1 Sept. 1863. Discharged 16 Dec. 1864.

Kittel Olson, Ridgeway, IA, 16 Jan. 1861, died at Stevenson, Ala., 10 Oct. 1863.

Peter Olson, Greenfield, 26 Feb. 1864, fell at New Hope Church 27 May 1864.

John Peters, Primrose, 11 Nov. 1861, Sergeant, discharged 20 Dec. 1864. Appointed Second Lieutenant, 1867 from 1863.

Andrew Peterson, Ziyette, 25 Dec. 1861, died at Bardstown, Ky., 6 Nov. 1862.

Borre Peterson, La Crosse, 26 Dec. 1862, died at Louisville, Ky., 10 May 1864.

Iver Ramsaas, Viroqua, 16 Dec. 1861, died at Chattanooga, Tenn., 1 Dec. 1863.

Mads Rosum, Argyle, 15 Nov. 1861, wounded and taken prisoner at New Hope Church 27 May 1864, died in prison.

Ostein Rulland, Portland, 5 Dec. 1861, discharged sick 11 Oct. 1862.

Christian Ruste, Blue Mounds, 9 Jan. 1862, died at Island No. 10, 2 May 1862.

Asbjørn Sachariason, Rushford, Minn., 18 Dec. 1861, discharged 20 Dec. 1864.

Aadne Sandmark, 19 Dec. 1861, discharged sick 16 July 1862.

Christian Simonson, Gule, 26 Feb. 1864, moved to I, 13th Infantry, discharged 24 Nov. 1865.

John O. Sorum, Jackson, 14 Nov. 1861, discharged sick 3 Feb. 1863.

Johannes H. Stokke, Hamburg, 5 Dec. 1861, discharged 20 Dec. 1864.

Thor P. Sloan, La Crosse, 11 Dec. 1861, taken prisoner at Stone River 31 Dec. 1862.[2]

Ole Steensland, Moscow, 28 Oct. 1861, discharged 30 May 1865.

Ole Storland, Ridgeway, IA, 24 Dec. 1861, from Co. C, 1 May 1862, discharged 20 Dec. 1864.

Bryndal Syverson, York, 2 Nov. 1861, discharged sick 9 April 1863.

Lars Thomaseth, Moscow, 16 Dec. 1861, died at Jackson, Tenn., 11 Sept. 1862.

Thomas C. Thompson, Preston, Minn., 25 Nov. 1861, Sergeant, discharged sick 23 March 1863.

Christian Thompson, Spring Grove, 25 Jan. 1862, died in Andersonville, Ga., 1 June 1864.

Job Tjerans, Primrose, 1 Nov. 1861, died at Murfreesboro 15 May 1863.

Johannes Tysdal, Perry, 23 Oct. 1861, discharged 27 Jan. 1865.

Co. F:

Charles Gustafson, Manitowoc, 13 Dec. 1861, Captain, Major 21 Feb. 1865, discharged 14 June 1865.

Thor Simonson, Christian Co., Ill., First Lieutenant 10 Jan. 1862, Captain 18 Feb. 1865, discharged 14 Jan. 1865.

Svend Samuelson, Eaton, 11 Jan. 1862, Second Lieutenant, discharged 15 Nov. 1863.

Einar Anderson, 25 Dec. 1861, discharged 20 Dec. 1864.

Anders Berg, 15 Dec. 1861 (?)

Johannes Bergman, Manitowoc Co., 27 Nov. 1861, discharged sick 21 April 1863.

Svend Bjorgason, Manitowoc Co., 5 Nov. 1861, discharged 12 July 1864.

Peter Bloom, Manitowoc Co., 10 Nov. 1861, discharged sick 22 Jan. 1863.

Ole Christianson, Manitowoc Co., 18 Nov. 1861, discharged 13 Jan. 1865.

Hans Christenson, Brown Co., 18 Nov. 1861, fell at New Hope Church 27 May 1864.

Ole L. Christianson, Iowa Co., 20 Dec. 1861, died at Island No. 10, 26 May 1862.

Olaus H. Dahl (?), 4 Dec. 1861, discharged sick 9 Oct. 1862.

Sigbjørn Edmunds, Dodgeville, 2 May 1864, moved to I, 13th Infantry, 13 Jan. 1865, died at Green Lake, Tex., 6 Sept. 1865.

Helge C. Ellingboe, Manitowoc Co., 8 Nov. 1861, discharged sick 13 Oct. 1863.

Elling Ellingson, (?) 25 Dec. 1861, discharged 10 Jan. 1865.

Knut Erickson, Manitowoc Co., 3 Oct. 1861, discharged for sickness from hospital at Cincinnati, Ohio, Reinstated Co. F, 26th Infantry, 4 Jan. 1864, moved to F, 3rd Infantry, 10 June 1865, discharged 18 July 1865.

Nels I. Gilbert, Manitowoc Co., 2 Oct. 1861, Sergeant, First Sergeant, promoted First Lieutenant, Co. A, 8 Oct. 1864. See Co. A.

John Flack, 25 Oct. 1861, fell at Stone River 31 Dec. 1862.

Gudbrand Gilberts, Manitowoc Co., 17 Oct. 1861 (?)

Tosten J. Gilberts, Manitowoc Co., 10 Nov. 1861, discharged 13 Jan. 1865.

Even Geraldson, Manitowoc Co., 21 Oct. 1861, Corporal, discharged sick 5 Nov. 1863.

Ole Gunstenson, Manitowoc Co., 4 Jan. 1862, taken prisoner at Chickamauga.

Ole Haldorson, Manitowoc Co., 5 Feb. 1862, died in Andersonville Prison 25 July 1864.

Nils Halvorson, Manitowoc Co., 23 Oct. 1861, discharged 13 Jan. 1865.

Bjørn Halvorson, Madison, 24 Feb. 1862, died at Chattanooga, Tenn., 15 Dec. 1863.

Hans Hanson, Manitowoc Co., 23 Oct. 1861, died at Nashville, Tenn., 1 Oct. 1862.

Knut Iverson, Door Co., 18 Jan. 1862, fell at Stone River 21 Dec. 1862.

Ole B. Johnson, Manitowoc Co., 7 Oct. 1861, Corporal, Sergeant, prisoner at discharge, commissioned Second Lieutenant 15 Nov. 1863.

John P. Johnson, Manitowoc Co., 19 Oct. 1861, Sergeant, discharged sick 11 Feb. 1863.

Gunder Jørgenson, Manitowoc Co., 5 Nov. 1861, died at Island No. 10, 4 May 1862.

Erick Knudson, Manitowoc Co., 1 Oct. 1861, Corporal, died at Cincinnati, Ohio, 2 Aug. 1862.

Ole Knudson Kirkeberg, Manitowoc Co., 28 Oct. 1861, musician, discharged sick 16 Feb. 1863.

Ole N. Knudson, (?) 2 Dec. 1861, fell at Stone River, 30 Dec. 1862.

Gullick Knudson, Manitowoc Co., 28 Dec. 1861, moved to Veterans Reserve Corps, 1 Sept. 1863.

Torry Larson, Manitowoc Co., 21 Jan. 1861, wagoner, brevet Captain, 19 Sept. 1863, discharged 13 Jan. 1863.

Christen J. Larson, Manitowoc Co., 3 Dec. 1861, Corporal Sergeant, died at Louisville, Ky., 24 Nov. 1862.

Michel Larson, (?) 5 Dec. 1861, discharged 18 Jan. 1865.

Hans H. Lerum, Bad Ax Co., 23 Nov. 1861, discharged sick 6 Oct. 1862.

Andrew Michelson, Manitowoc Co., 20 Oct. 1861?

Albert Mikkelson, Madison, 21 Jan. 1862, discharged 13 Jan. 1865.

Reinert G.T. Morbeck, Manitowoc, 17 Nov. 1861, discharged sick 17 June 1862.

Christian O. Morbeck, Door Co., 22 Feb. 1862, Corporal, moved to Co. H, discharged 13 March 1865.

Trond Knudson, Manitowoc, 21 Oct. 1861, discharged sick 2 Jan. 1863.

Carl Nielson, Door Co., 24 Feb. 1862, discharged sick 6 Aug. 1862.

Ole Nelson (?), 20 Dec. 1861, discharged for wounds 2 Dec. 1863.

Ole B. Olson, Manitowoc Co., 25 Oct. 1861, Second Lieutenant 7 April 1862, discharged 13 Jan. 1865.

Gustav Olson, 26 Oct. 1861 (?)

Albert Olson, Iowa Co., 26 Nov. 1861, Corporal, died at Knoxville 17 March 1864.

Thomas Olson (?), 20 Dec. 1861, died at Murfreesboro 10 March 1863.

Knut Olson (?), 20 Dec. 1861, prisoner at discharge.

Gudmund Olson Dalebek, Liberty, 31 Dec. 1861, discharged sick 9 Oct. 1862.

Ole S. Olson, Manitowoc Co., 8 Jan. 1862, wounded at discharge.

Ole W. Olson, Manitowoc Co., 8 Jan. 1862, Corporal Sergeant, prisoner at discharge.

Ole Olson, Cato, 18 Feb. 1864, Corporal, moved to I, 13th Infantry, discharged 30 June 1865.

Ole H. Olson, Cato, Manitowoc Co., 20 Feb. 1864, moved to I, 13th Infantry, detached at discharge.

Tosten O. Oppen, Manitowoc Co., 9 Jan. 1862, died at Columbus 2 Sept. 1862.

Salve Olafson, Manitowoc Co., 5 Oct. 1861, discharged 10 Jan. 1865.

Gilbert Paulson, Manitowoc Co., 25 Oct. 1861, Corporal, died at Danville, Va., 1 April 1864.

Ole Rundberg, Manitowoc Co., 21 Oct. 1861, died at Louisville, Ky., 4 Nov. 1862.

William Speckerman, Manitowoc Co., 8 Nov. 1861, died at Nashville, Tenn., 21 Nov. 1863.

Knut Syverson, Manitowoc Co., 8 Jan. 1862, died at Island No. 10, 10 April 1862.

Andrew Thompson, Manitowoc, 31 Oct. 1861, Corporal, fell at Bald Knob 24 June 1864.

Thomas Thompson, (?), 15 Dec. 1861, discharged sick 5 Oct. 1862.

Ole A. Thompson, Door Co., 19 Feb. 1862, moved to H, discharged 13 March 1865.

Tholak Tholackson, Dane Co., 22 Oct. 1861, moved to Veterans Reserve Corps 7 Jan. 1864, discharged 7 Nov. 1864.

Torger Torgerson, Door Co., 22 Feb. 1862, died at Murfreesboro 3 April 1863.

Tove Torkilson, (?), 26 Nov. 1861, discharged wounded 3 April 1863.

Knut Torrison Dovre, Manitowoc Co., 5 Nov. 1861, Sergeant, wagoner, sick at discharge.

Christian Tostenson, Manitowoc Co., 21 Oct. 1861, died at Louisville, Ky., 15 Nov. 1862.

Ole Torstenson, Manitowoc Co., 16 Nov. 1861, sick at discharge.

Gilbert Thronson, Manitowoc, 5 Nov. 1861, discharged 18 Aug. 1862, died at Corinth, Miss., 2 Sept. 1862.

Ole K. Vigen, Cato, Manitowoc Co., 1 Jan. 1862, discharged 13 Jan. 1865.

Peter Vinson, Chicago, 10 Oct. 1861, moved to U.S. Cavalry 27 Nov. 1862, died at Soldiers Home 1911.

Mads Williamson, Manitowoc Co., 5 Nov. 1861.

William Wilson, 8 Nov. 1861, discharged sick 26 April 1863.

Co. G:

Henry Hauff, Stoughton, 14 Dec. 1861, Captain. See Co. E.

Charles B. Nelson, Beloit, 27 Sept. 1861, First Sergeant, First Lieutenant 25 Jan. 1863, discharged 13 Jan. 1865.

John M. Brown, Christiana, 1 Nov. 1862, from Sergeant in Co. K, 3rd Regiment. Infantry Wisconsin. Moved 16 Dec. 1862, to Co. E. Died at La Crosse 1864.

Arne Amundson, Clinton, 8 Oct. 1861, Corporal, discharged 18 April 1865.

Anton Anderson, Clinton, 6 Oct. 1861, died at Island No. 10, 31 May 1862.

Christopher Anderson, Martel, 12 Nov. 1861, died at Island No. 10, 20 May 1862.

Hans Anderson, Martel, 12 Nov. 1861, died at Island No. 10, 10 June 1862.

Lewis Anderson, Martel, 5 Dec. 1861, discharged sick 25 Sept. 1864.

Ole Anderson, Wyoming, 4 Dec. 1861, discharged sick 30 Jan. 1863.

John Anderson, Perry, 8 Jan. 1862, discharged sick 20 Oct. 1862.

Lars Anderson, East Troy, 16 Jan. 1864, to Co. I, 13th Infantry at discharge.

Fredrick Boyeson, Madison, 4 Jan. 1862, Sergeant, discharged 13 Jan. 1865.

Olaus Broness, Belville, 11 Nov. 1861, died in Andersonville Prison 20 Jan. 1864.

Albert G. Brown, Beloit, 5 Oct. 1861, discharged 13 Jan. 1865.

Matias Christenson, Clinton, 3 Oct. 1861, died at Island No. 10, 25 May 1862.

John Christianson, Viroqua, 7 Nov. 1861, died at Columbus, Ky., 28 Sept. 1862.

Elias Christopherson, Primrose, 26 Nov. 1861, discharged 13 Jan. 1865.

Ole Colby, Primrose, 3 Jan. 1862, discharged 13 Jan. 1865.

Joseph L. Deremo, Beloit, 11 Dec. 1861, discharged 13 Jan. 1865.

Christian Erickson, Moscow, 13 Nov. 1861, died in Atlanta 12 July 1864.

Gudrick Erickson, Blue Mounds, 16 Dec. 1861, Corporal, discharged 13 Jan. 1865.

Nils Erickson, Mitomen, 26 Feb. 1864, moved to Co. I, 13th Infantry, discharged 24 Nov. 1865.

John Hanson, Belville, 15 Oct. 1861 (?)

Hans Hanson, Beloit, 22 Nov. 1861, Corporal, discharged 13 Jan. 1865.

Henry Hendrickson, Primrose, 11 Nov. 1861, Corporal, discharged 13 Jan. 1865.

Simon Hovland, Oxford, 7 Jan. 1862, discharged sick 10 Jan. 1863.

John Hovland, Spring Valley, 4 Jan. 1862, veterinarian, moved to Hancock Corps as Johan Jenson, Corporal, 13 Feb. 1865, discharged 13 Feb. 1866.

George Johnson, Beloit, 28 Sept. 1861, Sergeant, First Sergeant, discharged 13 Jan. 1865, commissioned Second Lieutenant, time of service counted from 1 Oct. 1862.

James Johnson, Chilton, 13 Oct. 1861, Corporal, discharged 13 Jan. 1865.

John H. Johnson, Primrose, 4 Nov. 1861, Sergeant, discharged 13 Jan. 1865.

George Johnson, New Centerville, 11 Nov. 1861, fell at Resaca, Ga., 14 May 1864.

Ole Johnson, Martel, 6 Dec. 1861, discharged 13 Jan. 1865.

Knut Knutson Skrautvold, Avon, 16 Oct. 1861, discharged sick 10 Oct. 1862.

Hans Olson Lanfelt, Clinton, died at Island No. 10, 10 Oct. 1862.

Torstein Larson, Coon Prairie, 12 Nov. 1861, discharged 13 Jan. 1865.

Erick Larson, Dodgeville, 4 Dec. 1861, fell at New Hope Church 27 May 1864.

Hans Larson, Dodgeville, 4 Dec. 1861, Corporal, discharged 13 Jan. 1865.

Lars Larson, Martel, 4 Jan. 1862, discharged 14 May 1862.

Nils K. Luraas, Springdale, 2 Nov. 1861, discharged 13 Jan. 1865.

Iver O. Myhre, Clinton, 3 Oct. 1861, Corporal, discharged 13 Jan. 1865.

Edgar A. Nelson, Beloit, 26 Nov. 1861, discharged 14 Aug. 1862.

Haakon Nelson, Madison, 10 Jan. 1862, died at Island No. 10, 2 June 1862.

Lewis Ogleson, Beloit, 11 Dec. 1861, discharged sick 1 Aug. 1862.

Helge Alfson, Onalaska, 20 Nov. 1861, died at Columbus, Ky., 28 April 1863.

Hans Olson, Beloit, 28 Sept. 1861, discharged sick 11 Aug. 1862.

Knut Olson, Beloit, 1 Oct. 1861, discharged sick 11 Aug. 1862.

Erick Olson, Coon Prairie, 6 Dec. 1861, sick at discharge.

Asmund Peterson, Martell, 11 Nov. 1861, discharged 13 Jan. 1865.

Christopher Peterson, Monroe, 11 Nov. 1861, discharged sick 11 Aug. 1862.

Samuel Sandahl, Beloit, 28 Sept. 1861, Corporal, died at Chattanooga 17 Nov. 1863.

John L. Sether, Moscow, 20 Nov. 1861, died at Island No. 10, 18 June 1862.

Ole Stenson, Beloit, 28 Sept. 1861, discharged sick 10 Oct. 1862.

Bernt Swenson, Beloit, 2 Oct. 1861, discharged 13 Jan. 1865.

Lewis Swenson, Clinton, 7 Jan. 1862, Corporal, discharged 1 Jan. 1865, died at Montevideo 1906.

John Thompson, Moscow, 4 Nov. 1861, drowned in Miss., April 1862.

Oscar Thompson, Beloit, fell at New Hope Church 27 May 1864.

Henry Thompson, Dodgeville, 4 Dec. 1861, discharged 13 Jan. 1865.

Knut Thoreson, Clinton, 25 Oct. 1861, discharged sick 11 Aug. 1862.

Fingar Thoreson, Newark, 9 Jan. 1864, moved to Co. I, 13th Infantry, sick at discharge.

Gilbert Tosten, Clinton, 11 Dec. 1861, Corporal, died at Island No. 10, 30 Oct. 1862.

Hans Tollefson, Martell, 11 Nov. 1861, sick at discharge.

Jens Tonneson, Martell, 4 Jan. 1862, moved to Veterans Reserve Corps 30 April 1864.

Torger Torgerson, Beloit, 28 Sept. 1861, Corporal, died in Andersonville as a prisoner 24 Sept. 1864.

Anders Torgerson, Sr., Martell, 5 Dec. 1861, died at Island No. 10, 18 May 1862.

Anders Torgerson, Jr., Madison, 14 Jan. 1862.

Hellick Tostenson, Beloit, 8 Sept. 1861, discharged 13 Jan. 1865.

Anders Tveit, Moscow, 9 Nov. 1861, discharged 13 Jan. 1865.

Ole Wold, Clinton, 21 Oct. 1861.

Chas. Black, Coon Prairie, 6 Nov. 1861, discharged 13 Jan. 1865.

Co. H:

Knut J. Sime, Cambridge, Captain. 17 Jan. 1862, discharged 3 May 1862.

George Wilson, Madison, Second Lieutenant, Co. B, promoted, Captain 3 May 1862, Major 11 March 1863.

Andrew Brown, Chicago, 14 Dec. 1861, First Lieutenant 7 Jan. 1862, Captain 27 May 1863, discharged 10 Feb. 1865.

E. Williams Cornelius, Cambridge, 3 March 1862, Second Lieutenant 10 Jan. 1862, First Lieutenant 27 May 1863, discharged 13 Feb. 1865.

John L. Johnson, Columbia Co., 17 Jan. 1862, discharged 15 May 1862, died at Hillsboro, N.D., 1910.

Martin A. Erickson, Sparta, 25 Oct. 1861, First Sergeant-Major 18 May 1862, Second Lieutenant 27 May 1863, discharged 20 April 1865.

Gabriel Ager, Freeborn Co., Minn., 29 Nov. 1861, died at Jefferson Barracks, Mo., 28 Aug. 1862.

Thorwald Anderson, Houston Co., Minn.., 13 Jan. 1862, discharged 5 May 1862.

Ole Anfinson, Lodi, 2 Oct. 1861, moved to Veterans Reserve Corps 25 March 1864, discharged 25 Sept. 1864.

Lars N. Berg, Deerfield, 22 Oct. 1861, Corporal, died at Island No. 10, Tenn., 22 May 1862.

Stener E. Bilstad, Christiana, 21 Oct. 1861, Sergeant, First Sergeant, discharged 13 Feb. 1865.

Knut Bjørnson, Cambridge, 12 Feb. 1862, died 4 Dec. 1864.

Christian E. Bolstad, Rising Sun, 22 Oct. 1861, moved to Veterans Reserve Corps 7 July 1864.

Gudbrand Christenson, Clearmont, 28 Jan. 1862, died 10 Aug. 1864.

Tobias Christianson, La Crosse, 16 Feb. 1862, from Co. A, died in Andersonville Prison 18 Oct. 1864.

Frans Christofferson, Clearmont, Iowa, 10 Jan. 1862, died at Island No. 10, 9 April 1862.

Lars O. Dokken, Perry, 2 Dec. 1861, died at Nashville 1 April 1863.

Knut O. Dokken, Perry, 23 Jan. 1862, died at Island No. 10, 7 May 1862.

Nels J. Eide, New Glarus, 10 Feb. 1862, Corporal, moved to Veterans Reserve Corps 25 March 1864.

Nils Einarson, Perry, 8 Nov. 1861, discharged 20 April 1865, died at Hillsboro, N.D., 1906.

Ole Evenson, Stoughton, 26 Nov. 1861, brevet Captain June 1864, discharged 13 Feb. 1865.

Carl C. Evenson, Madison, 5 March 1862, principal musician, discharged 13 March 1865.

Andrew L. Fosse, Deerfield, 7 Oct. 1861, Corporal, brevet Captain 31 Dec. 1862, fell at Stone River 31 Dec. 1862.

Ole L. Fosse, Deerfield, 7 Oct. 1861, wagoner, discharged 13 Feb. 1865.

Stephen L. Fosse, Leeds, 2 Nov. 1861, discharged 13 Feb. 1865.

Andrew P. Gjerdee, Deerfield, 20 Oct. 1861, musician, died in Andersonville Prison 18 June 1865.

Hans Gulbranson, Halfway Creek, 2 Oct. 1861, fell at Stone River 30 Dec. 1861.

Nils Halvorson, Christiana, 12 Nov. 1861, discharged 16 Oct. 1862.

Ole Halvorson, Sun Prairie, 18 Nov. 1861, discharged 20 March 1865.

Abraham Halvorson, Decorah, Iowa, 30 Dec. 1861, discharged 6 Aug. 1862.

Even Halvorson, Arendal, Minn., 28 Jan. 1862, discharged 9 Aug. 1862.

Lars P. Hauff, Christiana, 20 Dec. 1861, discharged 10 June 1863.

John Helgeson, Moscow, 25 Nov. 1861, discharged 13 Feb. 1865.

Arne Helgeson, Clearmont, Iowa, 20 Jan. 1862, discharged 13 Feb. 1865.

Ole S. Haugnes, Clearmont, Iowa, 10 Jan. 1862, died in Andersonville Prison 18 Jan. 1865.

Ole Iverson, Elgin, Iowa, 20 Jan. 1862, moved to Veterans Reserve Corps 4 Aug. 1863.

Markus Johnson, Columbia Co., 10 Dec. 1861, Corporal, Sergeant, died at Corinth, Miss., 22 July 1862.

Wm. Johnson, Christiana, 20 Dec. 1861, Corporal, died at Nashville 27 June 1864.

Engebret Johnson, Primrose, 17 Dec. 1861, died at Nashville 23 Dec. 1862.

Andrew Johnson, Sparta, 27 Jan. 1862, discharged 27 July 1863.

Knut Knutson, Clearmont, 27 June 1862, died at Louisville, Ky., 16 Oct. 1863.

Erick Knutson, Clearmont, 27 June 1862, died Island No. 10, 14 May 1862.

Hans C. Larmoe, Rising Sun, 25 June 1862, discharged 6 March 1865.

Lars Larson, Michicott, 5 Nov. 1861, discharged 4 Nov. 1862.

Knut Larson, Leeds Center, 27 Jan. 1862, died at Nashville 18 Jan. 1863.

Halvor Larson, Durand, Ill., 30 Jan. 1862, discharged 13 Feb. 1865.

Soren C. Larson, Norway, 12 Dec. 1862. See Co. C.

Torger Larson, Deerfield, 9 Feb. 1864, discharged 20 May 1865.

Ole Larson, Neshonoc, 29 Feb. 1864, from E, died at Nashville, Tenn., 10 Dec. 1864.

Berge O. Lee, Deerfield, 22 Oct. 1861, Corporal, discharged 13 Feb. 1865.

Sivert Lee, Deerfield, 25 Jan. 1864, discharged 24 Nov. 1865 in K Infantry.

Olaus H. Lokken, Madison, 24 Sept. 1861, Sergeant discharged 13 Feb. 1865.

Ole B. Lokken, Clearmont, Iowa, 28 Jan. 1862, discharged sick 22 Oct.

Tosten L. Mossefin, Cambridge, 10 Oct. 1861, discharged 13 Feb. 1865.

Knut Nilsen, Leeds Center, 21 Nov. 1861, died at Andersonville Prison 30 July 1864.

Lars Nelson, Neenah, 22 Dec. 1861, died at Nashville, Tenn., 25 Feb. 1863.

Osmund Nerison, Perry, 1 Dec. 1861, discharged sick 6 Oct. 1862.

Erick P. Oiene, Desota, 25 Jan. 1862, fell at New Hope Church 27 May 1864.

Tobias Olson, Cambridge, 18 Oct. 1861, died at Nashville 8 March 1863.

Ole Olson, Stoughton, 2 Nov. 1861, died at Chickamauga 10 Aug. 1864.

Ingebret Olson, Elgin, 1 Feb. 1862, died at Columbus, Ky., 9 Sept. 1862.

Svend Olson, Elgin, 3 Feb. 1862, discharged sick 6 Oct. 1862.

Anders Pederson, East Troy, 3 Feb. 1864, discharged in Co. I, 13th Infantry, 29 July 1865.

Peter Peterson, Freeborn Co., Minn., 22 Nov. 1861, discharged 13 Feb. 1865.

Ole H. Rome, Rising Sun, 25 Jan. 1862, discharged 13 Feb. 1865.

Andrew T. Rothe, Deerfield, 20 Oct. 1861, Corporal, died at McFarland 1906.

Sam Sampson, Leeds, 2 Oct. 1861, wounded at discharge.

Thomas A. Sandvig, Rising Sun, 26 Jan. 1862, discharged 13 Feb. 1865.

Ellend P. Sime, Cambridge, 23 Oct. 1861, discharged 13 Feb. 1865.

Gunder Sivertson, Primrose, 2 Dec. 1861, discharged sick 16 Dec. 1862.

Aslag Sivertson, Decorah, Iowa, 6 Jan. 1862, discharged 13 Feb. 1865.

Nils N. Slaaten, St. Ansgar, Iowa, 15 Jan. 1862, died at Nashville 14 Feb. 1863.

Sivert Starkson, Cambridge, 2 Jan. 1862, died at Danville, Ga., 3 April 1864.

Christopher Sundby, Chicago, 5 Dec. 1861, discharged sick 20 May 1862.

Lars Thomason, Clearmont, Iowa, 10 Jan. 1862, died at Columbus, Ky., 3 Nov. 1862.

Thomas Thompson, Utica, 28 Oct. 1861, Corporal, discharged with wounds 9 June 1863.

Andrew T. Thompson, Deerfield, 15 Nov. 1861, Sergeant, died at Island No. 10, 22 May 1862.

Anfin Thompson, Hampton, 15 Nov. 1861, discharged 13 Feb. 1865.

Stephen Torgerson, Christiana, 22 Dec. 1861, discharged sick 4 April 1862.

Asbjørn Torgerson, Spring Valley, 22 Feb. 1862, discharged 13 Feb. 1865.

Iver Torkelson, Melrose, 4 Dec. 1861, Sergeant, moved to Veterans Reserve Corps 20 Oct. 1863, discharged 19 Dec. 1864.

Ole Torstenson, Christiana, 14 Dec. 1861, Corporal, Sergeant, discharged 12 Feb. 1865.

Herbrand Troan, Rushford, 7 Dec. 1861, died at Bowling Green, Ky., 5 Oct. 1862.

Ole T. Westby, Bad Ax, 25 Dec. 1861, discharged 13 Feb. 1865, died 16 Feb. 1890.

Co. I:

August Gasman, Waupun, 15 Jan. 1862, Captain, discharged 8 Aug. 1863.

M. Gasman Lindonus, Ashippun, 6 Feb. 1861, First Sergeant, Veterinarian, Commissioned First Lieutenant 31 Oct. 1862, enlisted 7 Dec. 1862, discharged 10 Feb. 1865.

Christian Olson, Mt. Morris, 9 Dec. 1861, Sergeant, promoted Second Lieutenant 3 Nov. 1862, discharged 10 Feb. 1865.

Ole Amundson, New Hope, 10 Nov. 1861, died at Chickamauga of sickness 22 July 1864.

Bernhard Anderson, Chicago, 7 Oct. 1861, musician, discharged 10 Feb. 1865.

Herman Anderson, Scandinavia, 4 Nov. 1861, discharged 10 Feb. 1865.

Erick Anderson, Pepin, 4 Dec. 1861, died at Louisville, Ky., 22 Sept. 1863.

Jens Anderson, Chippewa, 9 Dec. 1861, discharged 10 Feb. 1865.

Ole P. Anderson, Scandinavia, 2 Jan. 1862, discharged 10 Feb. 1865, died at Granite Falls 1906.

Olaf Anderson, Mt. Morris, 29 Oct. 1861, discharged sick 30 Jan. 1863, enrolled again 9 Jan. 1864, moved to Veterans Reserve Corps 20 Dec. 1864.

Newton K. Andrew, Primrose, 15 Jan. 1862, Corporal, discharged 15 Feb. 1865.

Dreng Arneson, Scandinavia, 20 Nov. 1861, wagoner, died at Knoxville, Tenn., 4 Feb. 1864.

Ben Bendixon, Mt. Morris, 14 Jan. 1862, discharged 10 Feb. 1865.

Nels Bjornson, Spring Prairie, 20 Oct. 1861, died in Andersonville Prison 14 Nov. 1864.

Anton Boason, Halfway Creek, 18 Dec. 1861, discharged sick 7 Aug. 1862.

Ingebret O. Volstad, Primrose, 22 Oct. 1861, discharged 10 Feb. 1865.

Peter Clausen, Amherst, 10 Oct. 1861, died at Chattanooga 23 Nov. 1863.

Andrew Erickson, La Crosse, 18 Dec. 1861, veterinarian, moved to I, 13th Infantry, discharged 24 Nov. 1865.

Even H. Floen, Albert Lea, 6 March 1862, discharged sick 31 Dec. 1862.

Torger Gilbertson, Scandinavia, 16 Nov. 1861, Corporal, discharged 10 Feb. 1865.

Nels P. Gram, Stockholm, 5 Dec. 1861, discharged sick 16 June 1863

Andrew Gurud, Stockholm, 4 Jan. 1864, moved to I, 13th Infantry, discharged 24 Nov. 1865.

Lewis Gurud, Stockholm, 4 Jan. 1864, died in Andersonville Prison 11 Oct. 1864.

Hans Gunderson, Scandinavia, 12 Nov. 1861, Sergeant, died in Andersonville Prison 11 Oct. 1864.

Peter O. Harstad, Scandinavia, 2 Dec. 1861, Corporal, fell at Resaca, 8 June 1864.

Helge Halvorson, Scandinavia, 9 Nov. 1861, discharged sick 7 Aug. 1862.

Lars Halvorson, New Hope, 26 Nov. 1861, discharged 4 April 1863.

Hans Hanson, Stockholm, 6 Dec. 1861, discharged 10 Feb. 1865.

Casper Hanson, Eau Claire, 14 Dec. 1861, moved to Veterans Reserve Corps 6 April 1864.

Andrew Hanson, Mt. Morris, 14 Jan. 1862, discharged sick 30 June 1863.

Halvor E. Hove, Dodgeville, 15 Jan. 1862, discharged 10 Feb. 1865.

Julius Ingebretson, Iola, 20 Oct. 1861, Sergeant, discharged sick July 1864.

Andrew Ingebretson, Stockholm, 6 Dec. 1861, discharged 10 Feb. 1865.

Jacob Jackson, La Crosse, 25 Dec. 1861, discharged sick 6 Feb. 1863.

Christian Jacobson, Helvetia, 5 Nov. 1861, Corporal, discharged 10 Feb. 1865.

Martin Jenson, Scandinavia, 17 Nov. 1861, Corporal, discharged 10 Feb. 1865, died at Brandon, Minn., 1906.

Ole Johnson, Scandinavia, 4 Nov. 1861, discharged 10 Feb. 1865.

Søren Johnson, Iola, 11 Nov. 1861, fell at Resaca 15 May, 1864.

Amos Johnson, Waushara Co., 14 Jan. 1862, discharged 10 Feb. 1865.

Lars Jørgenson, Scandinavia, 4 Nov. 1861, discharged 21 May 1862.

Paul Kittilson, Gallagher, Iowa, 14 Jan. 1862, discharged sick 27 Sept. 1862.

Samuel Knutson, Scandinavia, 5 Nov. 1861, died at Mound City, 26 Oct. 1862.

Tollef Knutson, Scandinavia, 10 Nov. 1861, died at Mound City, 28 Oct. 1862.

Arne Knutson, Mower Co., Minn., 6 March 1862, moved to 24th Wisconsin Infantry, discharged 13 March 1865.

Peter Larson, Scandinavia, 15 Feb. 1864, musician, discharged 2 Feb. 1866.

Jens Lorentson, Scandinavia, 18 Nov. 1861, discharged 10 Feb. 1865.

Ole J. Lorentson, Chicago, 28 Oct. 1861. See Co. A.

Peter A. Myhre, St. Lawrence, 16 Nov. 1861, discharged 10 Feb. 1865.

Simon A. Myhre, St. Lawrence, 9 Dec. 1861, Corporal, died in Andersonville Prison.

Hans A. Myhre, St. Lawrence, 9 Dec. 1861, discharged 10 Feb. 1865.

James K. Nelson, Dover, 5 Feb. 1864, moved to K, 13th Infantry, discharged 24 Nov. 1865.

John Nelson, Waupaca, 20 Oct. 1861, discharged 10 Feb. 1865.

Ben Nelson, Dane Co., 8 Nov. 1861, discharged 10 Feb. 1865.

Martin J. Nordre, Scandinavia, 20 Nov. 1861, Sergeant, First Sergeant, discharged 10 Feb. 1865.

Hans Olson, Scandinavia, 9 Nov. 1861, discharged 21 May 1862.

Knut Olson, Scandinavia, 9 Nov. 1861, fell at New Hope Church 27 May 1864.

Olaus Olson, Scandinavia, 9 Nov. 1861, discharged 10 Feb. 1865.

Albert Olson, New Hope, 19 Nov. 1861, died at Island No. 10, 24 May 1862.

Tollef Olson, Primrose, 16 Dec. 1861, discharged sick 24 June 1862.

Iver Olson, Albert Lea, Minn., 8 March 1862, died 1864 at Chattanooga.

Martin Olson, Mt. Morris, 3 Sept. 1864, moved to I, 13th Infantry, 10 June 1865, discharged 24 July 1865.

Charles Olson, Stockholm, 5 Dec. 1861, discharged 10 Feb. 1865.

Peter Simonson, Scandinavia, 9 Nov. 1861, Corporal, died in Andersonville Prison 27 Nov. 1864.

Samuel Peterson, Scandinavia, 6 Dec. 1861, discharged 10 Feb. 1865.

John Peterson, Scandinavia, 9 Dec. 1861, discharged 10 Feb. 1865.

Ole Peterson, St. Lawrence, 4 Nov. 1861, in prison at discharge.

Daniel Peterson, Porter, 9 Nov. 1861, died 23 June 1864.

John P. Peterson, Mt. Morris, 4 Dec. 1861, discharged sick 4 Oct. 1862.

John Ranbeck, New Hope, 30 Oct. 1861, Corporal, discharged sick 20 Aug. 1862, died in Andersonville Prison 5 Sept. 1864.

Elias Peterson, La Crosse, 4 Jan. 1864, moved to I, 13th Infantry, 10 June 1865, discharged 24 July 1865.

Ole Peterson, La Crosse, 14 Jan. 1864, moved to K, 13th Infantry, 10 June 1865, sick at discharge.

John L. Rambeck, Springfield, 22 Jan. 1864, discharged 5 June 1865.

Ole H. Ruste, Mitchell Co., Iowa, 18 Feb. 1862, discharged 13 March 1865.

Casper Simonson, Scandinavia, 9 Nov. 1861, sick at discharge.

John Sorenson, Sparta, 18 Dec. 1861, died at Birds Pt., Mo., 7 April 1862.

Nils Stenerson, Chicago, 10 Oct. 1861, died at Chattanooga, 8 July 1864.

Nils Starkson, Norway Grove, 16 Nov. 1861, discharged 10 Feb. 1865.

Bjorn Thompson, Chippewa, 5 Nov. 1861, discharged 10 Feb. 1865, died 1909.

Michael Thompson, Scandinavia, 18 Nov. 1861, Corporal, Sergeant, discharged 10 Feb. 1865, died at St. Ansgar 1906.

Gullick O. Tilden, Nevada, Minn., 1 March 1862, discharged sick 16 Nov. 1862.

Andrew Torkilson, Scandinavia, 5 Nov. 1861, wounded at discharge.

Arne Torkelson, Spring Grove, 9 Nov. 1861, sick at discharge.

Edward Thoreson, Pepin, 10 Dec. 1861, discharged 10 Feb. 1865.

Ole E. Troan, Madison, 27 Sept. 1861, discharged 10 Feb. 1865.

John Waserud, St. Lawrence, 4 Dec. 1861, Corporal, Sergeant, discharged 10 Feb. 1865.

Robert Watson, Primrose, 18 Feb. 1864, moved to I, 13th Infantry, discharged 14 July 1865.

John O. Wraalstad, New Hope, 8 Nov. 1861, Sergeant, discharged 10 Feb. 1865.

Co. K:

Mons Grinager, Captain, Freeborn Co., 30 Jan. 1862, discharged 10 Feb. 1865.

Ole Peterson, Freeborn Co., 30 Jan. 1862, First Lieutenant, discharged 31 Aug. 1862.

Andrew Clement, Waupun, 5 Oct. 1861, First Sergeant, promoted First Lieutenant 10 Oct. 1862, died 23 Sept. 1864 at Briggsville, Wis.

Ellend Erickson, Albert Lea, 22 Nov. 1861, Corporal, Sergeant, promoted Second Lieutenant 27 May 1862, First Lieutenant 10 Nov. 1864, without review, discharged 10 Feb. 1865.

Olaus Solberg, Freeborn Co., 30 Jan. 1862, discharged 27 May 1862, Second Lieutenant.

John E. Irgens, St. Ansgar, 1 March 1862, First Sergeant, promoted Second Lieutenant 5 June 1862, discharged 3 Sept. 1862.

Simon Annenson, Winneshiek Co., Iowa, 26 Jan. 1862, died at Dennison, Ohio, 23 Aug. 1862.

Engebret Amundson, Freeborn Co., 20 Jan. 1862, died at Island No. 10, 6 May 1862.

Knut Amundson, Nevada, Minn., 29 Jan. 1862, Corporal, moved to Veterans Reserve Corps 1 Sept. 1863.

Tollef Anderson, Worth Co., Iowa, 11 Dec. 1862, discharged 10 Feb. 1865.

Torger Aslakson, Worth Co., Iowa, 10 Dec. 1861, died at Island No. 10, 2 June 1862.

Halvor Aslakson, Freeborn Co., Minn., 18 Jan. 1862, died at Nashville 11 Nov. 1862.

Ole Asleson, Winneshiek Co., Iowa, 6 Jan. 1862, prisoner at discharge.

Peter Bjerk, Freeborn Co., Minn., 28 Dec. 1861, discharged 10 Feb. 1865.

Ole Christianson, Vindson, 5 Jan. 1864, moved to I, 13th Infantry, died at Green Lake, Tex., 27 July 1865.

Fingal Christopherson, Worth Co., Iowa, 12 Dec. 1861, discharged sick 22 July 1862.

Iver G. Dahl, Worth Co., Iowa, 20 Nov. 1861, died at Richmond, Va., 10 March 1864.

Ole N. Danness, Freeborn Co., Minn., 18 Dec. 1861, Corporal, fell at Chickamauga, 10 Sept. 1863.

Jens Enger, Fillmore Co., Minn., 26 Jan. 1862, died in Andersonville Prison 24 June 1864.

Tosten Erickson, Freeborn Co., 30 Nov. 1861, Sergeant, discharged sick 28 July 1862.

Erick Erickson, Lafayette Co., 22 Jan. 1862, died at Bowling Green, Ky., 1 Dec. 1862.

Helge Erickson, Fillmore Co., 22 Jan. 1862, died at Jackson, Tenn., 26 Sept. 1865.

Ole Evenson, Freeborn Co., 18 Jan. 1862, discharged 10 Feb. 1865.

Christian Guldbrandson, Worth Co., Iowa, 20 Jan. 1862, discharged sick 10 Oct. 1862.

Anders Gudbrandson, Green Co., 21 Jan. 1862, Corporal, moved to Veterans Reserve Corps, 1 March 1864.

Knut Gullickson, Mitchell Co., Iowa, 28 Jan. 1862, discharged sick 9 Dec. 1862.

Halvor Gullickson, Winneshiek Co., Iowa, 25 Jan. 1862, discharged sick 11 March 1863.

Lars Halvorson, Freeborn Co., 17 Jan. 1862, died at Farmington, Miss., 30 Aug. 1862.

Jens Hanson, Calumet Co., 16 Nov. 1861, Captain, 20 Sept. 1863, prisoner at discharge.

Ole Hanson, East Troy, 15 Jan. 1864, moved to I, 13th Infantry, veterinarian, discharged.

John F. Hauff, Windsor, 31 Dec. 1863, discharged sick 2 Nov. 1864.

Peter Helgeson, Freeborn Co., 18 Dec. 1861, discharged sick 15 Oct. 1862.

Nils Helgeson, Worth Co., 18 Jan. 1862, discharged sick 22 June 1863.

Gudbrand Helgeson, Worth Co., 1 March 1862, died at Island No. 10, Tenn., 3 April 1862.

Hans J. Helgeson, Mitchell Co., Iowa, 23 Jan. 1862, died at Nashville, Tenn., 10 March 1863.

Halvor Holland, Winneshiek Co., 25 Jan. 1862, Sergeant, First Sergeant, died in Andersonville, Ga., 2 July 1864.

Theodore E. Hundeby, Worth Co., Iowa, 10 Dec. 1861, wagoner, Sergeant, discharged 10 Feb. 1865, died in Northwood, Iowa, 1906.

Jens Jacobson, Freeborn Co., 3 Nov. 1861, Sergeant, died at Richmond, Va., 16 Feb. 1864.

Iver Jacobson, Freeborn Co., 24 Nov. 1861, discharged 13 May 1863.

Ole Jenson, Freeborn Co., 18 Jan. 1862, died at Chattanooga 2 Jan. 1864.

Jens Jenson, Freeborn Co., 20 Jan. 1862, wagoner, discharged 10 Feb. 1865.

Ole Jenson Twenge, Freeborn Co., 7 Feb. 1862, discharged 10 Feb. 1865.

Martin Jenson, Filmore Co., 25 Jan. 1862, discharged sick 3 Feb. 1863.

Halvor Jenson, Fillmore Co., 11 Feb. 1862, discharged sick 3 Feb. 1863.

Iver Johanneson, Winneshiek Co., 21 Jan. 1862, discharged sick 30 Dec. 1862.

Christopher Johnson, Freeborn Co., 26 Nov. 1861, discharged 10 Feb. 1865.

John Johnson, Worth Co., 23 Dec. 1861, fell at New Hope Church 27 May, 1864.

Osmund Johnson, Fillmore Co., 11 Feb. 1862, discharged 30 May 1865.

Christen Knutson, Fillmore Co., 11 Feb. 1862, prisoner at discharge.

Lars A. Larson, Freeborn Co., 12 Dec. 1861, Corporal, Sergeant, discharged 20 Feb. 1865, commissioned Second Lieutenant 25 Feb. 1867, time of service counted from 10 Nov. 1864.

Gunder Larson, Lafayette Co., 22 Jan. 1862, died at Island No. 10, 22 May 1862.

Thos. Larson, Lafayette Co., 22 Jan. 1862, died at Lebanon, Ky.

Severt Larson, Emmet Co., Iowa, 3 Feb. 1862, discharged 10 Feb. 1865.

Lars Leufson, Deerfield, 10 Feb. 1864, fell at New Hope Church 27 May 1864.

Peder E. Lomo, Pierce Co., 12 Nov. 1861, Sergeant, moved to Veterans Reserve Corps 1 Sept. 1863.

Isak Lundegaard, Winneshiek Co., 6 Jan. 1862, discharged 15 Nov. 1862.

Andrew Madson, Freeborn Co., 18 Jan. 1862, moved to Veterans Reserve Corps 1 Sept. 1863, discharged 11 Feb. 1865.

Johannes Martinson, Mower Co., 3 Feb. 1862, fell at Stone River 30 Dec. 1862.

Ole Mickelson, Winneshiek Co., 15 Jan. 1862, discharged sick 22 July 1862.

Ole T. Morck, Mitchell Co., Iowa, 8 Feb. 1862, prisoner at discharge.

Nels Nelson, Freeborn Co., Minn., 19 Dec. 1861, died at Eaglefield Jct., Tenn., 15 Nov. 1862.

Laurits Nilson, Winneshiek Co., Iowa, 21 Jan. 1861, discharged sick 2 Oct. 1862.

Erick Nelson, Green Co., Wis., 24 Jan. 1862, died at Louisville, Ky., 9 April 1864.

Iver Nelson, Fillmore Co., Minn., 11 Feb. 1862, died in Fillmore Co., 18 Sept. 1863.

Rasmus Nilson, East Troy, Wis., 28 Jan. 1864, Sergeant, moved to Co. I, 13th Infantry, discharged 30 June 1865.

Jacob Olson, Freeborn Co., Minn., 10 Dec. 1861, discharged sick 15 Aug. 1862.

Helge Olson, Freeborn Co., Minn., 18 Dec. 1861, discharged sick 11 Oct. 1862.

Knut Olson, Freeborn Co., Minn., 18 Dec. 1861, discharged sick 12 Nov. 1862.

Christen Olson, Avoca, 9 Jan. 1862, died at Chickamauga 12 Nov. 1863.

Kittel Olson, Worth Co., Iowa, 18 Jan. 1862, discharged 22 July 1862.

Gudbrand Olson, Freeborn Co., 18 Jan. 1862, discharged 28 Nov. 1864.

Ole Olson, Freeborn Co., 20 Jan. 1862, died at Farmington, Miss., 24 Aug. 1862.

Lars Olson, Winneshiek Co., Iowa, 25 Jan. 1862, discharged sick 31 May 1862.

Knut R. Olson, Winneshiek Co., 25 Jan. 1862, First Sergeant, died at Murfreesboro 9 Jan. 1863.

Charles Oleson, Vernon, 11 Jan. 1864, moved to Veterans Reserve Corps 20 Dec. 1864, discharged 18 Sept. 1865.

Paul M. Paulson, Worth Co., Iowa, 10 Dec. 1861, died at Richmond, March 1864.

Axel Peterson, Worth Co., Iowa, 20 Nov. 1861, Corporal, died in Andersonville Prison 3 July 1864.

Narve Peterson, Freeborn Co., 18 Jan. 1862, died at Eaglefield Jct. 19 Nov. 1862.

Haagen Peterson, Freeborn Co., 20 Jan. 1862, sick at discharge.

Syvert Peterson, Winchester Co., Iowa, 25 Jan. 1862, brevet Captain 31 Dec. 1862, died in Andersonville Prison 5 Sept. 1864.

Soren Peterson, East Troy, 23 Jan. 1864, taken prisoner at New Hope Church, died.

Aslak Rasmussen, Fillmore Co., 11 Feb. 1862, died at St. Louis, Mo., 6 Aug. 1862.

Albert E. Rice, East Troy, 12 Jan. 1864, moved to Co. H, discharged 3 June 1865.

Bernt Sanders, Winneshiek Co., 6 Jan. 1862, Corporal, died at Jacinto Jct. 21 July 1862.

Kittel Sanderson, Winneshiek Co., 21 Feb. 1862, moved to Veterans Reserve Corps 1 March 1864.

Lars Sebjornson, Freeborn Co., 18 Jan. 1862, discharged sick 11 March 1863.

Johannes Sorenson, Worth Co., Iowa, 10 Dec. 1861, wounded 30 April 1863, reported dead.

Lars L. Slettum, Winneshiek Co., 25 Jan. 1862, discharged sick 9 Oct. 1862.

Otto F. Steen, Winneshiek Co., 21 Jan. 1862, Corporal, Sergeant, discharged 14 April 1865.

Ole Thompson, Winneshiek Co., 23 Jan. 1862, Corporal, discharged 10 Feb. 1864.

Charles Thompson, Winneshiek Co., 2 Jan. 1862, died at Jackson 7 Oct. 1862.

Peter Thompson, Winneshiek Co., 23 Jan. 1862, died at Bowling Green, Ky., 8 Jan. 1863.

Ole G. Thompson, Green Co., Wis., 22 Jan. 1862, discharged 10 Feb. 1864.

Anders Thompson, Fillmore Co., 11 Feb. 1862, discharged sick 22 April 1863.

Anders Tobiason, Winneshiek Co., 18 Jan. 1862, Corporal, discharged 2 May 1863.

Rollef Tykeson, Freeborn Co., 20 Jan. 1862, moved to Veterans Reserve Corps 1 Sept. 1862.

Ole K. Wingaard, Winneshiek Co., 23 Jan. 1862, discharged 27 April 1863.

NOTES

1. In this regiment there were many commissioned officers who were promoted without review because they were heavily involved in military action.

2. Lieutenant N.J. Gilbert relates about Sloan that he was able to escape from his imprisonment and that he was sent home as a recruiting officer, and that he returned with people who were attacked by a battery at Kennesaw Mountain on June 21, 1864. The enemy was forced to flee and the battery with four cannons was taken. Thereafter while they sat down to drink a cup of coffee, a bombshell came hurtling and hit the coffee pot and exploded. Sloan was hit and died four days later.

Index

Stone's River, Battle of, 5, 26, 147,
    158–161, 201
Stub, H.A., 196
Svandsen, Ole, 125
Swenson, Lewis, 207–208

Tandberg, Lieut. Christian, 60
Thoe, John Johnson, 112–120
Thoe, Margit Johnson, 116–117, 119
Thoe, Nils Johnson, 140
Thomas, General George Henry:
    "Rock of Chickamauga," 31, 62;
    outwits Gen. Longstreet, 34–35,
    37; at Rocky Face, 41; near
    Atlanta, 47; at Orchard Knob,
    178; mentioned, 40, 43, 134,
    159, 177
Thompson, Anders (Andrew), 65,
    79, 80
Thompson, Bjørn (Ben), 12, 51
Thompson, Chris, 148
Thompson, Elias, 207
Thompson, Michael, 51, 207
Thompson, Lieut. Oliver, 61, 66
Thompson, Oscar, 191
Thompson, Th. (Thomas?), 208
Thoresen, Edvard, 39, 51
Thorkelsen, Arne, 19, 27, 51
Thorkildsen, Captain Andrew,
    185–186
Tofte, A.A., 207

Tollefsen, Ole, 121
Troyan, O.E., 51

Union City, Tennessee, 5, 15, 63, 147
Urness (Urnæs), Anders, 58, 173,
    174, 210
Urness, Ole, 210
Urness, Peter 210

Volstad, Hans, 105

Wasrud, John, 137
Westby, Ole P., 21, 51
Wheeler, General Joseph, 131, 141
Williams, Z., 51
Willich, General Augustus: at New
    Hope Church, 7, 166; at Rocky
    Face, 41; popularity with soldiers,
    79, 81–82, 188; wounded, 84; at
    Pickett's Mill, 170; mentioned,
    168, 173
Wilson, Major Geroge: heroism at
    New Hope Church, 7, 170, 173;
    praise of, 93, 168, 174; wounded
    at Murfreesboro, 111, 161; men-
    tioned, 172, 178
Wirz, Captain Henry, 154
Wood, General T.J.: at Chickamauga,
    56, 61; at Chattanooga, 177; men-
    tioned, 38, 79, 166, 168, 188
Wrolstad (Wraalstad), John Olson,
    6–7, 41, 50, 106–109